Deutsch heute

Arbeitsheft

8TH EDITION

Arbeitsheft

Deutsch heute

INTRODUCTORY GERMAN

Workbook
Lab Manual
Self-Tests
Video Workbook

Moeller

Adolph

Hoecherl-Alden

Berger

Lalande

Simone Berger
Rösrath, Germany

Jack Moeller
Oakland University

Houghton Mifflin Company
Boston   New York

Publisher: Rolando Hernández
Sponsoring Editor: Van Strength
Development Manager: Sharla Zwirek
Project Editor: Harriet C. Dishman
Senior Manufacturing Coordinator: Priscilla J. Bailey
Senior Marketing Manager: Tina Crowley Desprez
Marketing Manager: Claudia Martínez

Credits

The authors and editors of the **Deutsch heute, Eighth Edition,** *Arbeitsheft* would like to thank the following companies and organizations for granting permission to reproduce or adapt copyrighted material:

p. 3   From Volkshochschule Tübingen

p. 4   © Bryn Colton/Assignments Photographers/CORBIS

p. 5   BOSE, Nordhorn

p. 20   Deutsche Welle, Köln

p. 30   © Dave Bartfuff/CORBIS

p. 37   Courtesy Fleesensee

p. 38   Universität Heidelberg

p. 49   AP/Wide World (photo left)

p. 49   AP/Wide World (photo right)

p. 49   Austrian Tourist Office (text)

p. 52   Egon Schiele Museum, Tulln

p. 56   Courtesy Caroline Link

p. 62   From IKEA room magazine, September-November 2002, pg. 15. Reprinted by permission.

p. 72   Reprinted with permission of FOCUS, 25, 2000.

p. 78   Reprinted with permission of FOCUS, 13, 2002.

p. 79   Reprinted with permission of FOCUS, 13, 2002.

p. 84–85   Courtesy Franzz Magazine

p. 87   New Glarus Chamber of Commerce, New Glarus, WI

p. 91   Courtesy Komodie Theater

p. 95   Allgemeiner Deutscher Fahrrad-Club e.V.

p. 97   Léon von Roy, Belgien, © Frick Friedrich

p. 101   Courtesy Franzz Magazine

p. 103   Hörzu

p. 104   Reprinted with permission of Deutsche Welle.

p. 105   Diogenes Verlag, Zürich

p. 114–115   Copyright © 1984 Fischer Taschenbuch Verlag GmbH, Frankfurt am Main.

p. 117   Horn

p. 117   Impressum, Frankfurter Societäts-Druckerei GmbH, Frankfurt am Main

p. 165   GLOBUS-Kartendienst GmbH, Hamburg

Drawings by George Ulrich, Anne Burgess, Tim Jones, and Anna Veltfort.

Printed in the U.S.A.

ISBN: 0-618-33831-4

6789-POO-08 07

Contents

SELF-TESTS

SELF-TESTS ANSWER KEY

VIDEO WORKBOOK

GERMAN-ENGLISH VOCABULARY

Introduction

The *Arbeitsheft* to accompany ***Deutsch heute: Introductory German, Eighth Edition,*** is designed to help you improve your reading and writing skills, reinforce your listening comprehension skills, and enhance your cognition of grammatical features of German. The *Arbeitsheft* consists of four components: (1) the Workbook, (2) the Lab Manual, (3) Self-Tests with an Answer Key, and (4) the Video Workbook.

Workbook

The Workbook provides guided practice in writing German. Exercises include completing dialogues or sentences, rewriting sentences, answering questions, building sentences or paragraphs from guidelines, and creating short compositions. Some exercises encourage you to express your own moods, opinions, and ideas and to speculate on what you would do in a particular situation. Other exercises are based on line art and realia, including maps, photos, ads, and charts; some activities offer extra reading practice and new cultural information. Vocabulary sophistication is developed by exercises that require you to supply synonyms, antonyms or definitions, or to form new words with suffixes and prefixes. In general the exercises are based upon a situation that presents the language in a realistic and natural context. Many of the situations involve the characters you have become familiar with in the textbook. For the instructor's convenience, an Answer Key to the exercises in the Workbook is provided as a separate print ancillary, as well as on the *Deutsch heute Instructor Class Prep CD-ROM*.

Lab Manual

The Lab Manual contains material that is coordinated with the **Übungen zum Hörverständnis** in the Audio Program. The exercises consist of new oral material based on the dialogues and readings in each chapter of the text. Exercises include true/false statements about the **Lesestück** and about conversations and stories heard on the recordings, and logical/illogical response. In general, responses to the recorded material consist of checking off correct answers or writing short answers in the Lab Manual. For the instructor's convenience, the script for the listening comprehension exercises and an Answer Key are provided on the *Instructor Class Prep CD-ROM*.

Self-Tests

The Self-Tests are provided to help you determine whether you are ready for the chapter test by giving you an opportunity to review structures and vocabulary. Doing the Self-Tests, either individually or in class, will enable you to see whether you have understood the grammatical features introduced in the chapter and whether you can apply your understanding of the grammatical principles. You will need to use a separate answer sheet for the Self-Tests. An Answer Key to the Self-Tests follows the Self-Tests.

Video Workbook

The Video Workbook contains activities designed to be used in conjunction with the video *Unterwegs!*

The Video Workbook is divided into twelve segments that correspond to the scenes of the video. Each segment of the Video Workbook takes you through a series of steps. Step one prepares you to view the video. Step two has you view the video with the sound off. Step three has you view the video with the sound on. And step four helps you assimilate what you have seen.

Step one contains three sections. The **Vorschau** *(preview)* contains questions in English that should help you bring focus to your viewing of the module. **Besondere Ausdrücke** *(special expressions)* introduces some words and expressions in the scene that may be unfamiliar to you but are crucial for your understanding of the dialogue. **Landeskunde** *(cultural information),* which occurs in Scenes 2–12, points out cultural details in the video and helps you understand it.

In step two you will be asked to view the video scene with the sound off, so that you can concentrate on visual cues. When you watch a TV program in English without the sound on, you can often still tell what is happening. You will find that the same is true when you are watching the video in German. Body language, people's facial expressions, and the scenery in the background all combine to let you know what is going on and anticipate what people are saying.

The activities in step three progress from asking you to identify actual statements you hear in the video to checking your understanding of the language and action.

The post-viewing activities of step four encourage you to expand on what you have seen in the video and to call on your own experience and imagination, e.g., you may be asked to create a dialogue, a role-play, or to give your opinion about one of the characters or their relationships to others.

An Answer Key to the Video Workbook is included on the *Instructor Class Prep CD-ROM.*

Workbook

Name _____   Datum _____

EINFÜHRUNG   Wie heißt du?

A. Wie heißt du? Markus is attending his first lecture at the university. While waiting for the professor to appear, he gets acquainted with the student next to him. Complete their dialogue by writing in the appropriate responses from the column on the right.

1. Hallo, ich heiße Markus. Wie heißt du?

   _____

2. Hmm. Wie schreibt man das?

   _____

3. Wie ist deine Telefonnummer?

   _____

4. Und wie ist deine Adresse?

   _____

a. 68 90 74.

b. Nauklerstraße 72.

c. eff ah üppsilon err ih enn ih ess ess ah.

d. Hallo. Mein Name ist Fayrinissa.

B. Farben. Fill in the correct color.

1. Ein Elefant ist _____.

2. Ein Tiger ist _____ und _____.

3. Ein Kamel ist _____.

4. Ein Krokodil ist _____.

5. Eine Tomate ist _____.

6. Moby Dick war° _____.   was

7. Eine Banane ist _____.

8. Eine Pflanze ist _____.

9. Der Ozean ist _____.

10. Die Grundfarben° sind _____, _____   primary colors

    und _____.

11. Mein Telefon ist _____.

12. Mein Rucksack ist _____.

13. Die Wand in meinem Zimmer ist _____.

14. Meine Lieblingsfarbe° ist _____.   favorite color

C. Welcher Artikel? You have already learned a number of nouns. Since the gender of nouns is very important in German, categorize them by their *definite articles*.

Frau   Professorin   Woche   Stuhl   Papier
Tag   Buch
Mädchen   Bleistift   Farbe   Telefon   Computer

der	das	die
_____	*das Buch*	_____
_____	_____	_____
_____	_____	_____
_____	_____	_____

D. Wie ist ... ? Alex and Gisela are talking about the following people and things. For each item, first complete the question by supplying the pictured *noun and its definite article*. Then give an answer, using a complete sentence with the cue in parentheses.

(47)

(Alex)

→ Wie alt ist der Mann?
Er ist siebenundvierzig Jahre alt.

1. Wie heißt _____?

_____

_____

(braun)

2. Welche Farbe hat _____?

_____

_____

(Gisela)

3. Wie heißt _____?

_____

_____

4. Wie alt ist _____?

(80)

_____

_____

(schwarz)

(alt)

(neu)

5. Welche Farbe hat _____?

_____

_____

6. Wie ist _____?

_____

_____

7. Wie ist _____?

_____

_____

E. Volkshochschule° Tübingen. Look at the ad from the adult education center in Tübingen and answer the following questions.

adult education center

```
        Tübingen
      ┌──────┐
      │ vhs  │
      └──────┘
volkshochschule tübingen

Katharinenstraße 18
72072 Tübingen

Telefon (0 70 71) 56 03 0
Fax     (0 70 71) 56 03 28
www.vhs-tuebingen.de

Öffnungszeiten:
Mo.-Fr.  09:00 bis 12:30 Uhr
         14:00 bis 17:30 Uhr
```

1. Wie heißt die Abkürzung° für „Volkshochschule"? _____   abbreviation

2. Wie ist die Adresse? _____

3. Wie ist die Telefonnummer? _____

4. An welchen Tagen ist die Volkshochschule offen°?   open

   Sie ist offen am Montag, am _____, am

   _____, am _____ und am

   _____.

5. An welchen Tagen ist sie nicht offen?

   Am _____ und am _____.

6. Wie ist das vhs-Haus°? Alt oder neu? _____ building

F. Das Zimmer. Gisela sends you a picture of her room in Tübingen. A friend of yours is planning to go to Germany next summer, so you tell her on the phone about Gisela's room.

1. Name six items with the indefinite article. If there is more than one of an item, name only one.

➡ *In Giselas Zimmer ist ein Stuhl, ...* _____

_____

_____

2. Your friend is curious and wants to know what the room and the things in the room look like. Using various *modifiers* (colors, size, age), write five sentences describing the room and the objects in it.

➡ *Der Stuhl ist neu.* _____

_____

_____

_____

_____

Name _____   Datum _____

G. Deutsch ist leicht°! You may be surprised to discover how much   easy
German you can understand without knowing every word. Since German
and English are closely related linguistically, you will find many cognates
that will help you get the gist of a reading. Look at the ad *Ja, Bose ist Musik*
in meinen Ohren and answer the questions below.

```
╔══════════════════════════════════════╗
║          Ja, Bose ist                  ║
║     Musik in meinen Ohren.             ║
║  Bitte senden Sie mir weitere Informationen ║
║       über das Bose Wave® Radio zu.    ║
║                                        ║
║  Name_____ Herr/Frau      ║
║                                        ║
║  Telefon_____ tagsüber      ║
║                                        ║
║  _____ abends       ║
║                                        ║
║  Straße_____         ║
║                                        ║
║  PLZ/Ort°_____         ║
║                           3050         ║
║                                        ║
║  Bitte in unfrankiertem Umschlag zurück an: ║
║  Bose, Postfach 1468, 48504 Nordhorn oder  ║
║  als Fax an folgende                   ║
║  Nummer:         BOSE®                  ║
║  05921 - 833 250.  Better sound through research. ║
╚══════════════════════════════════════╝
```
postal code / place (city)

1. List six German words you already know.

    _____   _____

    _____   _____

    _____   _____

2. List five German words that look *similar to* English words.

    _____   _____

    _____   _____

    _____

3. What is this ad about? _____

4. In the ad, fill in the requested personal details so that you can receive
    more information from *Bose*.

5. Wie heißt die Firma°? _____   company

6. Wie heißt die Stadt°? _____   city

7. Wie ist die Faxnummer? _____

H. Am Telefon. In order to get information about the University of Tübingen you call the office for international students. The person on the phone promises to send the information and asks for your address. Answer her/his questions.

1. Wie heißen Sie?

   _____

2. Wie ist Ihre Adresse? Die Straße?

   _____

3. Und die Stadt° und die Postleitzahl°?   city / postal code

   _____

4. Ihre E-Mail-Adresse?

   _____

5. Danke, Herr / Frau _____

I. Cognates. Look at the following groups of cognates and cross out the one word in each group that doesn't belong.

➔   der Elefant   das Känguru   ~~die Lampe~~   die Maus

1. der Arm   der Finger   die Hand   die Socke
2. blau   dumm   grün   rot
3. der Ball   die Klarinette   die Trompete   die Violine
4. das Bett   die Couch   das Sofa   das Telefon
5. der Film   die Musik   die Politik   das Theater

J. *Kulturelle Notizen°.* You plan to visit Germany, Austria, or   cultural notes
Switzerland next year. To prepare for the trip, you keep a diary about
cultural differences between these countries and the United States. Provide
brief responses in English.

1. Compare American postal codes with German, Austrian, and Swiss postal codes.

   _____

   _____

2. Give three reasons why German is an important world language.

   _____

   _____

3. Compare what you say when you answer the phone at home with how it is typically done in Germany.

   _____

   _____

KAPITEL 1   Guten Tag! Wie geht's?

A. Gehen wir ins Kino? Melanie and Michael have classes in the same building. When they run into each other, they talk about their plans for the evening. Make up their conversation by writing the following sentences in a meaningful sequence.

—Nichts Besonderes. Was machst du?
—Tschüs. Bis dann.
—Gisela und ich, wir gehen ins Kino, in *Herr der Ringe*. Kommst du auch?
—Gut, dann bis halb acht. Ciao.
—Au ja, ich komme gern. Ich glaube, der Film ist toll. Wann geht ihr?
—Was machst du heute Abend?
—So um halb acht.

MICHAEL: Was machst du heute Abend?

MELANIE: _____

MICHAEL: _____

MELANIE: _____

MICHAEL: _____

MELANIE: _____

MICHAEL: _____

B. Was machst du? Gisela and Michael meet in the lounge of their dormitory. Choose Michael's lines from the list provided and write them in the spaces provided.

Also, bis später. Ciao. ■ Ich gehe schwimmen. Was machst du? ■ Spielst du gut? ■ Wann spielt ihr?

GISELA: Hallo Michael. Na, was machst du heute Nachmittag?

MICHAEL: _____

GISELA: Ich spiele Tennis mit Alex.

MICHAEL: _____

GISELA: Nein, nicht so gut. Aber ich spiele sehr gern Tennis.

MICHAEL: _____

GISELA: Um halb vier.

MICHAEL: _____

GISELA: Ja, tschüs, Michael. Bis dann.

C. Wie sind Sie? You're participating in a survey of the Department of Psychology dealing with the relationship between the generations. Complete the chart for yourself and others. For each person select three *adjectives* from the following list and enter them.

traurig ■ glücklich ■ froh ■ kritisch ■ sympathisch ■ unsympathisch ■ intelligent ■ praktisch ■ lustig ■ ernst ■ ruhig ■ laut ■ tolerant ■ freundlich ■ unfreundlich ■ egozentrisch

	sehr	manchmal°	nicht	
→ ich bin	[kritisch]	[praktisch]	[unfreundlich]	sometimes
1. meine Mutter° ist				mother
2. mein Vater° ist				father
3. meine Freundin ist				
4. mein Freund ist				
5. meine Professorin ist				
6. mein Professor ist				

D. Wann? You are visiting your Swiss friend Sabine. For today you have planned an excursion on the lake near Luzern. Ask the steamship employee about *departure and arrival times*. He looks up the times in the steamer schedule and gives you the official time (use Method 1 as in a). You tell Sabine the time in conversational German (use Method 2 as in b).

Luzern	(ab)	9.30
WEGGIS X	(an)	10.09
	(ab)	10.32
KEHRSITEN X	(an)	10.50
	(ab)	11.00
ALPNACHSTAD	(an)	12.00
	(ab)	15.10
Luzern	(an)	16.45
	ab	

→ Wann fahren wir von° Luzern ab°?   from / **fahren ab:** depart
  a. Um *neun Uhr dreißig* .
  b. Um *halb zehn* .

1. Wann kommen wir in Weggis an°?   **kommen an:** arrive

   a. Um _____ .

   b. Um _____ .

2. Wann fahren wir von Kehrsiten ab?

   a. Um _____ .

   b. Um _____ .

3. Wann kommen wir in Luzern an?

   a. Um _____ .

   b. Um _____ .

E. Wer ich bin und was ich gern mache. Peter is spending a year as an exchange student in Berlin. For his German class, he has to write a short essay about himself, including his hobbies. Complete each paragraph of Peter's report with the appropriate form of the verbs listed.

Verbs: kommen ■ sein *(5x)* ■ studieren

Ich _____[1] 22 Jahre alt und ich _____[2]

aus° Boston. Dort° _____[3] ich an der Boston University.   from / there

Jetzt° _____[4] ich für ein Jahr als° Austauschstudent° in   now / as / exchange student

Berlin. Berlin _____[5] toll und total interessant. Ich wohne°   live

im Wohnheim°. Mein Zimmer _____[6] klein, aber okay. Die   dorm

Studenten im Wohnheim _____[7] auch ganz nett, vielleicht

ein bisschen reserviert.

Verbs: machen ■ schwimmen ■ sein ■ spielen ■ wandern ■ wandern gehen *(fills 2 blanks)*

Und ich? Ich _____[8] natürlich freundlich, sympathisch,

intelligent, sportlich, tolerant und ziemlich° ironisch! Ich   rather

_____[9] Basketball und ich _____[10]

Fitnesstraining. Im Sommer _____[11] ich auch oft und ich

_____[12] gern. Meine Freunde und ich _____[13]

oft in Vermont _____[14].

Verbs: arbeiten ■ glauben ■ haben *(2x)* ■ machen ■ tanzen gehen
(fills 2 blanks)

An der BU _____ [15] ich Musik in einer Band. Ich

_____ [16] hier in Berlin zwei gute Freunde, Monika und

Stefan. Heute Abend _____ [17] wir _____ [18].

Stefan _____ [19] in einem Club, dem „Cinderella". Am

Wochenende _____ [20] wir Karten für ein Konzert in dem

Club. Ich _____ [21], die Band ist super!

F. Gespräche°. Gisela's parents, Mr. and Mrs. Riedholt, have come to
Tübingen to visit her for the weekend. On Saturday evening they invite
Gisela and her new friends Alex and Michael out for dinner. During dinner
there are lots of questions and answers as they all get acquainted. Use the
cues provided to write a question addressed to the person listed. Then
make up an answer for that person. You may answer in short phrases,
which is normal in conversation. Pay attention to the appropriate use of **du,
ihr,** or **Sie.** Since Mr. and Mrs. Riedholt are meeting Alex and Michael for
the first time, they address them formally **(Sie),** but use first names because
they are friends of Gisela's. Note that specific questions as well as yes/no
questions are being used.

conversations

→ HERR RIEDHOLT: Alex, _gehen Sie gern ins Kino_ ? (gehen / gern / ins Kino?)
   ALEX: Nein, nicht sehr gern.

1. GISELA: Alex, _____? (wann / machen / Fitnesstraining?)

   ALEX: _____.

2. MICHAEL: Herr Riedholt, _____? (wandern / gern?)

   HERR RIEDHOLT: _____.

3. GISELA: Alex und Michael, _____?
   (gehen / am Wochenende /inlineskaten?)

   ALEX UND MICHAEL: _____.

4. FRAU RIEDHOLT: Michael, _____? (spielen / oft / Gitarre?)

   MICHAEL: _____.

5. ALEX: Gisela, _____? (hören / gern Musik?)

   GISELA: _____.

6. HERR RIEDHOLT: Alex, _____? (sein / musikalisch?)

   ALEX: _____.

G. Was? Wann? Your Austrian neighbor, Andrea, asks you about various activities. Check your calendar and respond in German using complete sentences with **Ja, ...** or **Nein, ...** and the correct activity.

→   *Freitag:* Wir gehen schwimmen, nicht?   *Nein, wir gehen tanzen.*

1. *Montag:* Wir spielen Fußball, nicht? _____

2. *Dienstag:* Du spielst Schach, nicht? _____

3. *Mittwoch:* Gehst du heute Abend schwimmen? _____

4. *Donnerstag:* Gehen wir ins Kino? _____

5: *Samstag:* Spielen wir heute Morgen Tennis? _____

6. *Sonntag:* Du arbeitest heute viel, nicht? _____

H. Wer sind Sie? You're going to be an exchange student in Germany for a year. The study abroad agency wants you to provide information about yourself so that your German host family will know who you are and what you like to do. Complete the questionnaire they have sent.

Eigenschaften°   **Hobbies/Aktivitäten**   °characteristics

klein	freundlich	wandern		schwimmen
groß	ruhig	tanzen		Sport treiben
ernst	kritisch	Volleyball		schreiben
fleißig	praktisch	Tennis	spielen	Musik hören
tolerant	nett	Basketball		Gitarre spielen
intelligent	sportlich	Schach		Videospiele spielen
lustig	musikalisch	joggen		inlineskaten gehen

Wer sind Sie?

Adresse

Nachname: _____

Vorname(n)°: _____

Wohnort°: _____

Straße und Hausnummer: _____

Telefonnummer: _____

Alter°: _____

Persönlichkeit°

Welche Eigenschaften° haben Sie? _____

_____

Was machen Sie gern? _____

_____

Was machen Sie nicht gern? _____

_____

first name(s)

city

age

personality

character traits

I. Lieber° Thomas! Michael is back in Tübingen and is writing a brief note to his friend Thomas in Hamburg. Read the letter and answer the questions below.

dear

Lieber Thomas,

wie geht's? Heute ist Donnerstag und ich bin jetzt wieder° in Tübingen. Meine neue Adresse ist Pfleghofstraße 2, 72072 Tübingen. Meine Nachbarin heißt Gisela. Gisela studiert auch Englisch und sie ist sehr sympathisch und freundlich. Heute Abend um sieben Uhr spielen wir zusammen Schach. Und am Samstagnachmittag gehen Gisela, Alex und ich schwimmen und am Abend tanzen. Ich weiß°, du tanzt nicht gern. Aber ich tanze sehr gern. Oh je°, es ist schon° Viertel vor sieben und Gisela kommt in fünfzehn Minuten.

again

know

oh dear / already

Viele Grüße

dein° Michael

your

1. Wo ist Michael? _____

2. Welcher Tag ist heute? _____

3. Was machen Michael und Gisela heute Abend? _____

4. Wer geht am Samstag schwimmen und später tanzen? _____

5. Tanzt Thomas gern? _____

6. Wer kommt gleich°? _____

right away (in a minute)

J. *Kulturelle Notizen.* You plan to visit Germany, Austria, or Switzerland next year. To prepare for the trip, you keep a diary about cultural differences between these countries and the United States. Provide brief responses in English.

1. Give several reasons for the saying "Tübingen hat keine Universität. Tübingen ist eine Universität."

   _____

   _____

   _____

   _____

2. What are the general guidelines for using **du** and **Sie?** Is there a distinction between formal and informal forms of address in English?

   _____

   _____

   _____

3. Compare how people in Germany and people in your country may participate in competitive sports.

   _____

   _____

   _____

KAPITEL 2   Alles ist relativ

A. Das Wetter. You and your friends are talking about the weather. Finish the following dialogue with appropriate replies.

1. IHRE FREUNDIN: Schönes Wetter, nicht wahr?

   SIE: _____

2. IHR FREUND: Heute ist es wirklich kalt.

   SIE: _____

3. IHR FREUND: Vielleicht schneit es morgen.

   SIE: _____

4. IHRE FREUNDIN: Es sind nur drei Grad Celsius.

   SIE: _____

B. Wetterprobleme. Gisela and Monika are talking on the phone and they find out that the weather is quite different in Tübingen and in Berlin. Rewrite each sentence, beginning with the cued word. Be sure not to delete any of the original words in rewriting the sentences. Note that in one sentence you have to change the verb from present tense to simple past.

→   Das Wetter ist selten° schön. (im November)   seldom
    Im November ist das Wetter selten schön.

1. Der Wind ist sehr kalt. (in Berlin)

   _____

2. Es regnet in Berlin. (leider)

   _____

3. Es schneit bestimmt. (morgen)

   _____

4. Es ist sonnig und warm in Tübingen. (gestern)

   _____

5. Der Frühling kommt. (bald)

   _____

C. Was machst du (nicht) gern? Write down two things you like to do and two things you do not like to do. Then tell about your friends. The following expressions will give you some ideas.

> Gitarre spielen ■ Gewichte heben ■ joggen ■ Schach spielen ■ Tennis spielen ■ tanzen ■ wandern ■ arbeiten ■ Musik (Rock 'n Roll, Jazz, Rap) hören ■ schwimmen ■ Sport treiben ■ Basketball/Volleyball/Fußball spielen ■ Aerobic/Fitnesstraining machen ■ inlineskaten gehen ■ auf° eine Party gehen ■ auf ein Konzert gehen ■ ein Picknick machen

to

➜ *Ich jogge gern.*

1. _____

2. _____

➜ *Ich höre nicht gern Jazz.*

3. _____

4. _____

➜ *Meine Freunde heben gern Gewichte.*

5. _____

6. _____

D. Etwas über Deutschland. You have read a brochure about Germany and you exchange some facts with a friend in your German class. In each statement, underline the *subject* once. Some of the sentences contain a predicate noun. Underline each *predicate noun* twice.

➜ <u>Berlin</u> ist <u>die Hauptstadt</u> von Deutschland.

1. In Deutschland ist das Wetter anders als in Amerika.

2. Im Sommer ist es in Amerika oft sehr heiß.

3. In Deutschland ist der Sommer relativ kühl.

4. Österreich ist ein Nachbarland von Deutschland.

5. Im Süden von Deutschland liegt die Schweiz.

6. Die Deutschen spielen gern Fußball.

7. Gerhard Schröder ist der Bundeskanzler° von Deutschland.

chancellor

8. John F. Kennedy war im Sommer 1963 in Berlin.

> ## Es gibt kein schlechtes Wetter, nur falsche Kleidung°.

clothing

E. Wer hat was? Gisela, Alex, Uwe, Melanie, and Michael are comparing items in their apartments. Using the following chart, write statements about who owns how many of what. You will find the plural forms of the various nouns in the end vocabulary of your textbook.

	Gisela	Alex und Uwe	Melanie	Michael
das Bild	4	7	2	6
der Fernseher	—	2	1	2
das Telefon	1	2	1	—
das Buch	30	80	20	60
das Bett	1	2	1	1
der Computer	—	2	2	1
der Stuhl	2	4	3	4
das Videospiel	—	5	10	2

→   das Bild: Gisela; Michael   *Gisela hat vier Bilder. Michael hat sechs Bilder.*
→   das Telefon: Alex und Uwe   *Alex und Uwe haben zwei Telefone.*

1. das Buch: Alex und Uwe   _____

    _____

2. der Fernseher: Michael; Alex und Uwe   _____

    _____

3. das Videospiel: Melanie; Michael   _____

    _____

4. der Stuhl: Gisela; Michael   _____

    _____

5. der Computer: Alex und Uwe   _____

    _____

6. das Bett: Alex und Uwe; Gisela   _____

    _____

7. das Telefon: Melanie; Alex und Uwe   _____

    _____

F. Am Telefon. Monika and Stefan have started their first semester in Berlin and are sharing an apartment. Their mother calls to see how they have settled in. Complete their phone conversation with the correct form of the appropriate possessive adjectives: **mein, ihr, sein, unser, euer, ihr.** In one blank, you'll use the possessive form of **Alex.**

FRAU BERGER: Und was macht ihr zwei, du und Stefan? Seid ihr glück-

lich in Berlin? Wie sind ____eure____ Zimmer?

MONIKA: _____[1] Zimmer ist schön und ich bin sehr froh.

Stefan ist nicht so glücklich. _____[2] Zimmer ist

relativ groß, aber ein bisschen laut. Es geht zur Straße°.

Es ... Straße: It faces the street

FRAU BERGER: Und wie ist euer Garten?

MONIKA: _____[3] Garten ist toll! Leider sind

_____[4] Nachbarn nicht so nett. Sie denken, es

ist nur _____[5] Garten. Das ist aber falsch.

FRAU BERGER: Was hörst du von Gisela in Tübingen? Geht es ihr gut?

MONIKA: Ja, alles okay. … nur _____[6] Zimmer ist etwas

klein.

FRAU BERGER: Hat sie nette Freunde in Tübingen?

MONIKA: Ja, _____[7] Freund Alex ist sehr nett. Alex ist

schon° drei Jahre in Tübingen. Er und _____[8]

already

Freunde machen viel. Und Gisela ist oft dabei°.

ist dabei: goes along

_____[9] Freunde sind jetzt schon

_____[10] Freunde.

FRAU BERGER: Das ist schön. Und du und Stefan? Wie sind

_____[11] Freunde?

MONIKA: _____[12] Freunde sind auch sehr nett. …

Ist der Oktober warm und fein,
kommt ein harter Winter rein°
Ist der Oktober aber nass und kühl,
mild der Winter werden will°.

in

werden will: will be

G. Ja, so ist es. Michael is home in Hamburg for the weekend, where he meets his friend Thomas. They have kept in touch by e-mail since Michael went to Tübingen, so Thomas knows quite a bit about Michael's life and friends there. They are looking at pictures that Michael took in Tübingen and Thomas is commenting on them. Take Michael's place and respond in the affirmative, replacing the noun phrase with the corresponding *demonstrative pronoun*.

➔ Alex ist sehr sportlich, nicht?   *Ja, der ist sehr sportlich.*

1. Dein Zimmer ist ziemlich klein, nicht?

   Ja, _____.

2. Gisela studiert auch Englisch, nicht?

   Ja, _____.

3. Deine Freunde gehen oft tanzen, nicht?

   Ja, _____.

4. David kommt aus Washington, D.C., nicht?

   Ja, _____.

5. Die Uni ist relativ groß, nicht?

   Ja, _____.

6. Die Stadt ist ziemlich klein, nicht?

   Ja, _____.

H. Stefans Zimmer. Stefan has not completely furnished his room in Berlin. From the list below state which items are there and which are not. Remember to include the correct form of **ein** or **kein** with each item.

~~Bett~~ ■ ~~Bild~~ ■ Bücherregal ■ Computer ■ Fernseher ■ Gitarre ■ Lampe ■ Pflanze ■ Radio ■ Stuhl ■ Tisch ■ Uhr

1. Im Zimmer von Stefan ist *ein Bett* ,

   _____ ,

   _____ ,

   _____ und

   _____ .

2. Im Zimmer ist *kein Bild* , _____ , _____

   _____ , und _____ .

I. Wie ist das Wetter? Wie viel Grad ist es? Have a look at the weather map below and familiarize yourself with the symbols. Then answer the questions in complete sentences.

heiter	*pleasant*	bewölkt	*partly cloudy*	bedeckt	*cloudy*
Nebel	*fog*	Schauer	*showers*	Gewitter	*thunderstorms*

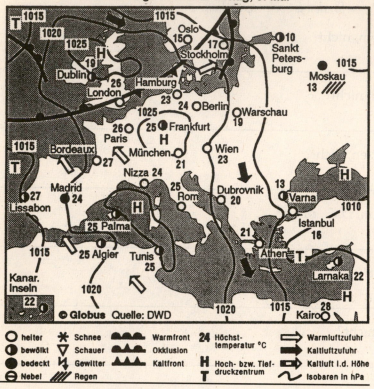

Heute noch warm und trocken, allmähliche Bewölkungszunahme

Vorhersage für heute Mittag, 5. Mai

→ Wie ist das Wetter in Moskau?   *Es ist in Moskau bedeckt. / In Moskau ist es bedeckt.*
→ Wie viel Grad sind es in Paris?   *Es sind in Paris 26 Grad. / In Paris sind es 26 Grad.*

1. Wie ist das Wetter in München? _____

2. Wie viel Grad sind es in Hamburg? _____

3. Wie ist das Wetter in Frankfurt? _____

4. Wie viel Grad sind es in Oslo? _____

5. Wo regnet es? _____

6. Wo ist es sehr warm? _____

7. In Berlin sind es 24 Grad. Wie viel Grad Fahrenheit sind das? *(Use the quick estimate.)* _____

_____

J. Deutsche Städte. Identify the five rivers° and fifteen cities marked on the   **Flüsse**
map of Germany. Refer to the map on the inside cover of your textbook as
necessary.

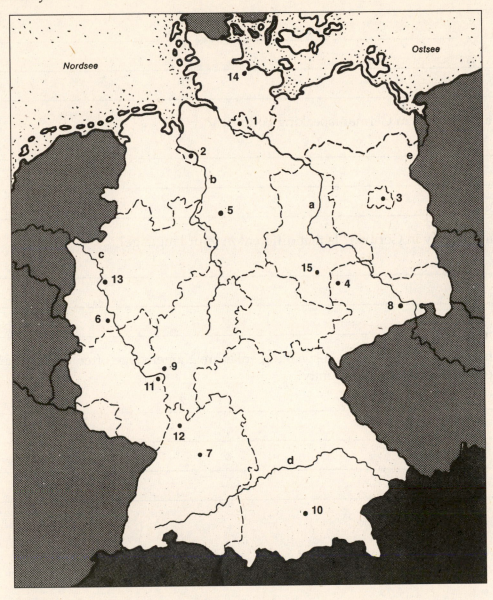

Flüsse   **Städte**

a. _____   1. _____   6. _____   11. _____

b. _____   2. _____   7. _____   12. _____

c. _____   3. _____   8. _____   13. _____

d. _____   4. _____   9. _____   14. _____

e. _____   5. _____   10. _____   15. _____

K. *Kulturelle Notizen.* In preparation for your trip to a German-speaking country, you go on taking notes about cultural and political aspects of these countries. Provide brief responses in English.

1. List several things you find interesting about Berlin.

   _____

   _____

   _____

   _____

2. When is **Hochdeutsch** used in German-speaking countries?

   _____

   _____

   _____

3. What role do dialects play in German? Is that different in your language?

   _____

   _____

   _____

4. What are **Namenstage?** In which German-speaking areas are **Namenstage** often celebrated? Are such days celebrated in your community?

   _____

   _____

   _____

   _____

Berlin ist eine Reise wert°.

eine ... wert: worth a trip

KAPITEL 3   Was brauchst du?

A. Wo kauft man was? Monika and Stefan are preparing for the visit of Diane and Joan. They need to stock up on their food and household supplies. Make up their shopping list, organizing it by store and item. For each store, list at least three items they can purchase there.

Apfelsaft	Brötchen	Hähnchen	Käse	Obst	Spaghetti
Aspirin	Butter	Hefte	Kuchen	Orangensaft	Tomaten
Bananen	Eier	Kaffee	Make-up	Rinderbraten	Trauben
Bier	Fernseher	Kämme	Margarine	Salat	Videospiele
Bleistifte	Gemüse	Karotten	Milch	Schinken	Wein
Brot	Gurken	Kartoffeln	Nudeln	Shampoo	Wurst

Beim Bäcker

Brötchen
_____
_____

Beim Metzger

_____
_____
_____

In der Drogerie

_____
_____
_____

Im Supermarkt

_____
_____

Auf dem Markt

_____
_____

Im Kaufhaus

_____
_____

B. Neue Wörter. Expand your newly acquired vocabulary without learning new words by forming a compound from each pair of nouns. Write the compound with its definite article and give the English equivalent.

		Compound	English Equivalent
→ der Kaffee und das Haus	_das_	_Kaffeehaus_	_coffee shop, café_
1. die Wand und die Uhr	_____	_____	_____
2. die Butter und das Brot	_____	_____	_____
3. der Sommer und der Abend	_____	_____	_____
4. der Frühling (+ s) und der Tag	_____	_____	_____
5. das Haus und die Tür	_____	_____	_____
6. der Herbst und der Wind	_____	_____	_____
7. der Geburtstag (+ s) und das Kind	_____	_____	_____

C. Im Café Engel. You and a friend are having breakfast at the Café Engel and are looking at the menu. Complete the following conversation between you and your friend. You may choose responses from the list provided or make up your own.

Bäckerei Café Engel
Odenthalerstraße 14
51465 Bergisch Gladbach

Frühstück

Nr. 1
Tasse Kaffee oder Schokolade, 1 Brötchen, Brot, Butter und
Marmelade oder ein Käsebrötchen .... 4.20 Euro

Nr. 2
Kännchen Kaffee, Tee oder Schokolade, 2 Brötchen, Brot,
Butter, Marmelade und ein Glas Orangensaft .... 8.40 Euro

Nr. 3
Milchkaffee, 2 Croissants, Butter, Marmelade und ein Glas Orangensaft........ 6.80 Euro

Nr. 4
Tasse Kaffee, Tee oder Schokolade, Müsli mit Jogurt und frischem Obst .... 7.30 Euro

Nr. 5
Kännchen Kaffee, Tee oder Schokolade, 2 Brötchen, 1 Croissant, Butter,
Marmelade, 2 Eier, Käse, Schinken .... 9.20 Euro

Possible responses:

Ja, ich auch.
Bist du so hungrig°?
Nein, ich trinke keinen Tee.
Ich glaube, ich nehme die
   Nr. 5.

Ja, bitte. Ich trinke gern Apfelsaft.
Aber du magst doch keine Würstchen!   hungry
Ich nehme die Nr. 1. – Kaffee und ein
   Käsebrötchen.
Ich mag schon Orangensaft. Aber
   morgens noch nicht.

1. IHR FREUND: Hmmm, es riecht hier toll nach frischen Brötchen. Was nimmst du?

   SIE: _____

2. IHR FREUND: Das ist aber nicht viel. Ich glaube ich nehme Nr. 3. Ich esse sehr gern

   Croissants. Aber Orangensaft mag ich nicht. Möchtest du ihn?

   SIE: _____

3. IHR FREUND: Hmmm, dann nehme ich vielleicht Nr. 5.

   SIE: _____

4. IHR FREUND: Ja, und ich brauche jetzt auch schnell einen Kaffee.

   SIE: _____

Name _____   Datum _____

D. Gespräche. Diane and Joan are visiting Monika and Stefan in Berlin, and they are talking about all kinds of things. Complete their conversations by choosing the appropriate verb from the list. Use it in the correct form, which may be either *present tense* or *imperative*. Note that some verbs change their stem-vowel.

essen ■ finden ■ fragen ■ geben ■ haben ■ kommen ■ nehmen ■ sein

➜ DIANE: Stefan, isst du oft Salat?

1. STEFAN: Monika, _____ du mir° bitte das Brot?   me

   MONIKA: _____ du Weißbrot oder Brötchen?

   STEFAN: _____ mir bitte das Weißbrot.

2. STEFAN: Was _____ es morgen zum Abendessen?

   MONIKA: Vielleicht Fisch. _____ ihr gern Fisch, Joan

   und Diane?

   JOAN: Ja, ich _____ gerne Fisch, aber Diane

   _____ Fisch nicht so gern.

3. JOAN: Ich _____ Kopfschmerzen.

   DIANE: _____ doch eine Tablette.

   JOAN: Ich _____ leider kein Aspirin hier.

   STEFAN: _____ mal Monika. Sie _____ immer

   Kopfschmerztabletten.

4. MONIKA: Wie _____ ihr Berlin eigentlich?

   JOAN: Ich _____ es toll und so interessant. Aber eine

   Woche hier _____ einfach nicht genug. In vier Tagen

   _____ wir schon wieder in Chicago. ... oh je.

   DIANE: _____ nicht sentimental, Joan! Wir

   _____ doch mal wieder nach Berlin.

   JOAN: Natürlich. Wir _____ immer gern Besuch!

Der Appetit kommt beim Essen.

E. Beim Einkaufen. Monika and Stefan are visiting Gisela in Tübingen and they go grocery shopping together. Underline each *subject* once and each *direct object* twice.

➔ Im türkischen Laden kennt <u>man</u> <u>Gisela</u>.

1. Gisela findet Herrn Özmir nett.

2. GISELA: Haben Sie den Käse aus der Türkei, Herr Özmir?

3. HERR ÖZMIR: Ja, wie viel Gramm Käse möchten Sie, Frau Riedholt?

4. Gisela, Monika und Stefan brauchen auch Kaffee, Butter und Marmelade aus dem

   Supermarkt.

5. Auf dem Markt bezahlt Monika die Blumen.

6. Dort kauft Gisela noch Fisch fürs Abendessen.

F. Der Nachbar. Gisela is visiting her parents in Mainz. While Gisela and her father are sitting on the balcony, the son of the new neighbor leaves his house. Gisela's father tells Gisela a little about him. Complete each sentence with the correct form of the word or phrase in parentheses.

GISELA: Kennst du _den Jungen_ da? (der Junge) Er geht durch

_____[1]. (unser Garten)

HERR RIEDHOLT: Ja, er ist seit Januar _____[2]. (unser Nachbar)

GISELA: Findest du _____[3] nett? (dein Nachbar)

HERR RIEDHOLT: Nein, nicht sehr.

GISELA: Aber er ist doch sympathisch, nicht? Was hast du denn gegen

_____[4]? (euer Nachbar)

HERR RIEDHOLT: Ich finde _____[5] ein bisschen unfreundlich. (er) Er sagt nie

„Guten Tag". Er geht nie ohne _____[6] aus dem Haus. (sein

CD-Player) Und die Musik ist immer sehr laut. Hmm, jetzt geht er schon

wieder um _____[7]. (unser Haus)

GISELA: Und _____[8] findest du eigentlich nett hier in der Straße?

(wer)

G. Was gibt's zum Abendessen? Michael and Gisela's dormitory has a kitchen where they often prepare meals together. They have invited Alex for dinner and while shopping they debate about the meal. Negate the italicized words by using **nicht** or a form of **kein**.

➔ MICHAEL: Im Supermarkt finde ich Wurst und Fleisch *gut*.
  Im Supermarkt finde ich Wurst und Fleisch nicht gut.

➔ GISELA: Aber es gibt hier *eine* Metzgerei.
  Aber es gibt hier keine Metzgerei.

Name _____   Datum _____

1. MICHAEL: Gisela, Alex isst doch *Würstchen*.

   _____

2. GISELA: Ach ja, und er trinkt auch *Bier*.

   _____

3. MICHAEL: Isst er *gern* Spaghetti?

   _____

4. GISELA: Ja, das stimmt. Also gut, dann kaufen wir *Würstchen*.

   _____

5. MICHAEL: Kaufen wir Spaghetti und Tomatensoße. Die macht Alex oft zu Hause. Und in der Mensa finde ich sie *gut*.

   _____

6. GISELA: Okay. *Bezahlst* du heute die Lebensmittel?

   _____

7. MICHAEL: Oh je, ich finde mein Geld nicht. Hast du *Geld*, Gisela?

   _____

H. Im Café. After class students often have coffee together in the student cafeteria. Complete their various conversations with the appropriate personal pronouns or possessive adjectives. Use nominative or accusative case as required. One blank requires nothing.

➔ FRANCO: Trinkst du dein*en*___ Kaffee nicht?
   SANDRA: Nein, möchtest du ___*ihn*___ trinken?

1. GISELA: Michael, du bezahlst immer unser_____ Getränke. Heute bezahle ich

   _____ mal.

   MICHAEL: Ja, gern. Danke. _____ kosten 5,60 Euro.

2. MIRIAM: Christian, isst du dein_____ Kuchen nicht?

   CHRISTIAN: Nein, ich mag _____ nicht. Er ist zu trocken. Möchtest du

   _____ essen?

   MIRIAM: Au ja, ich nehme _____ gern.

3. BRIAN: Oh, da ist ja Davids Freundin. Wie findest du _____?

   CLAUDIA: Hmm, ich finde _____ nicht so sympathisch.

   SYBILLE: Ich kenne _____ von der Uni. _____ ist ein bisschen reserviert,

   aber sehr nett.

4. JANE: Tom, brauchst du heute Abend dein_____ Deutschbuch?

   TOM: Nein, ich brauche _____ nicht. Warum fragst du? Wo

   hast du dein Buch?

   JANE: Frag _____ nicht. Seit drei Tagen suche _____

   es schon. Ich glaube, _____ ist weg°.   gone

5. MICHAEL: Anja und Tim, da seid _____ ja! Gisela sucht

   _____.

   ANJA: Warum sucht sie _____ denn?

   MICHAEL: Ich glaube, sie braucht eur_____ Telefonnummern.

                                                                         main train station

I. Hauptbahnhof° Tübingen. Look at this ad for the **Hauptbahnhof Tübingen,** a place where one can eat and attend cultural events. Answer the following questions.

H·A·U·P·T
Bahnhof
Gastronomie & Kultur

Europaplatz 19
72072 Tübingen
Tel. 07071/31816

täglich von
10.00 - 2.00 Uhr
geöffnet

• jeden Freitag Live Musik
• Täglich Frühstück von 10 bis 14 Uhr
• Sonntags großes Frühstücksbuffet
• Durchgehend warme Küche von 10 bis 24 Uhr
• täglich wechselnder Mittagstisch, auch vegetarisch, für € 5,00 und € 5,50
• Große Auswahl an frischen Salaten

1. Was gibt es immer freitags? _____

2. Von wann bis wann gibt es warmes Essen? _____

3. Was kostet ein Mittagessen? _____

4. Gibt es auch Essen ohne Fleisch? _____

5. Wann gibt es ein großes Frühstücksbuffet? _____

6. Welchen Tag finden Sie persönlich im Hauptbahnhof interessant? Warum?

   _____

J. Am Telefon. You and a friend are studying together and you are getting hungry. To save time you call a restaurant that has take-out sevice. Complete the following conversation between you and the person at the restaurant by writing the missing German words in the blanks.

—Was für Essen haben Sie denn heute? _____[1] Fisch? *(Is there)*

—Nein, heute haben wir leider _____[2]. *(no fish)*

—_____[3] nicht? *(Why)*

—Fisch haben wir nur _____[4]. _____[5]

   haben wir immer nur ganz frische Produkte. *(on Fridays and Saturdays / At Jeanette's)*

—Was haben Sie sonst?

—_____[6] sind sehr gut. _____[7] vielleicht Tortellini

   oder Spaghetti mit Käsesauce? Und Salat? Unser Frühlingssalat ist sehr gut. *(Our noodles /*

   Would you like)

—Gut, dann _____[8] zwei Portionen Tortellini, bitte. Aber

   _____[9], bitte. *(we'll take / without salad)*

K. Viele Fragen. While David and Alex are shopping together, David asks a number of questions about Alex's shopping and eating habits. Write down Alex's answers, using *demonstrative pronouns* to replace the direct object. Follow the model below.

➔   Findest du den Supermarkt gut? (Ja)   *Ja, den finde ich gut.*

1. Kaufst du das Brot beim Bäcker? (Ja)

    _____

2. Nimmst du den Kaffee aus Kolumbien? (Nein)

    _____

3. Magst du das Obst aus Spanien? (Ja)

    _____

4. Gibst du mir bitte den Geldbeutel°? (Ja)   wallet

    _____

5. Bekommst du die Blumen im Supermarkt? (Nein)

    _____

6. Isst du die Wurst zum Frühstück? (Nein)

_____

7. Brauchst du die Tabletten gegen Kopfschmerzen? (Ja)

_____

8. Kennst du die Metzgerei bei der Uni? (Nein)

_____

L. Hamburger, Currywurst oder Döner? Read the following text on fast food in Germany and answer the questions below. Some of the information appeared in the online edition of the German newspaper "taz."

Döner – Fastfood Nummer eins

Auch in Deutschland ist Fastfood populär. Hamburger isst man gern bei McDonald's oder bei Burger King. McDonald's ist mit 1200 Restaurants die Nummer 1 und Burger King mit 300 Restaurants die Nummer 2 in Deutschland. Und dann gibt es natürlich das traditionelle deutsche Fastfood, die Brat- oder Currywurst. Aber seit° ein paar Jahren ist der Döner das Fastfood Nummer 1. Döner – das ist eine Tasche aus Pitabrot, gefüllt mit gegrilltem Fleisch, Zwiebeln°, Tomaten, Salat und Knoblauch°-Jogurtsauce.

Der Döner entstand° vor etwa 160 Jahren° in der Türkei. 1971 machte° der 16jährige Migrant° Mehmet Aygün in Berlin den ersten° Döner und verkaufte° ihn in einer kleinen Imbissbude°.

1983 gab° es in Berlin schon etwa 200 Dönerverkaufsstellen°, Ende der 90er-Jahre 1300. Bald kam° der Döner-Boom auch in andere große Städte wie Frankfurt, Hamburg, Köln und München, dann auch in kleine Städte. Die Deutschen lieben° ihren Döner über alles und pro Jahr isst man in Deutschland etwa 720 Millionen Dönersandwiches. Ein Döner kostet etwa € 2,50 und hat 550 Kalorien. Guten Appetit!

since

onions / garlic

originated / **vor ... Jahren:** about 160 years ago / made / immigrant / first / sold / snack stand

there were / Döner shops and stands / came

love

1. Was für Gemüse braucht man für einen Döner?

_____

2. Was ist populärer? Döner oder Currywurst?

_____

3. Wann gab es den ersten Döner in Berlin?

_____

4. Wer machte ihn?

_____

5. Wie viele Dönerverkaufsstellen gab es 1983 in Berlin?

_____

6. Wie viele Dönersandwiches isst man in Deutschland pro Jahr?

_____

7. Was kostet ein Döner?

_____

8. Wie viele Kalorien hat er?

_____

M. *Kulturelle Notizen.* You plan to visit Germany, Austria, or Switzerland next year. To prepare for the trip, you keep a diary about cultural differences between these countries and the United States. Provide brief responses in English.

1. Name several practices connected to shopping in a German supermarket that are different from those in the store where you shop.

_____

_____

2. Name two things you would find particularly enjoyable about shopping at an outdoor market in a German-speaking country.

_____

_____

3. State two differences between weekend shopping hours in Germany and in your community.

_____

_____

KAPITEL 4   Was studierst du?

A. Fragen. David's American friend, Mark, has come for a visit. Mark would like to study at Tübingen University. So David has arranged for him to talk to his German friends Gisela and Michael. Form Mark's questions using the cues below.

➔ ihr / möchten / arbeiten / im Sommer / ?   *Möchtet ihr im Sommer arbeiten?*

1. du / mögen / Tübingen / ?

   _____

2. ihr / dürfen / studieren / zehn Semester / ?

   _____

3. Studenten / müssen / schreiben / viele Klausuren / ?

   _____

4. man / müssen / zurückzahlen / BAföG / ?

   _____

5. du / möchten / studieren / in Amerika / ?

   _____

6. wir / sollen / gehen / jetzt / in die Bibliothek / ?

   _____

B. Was machst du gern abends? Michael, Alex, and Gisela are talking about what they do when they want to relax in the evening. Complete their conversation by choosing the appropriate verb in the correct form.

   lesen ■ sehen ■ werden ■ wissen

➔ MICHAEL: _Liest_ du gern Romane, Alex?

1. ALEX: Was macht ihr abends immer, Michael und Gisela? _____ ihr oft fern?

2. MICHAEL: Nein, ich _____ nicht oft fern. Vom Fernsehen _____

   ich immer so müde. Ich _____ aber sehr viel. Krimis mag ich zum Beispiel

   sehr gern.

3. GISELA: Ich muss immer viel für Deutsch und Englisch _____. Ich

   _____ manchmal ganz nervös! Im Literaturstudium muss man so viele

   Romane kennen! Und du, Alex? _____ du manchmal ein Buch oder

   _____ du viel fern?

4. ALEX: Ich _____ eigentlich gern fern. _____ ihr eigentlich,

was heute Abend im Fernsehen kommt?

5. MICHAEL: Nein, ich _____ es nicht. Und ich spiele auch lieber Gitarre oder

_____ meinen Krimi fertig.

C. Wer ist denn das? You are showing family photos to your roommate. From your
account, she knows a lot about your family, but she mixes up most of the information.
Correct the mistaken identifications as you wish. Then supply your own answers concerning professions and nationality. (You may refer to the Supplementary Word Sets in
Appendix C in your textbook.)

→ Ist das deine Kusine?   *Nein, das ist meine Tante.*
  Ist sie Sozialarbeiterin?   *Nein, sie ist Professorin.*

1. Ist das dein Bruder?   _____

   Ist er Ingenieur?   _____

2. Das ist deine Mutter, nicht?   _____

   Ist sie Spanierin?   _____

3. Sind das deine zwei Vettern?   _____

   Sind sie Elektriker?   _____

4. Ist das dein Onkel?   _____

   Ist er Deutscher oder Schweizer?   _____

5. Das ist deine Kusine, nicht?   _____

   Was will sie werden?   _____

D. Weißt du, wo …? Claudia is in her first semester at Tübingen and would like to take an English literature course next semester. While looking for the English department, she is happy to run into Alex and Michael who have been there for several semesters. Complete their conversation with the correct form of **wissen** or **kennen**.

CLAUDIA: Alex, du _____¹ die Uni doch gut.

_____² du, wo die Englische Fakultät ist?

ALEX: Ich bin nicht sicher°, aber ich glaube, sie ist im Brecht-Bau. Du   sure

_____³ doch den Brecht-Bau, nicht?

MICHAEL: Dort habe ich gleich eine Vorlesung, Claudia. Komm doch mit!

Ich _____⁴ auch viele Anglistikprofessoren.

Ich habe vielleicht ein paar Tipps für dich. Professor Weyrich

ist besonders nett.

CLAUDIA: Ich _____⁵ Professor Weyrich nicht, aber ich

_____⁶ sein Buch über Englische Literatur.

_____⁷ ihr, wo die Bibliothek ist? Ich möchte

sein Buch gern leihen.

E. In der Mensa°. During coffee break after their seminars, students usu-   university cafeteria
ally talk about their courses and related matters. Complete the following
conversations by using an appropriate **der**-word in the correct form.

der-words: dies- ■ jed- ■ welch- ■ manch- ■ solch-

➔ BIRGIT: Wie findest du ____*diesen*____ Professor für Englische Literatur?

KARIN: ____*Welchen*____ Professor meinst du – Thompson oder Baumeister?

1. MARK: Viele Studenten machen Germanistik als Hauptfach. Aber

_____ Studenten nehmen Deutsch nur als Nebenfach.

WIEBKE: Weißt du, was _____ Studenten einmal° werden   later

wollen? Als Lehrer° am Gymnasium braucht man doch Germanistik   teacher

als Hauptfach.

2. SIMONE: Ich glaube, ich bereite kein Referat für _____ Seminar vor.

NILS: Hmmm, ich glaube, _____ Student muss ein Referat

vorbereiten.

SIMONE: Ach so.

3. AISHA: Findest du _____ Vorlesung in Biochemie auch so

   schwer?

   GIULIANO: Ja, aber _____ Fächer sind immer kompliziert.

4. BETTINA: In _____ Seminararbeit über deutsche Literatur

   hat Thomas eine eins°. _____ Noten möchte ich auch mal   one (the highest grade)

   haben.

   LARS: Na ja, aber er sitzt ja auch _____ Tag in der

   Bibliothek.

   BETTINA: Ja, _____ Leute arbeiten wirklich viel für ihr

   Studium.

F. Musst du arbeiten? Melanie and Gisela are talking about the work they have to do for
their German class. Express their conversation by using the cues below.

1. was / du / machen / heute Nachmittag / ?

   MELANIE: Hallo Gisela. _____

2. ich / müssen / schreiben / einen Artikel für mein Referat

   GISELA: _____ Und du?

3. ich / müssen / lesen / ein Buch für mein Referat

   MELANIE: _____

4. du / möchten / zusammen / arbeiten / ?

   GISELA: _____

5. dann / ich / kommen / um drei in die Bibliothek

   MELANIE: Gern. _____

6. und danach° / wir / können / spazieren gehen   afterwards

   GISELA: _____

7. leider / ich / müssen / durcharbeiten / meine Vorlesungsnotizen

   MELANIE: _____

8. aber / später / wir / fernsehen / zusammen

   GISELA: _____ Okay?

G. Ferien mit der Familie. Look at the following ad and complete the discussion between the family members based on the information that you find here.

Ihre **Frau möchte** Thalasso° Massagen und Dampfbäder° Ihr **Sohn will** Tennis spielen. Ihre **Tochter will** reiten° **sie wollen** golfen. Jetzt gibt's zwei Alternativen: Familienkrach° oder **Land Fleesensee.**

treatment that uses sea water and algae to cleanse the body cells

steam baths

ride

family quarrel

VATER: Was sollen wir denn in den Sommerferien machen? Wisst ihr schon, was ihr gern machen wollt?

MUTTER: _____

VATER: _____

TOCHTER: Das ist doch langweilig. Ich _____

SOHN: Das finde ich _____. Ich _____

_____

MUTTER: Seht, hier habe ich Informationen über Land Fleesensee.

VATER: _____

TOCHTER: _____

H. Ich brauche deine Notizen. Write a note to Ina asking if she can lend you her lecture notes. Tell her you have to prepare your report, and that you were sick yesterday and still have a lot to do. Ask if she can bring the notes along tomorrow.

Liebe Ina,

_____

_____

_____

_____

dein/deine

_____

I. Deutsch oder amerikanisch? Decide which system of higher education and which culture each of the following statements describes. Write **a** for **amerikanisch** or **d** for **deutsch** in each blank.

1. _____ An den Unis gibt es viele Studentenjobs.

2. _____ Es gibt zu wenig Studienplätze.

3. _____ Es gibt viele Privatuniversitäten.

4. _____ Viele Professoren kontrollieren, welche Studenten in der Vorlesung anwesend° sind.   present

5. _____ Fast° alle Studenten müssen Kurse wie Englisch und Geschichte nehmen.   almost

6. _____ Es gibt keine Studiengebühren.

7. _____ Nur wenige Kurse haben jedes Semester Prüfungen.

8. _____ Man studiert nur ein oder zwei Fächer.

J. An der Uni Heidelberg. Your friend Jonathan is going to the University of Heidelberg for a year to study German Literature. Together, you look at the course schedule he has received from the German Department. Help him find classes that would be interesting for him. You will not be able to understand every word, but try to guess the general meaning of the entries from the words that you do know and the ones that are similar in English.

VORLESUNGSVERZEICHNIS				
STUDIENBERATUNG°: Dr. Peter Gebhardt, Raum 026, Do. 11-13 Uhr und n. V.				advisor
ALLGEMEINE° UND VERGLEICHENDE° LITERATURWISSENSCHAFT°				general / comparative / literary studies
V	Theater des 20. Jahrhunderts, 2st. Prof. Harth	Di	11.00-13.00 NUni HS 10	
OS	Die großen Filmregisseure° (II): Cocteau, Greenaway, Lynch, 4st. Prof. Gerigk, Dr. Hurst	Mi	10.00-21.00 PB SR 137	film directors
HpS	Komparatistische Forschungen°. Literatur und Musik, 2st. Prof. Harth	Mo	16.00-18.00 PB 133	research
HpS	Literatur und Holocaust 2st.	Mo	9.00-11.00 PB 038	

1. Jonathan geht gern ins Theater. Welche Vorlesung kann er besuchen°?   attend

_____

2. Wann ist diese Vorlesung und wie heißt der Professor?

_____

_____

3. Welchen Kurs gibt es über Filme?

_____

4. Welches Seminar finden Sie interessant?

_____

5. An welchem Tag ist das Seminar und wer ist der Professor?

_____

_____

K. Als Student in Dresden. The following account is by the exchange student Benoît who has lived in several countries and is now studying in Dresden. Read the text and answer the following questions.

Benoît, 21, Informatikstudent aus Frankreich: „Ich bin Franzose, aber ich studiere seit einem Jahr in Boston in den USA. In Dresden bin ich für ein Semester. Ich wohne hier in einem Studentenwohnheim und teile° mir mit drei Kommilitonen° eine Wohnung°. Dort bereite ich mir morgens in der Küche° mein Frühstück zu°. Selten° habe ich dafür länger als 5–10 Minuten

share
classmates / apartment
kitchen / **bereite zu:** prepare /
seldom

Frühstück bei Benoît im Studentenwohnheim

Zeit. Ich nehme fertigen Instant-Cappuccino, auf den ich nur heißes Wasser schütten° muss. Dazu gibt es Cornflakes mit frischer Milch. Sie ist in den USA besser, denn da gibt es spezielle Frühstücksmilch. Nach dem Abitur habe ich ein Jahr lang in Thailand gelebt°. Dort gab es morgens zum Frühstück Tintenfischsuppe°. Daran muss man sich erst einmal gewöhnen°! […]

pour

habe gelebt: lived
squid soup / **daran sich ge-**
wöhnen: get accustomed to

In Dresden esse ich mittags häufig° in der Mensa. Das Essen dort ist gut und billig. In den USA kostet das gleiche° Mensa-Essen 4-mal so viel. Außerdem stehen hier immer wieder typisch deutsche Gerichte° auf dem Speiseplan°. Ich persönlich finde zum Beispiel Schweinebraten° mit Rotkohl° und Klößen° sehr originell. Oft esse ich auf die Schnelle° einen Döner, den man in Dresden für wenig Geld fast an jeder Ecke° bekommt. Wenn ich mal ausgehe, dann abends mit Freunden, zum Italiener. Pizza mag ich nämlich ziemlich gerne! […]

Was mir in Deutschland fehlt°? Frisches Baguette wie in Frankreich!"

often
same
dishes / menu
roast pork / sour red cabbage
*dumplings / **auf die Schnelle**: on the run / corner*

miss

1. Was macht Benoît in Dresden?

   _____

2. Wo wohnt er dort?

   _____

3. Was ist sein Frühstück? Was isst und trinkt er?

   _____

   _____

4. Wie findet Benoît das Mensaessen in Dresden? Und in Amerika?

   _____

   _____

5. Was isst Benoît gern? Nennen Sie ein paar Essen, die Benoît mag.

   _____

   _____

6. Welche Länder kennt Benoît ganz gut? Machen Sie eine Liste und sagen Sie kurz, welche Verbindung° er zu jedem Land hat.

   connection

   Land   **Verbindung**

   _____*Deutschland*_____   _____*ist für ein Semester in Dresden*_____

   _____   _____

   _____   _____

L. *Kulturelle Notizen.* You plan to go to Germany as an exchange student, so you write down important information about the educational system there in contrast to your country. Provide brief responses in English.

1. Define the following types of classes briefly: **Vorlesung, Übung, Seminar.**

    _____

    _____

    _____

2. How good are your chances of being accepted at a German university? What would your costs be? Could you possibly take courses that are taught in English?

    _____

    _____

    _____

3. What is **BAföG?** Does your country have a similar law?

    _____

    _____

4. Name three reasons for Hamburg's position as one of the major cities of Germany.

    _____

    _____

Hansestadt Hamburg

KAPITEL 5   Servus in Österreich

A. Pläne. Gisela is going to Austria on her semester break. She and Alex are talking about her plans. Complete their conversation and add *articles* and *prepositions* as necessary.

➜   ALEX: du / haben / Pläne / für / Ferien / ?   *Hast du Pläne für die Ferien?*

GISELA: ja, / ich / fahren / nach / Österreich

_____

ALEX: du / fahren / mit / Zug / ?

_____

GISELA: nein, / ich / fliegen

_____

ALEX: wann / du / kommen / wieder / Hause / ?

_____

GISELA: ich / wissen / noch nicht

_____

B. Identifizieren Sie. David and Michael are talking on the phone. For the following sentences, underline each *independent clause* once and each *dependent clause* twice.

1. Weißt du, dass Gisela in den Ferien nach Italien fährt?

2. Fährt sie denn mit dem Zug oder fliegt sie?

3. Ich glaube, dass sie mit dem Zug fahren will.

4. Das ist sicher schön, weil sie dann viel vom Land sieht.

5. Ich hoffe, dass du heute noch vorbeikommen kannst.

6. Wenn Alex mir sein Auto leiht, komme ich gegen drei Uhr.

7. Um vier ist besser, denn ich muss noch in die Bibliothek.

8. Ich möchte ja gern kommen, aber um vier habe ich leider eine Vorlesung.

C. Ungarn. Ilona lives in Hungary, but she has relatives in several other European countries. Complete the sentences with **aber** or **sondern,** as appropriate.

1. Ilonas Großeltern kommen nicht aus Ungarn, _____ aus Österreich.

2. Ilona kann den österreichischen Dialekt verstehen, _____ sie kann ihn nicht gut sprechen.

3. Ihre Tante wohnt noch in Wien, _____ ihr Vetter wohnt jetzt in der Schweiz.

4. In den Ferien arbeitet Ilona nicht in Budapest, _____ sie fährt nach Wien und nach Salzburg.

D. Studium in England. Michael plans to study in London next year. For each of the numbered sentences 1–6 find the correct supplementary sentence in the list below. Combine the two sentences using the conjunctions **dass, wenn,** or **weil,** as appropriate.

> Busfahren findet er zu teuer.
> Er kann in England studieren.
> Er braucht Geld.
> Er macht ein gutes Examen.
> Er möchte besser Englisch lernen.
> Er hat genug Geld.
> Er will in Tübingen sein Examen machen.

→ Michael jobbt im Sommer.
  Michael jobbt im Sommer, weil er Geld braucht.

1. Er geht jetzt immer zu Fuß.

   _____

2. Im Herbst studiert er in London.

   _____

3. Es ist toll.

   _____

4. Er bleibt ein ganzes Jahr.

   _____

5. Nach dem Jahr in London kommt er nach Tübingen zurück.

   _____

6. Er findet vielleicht einen guten Job bei einer Exportfirma.

   _____

Name _____ Datum _____

E. Akkusativ and Dativ. For each of the following sentences identify the *subject*, the *direct object*, and the *indirect object* (when present), and write them into the following chart.

Sachertorte

1. Meine Mutter bringt mir aus Wien eine Sachertorte° mit.   famous Viennese cake
2. Hmm, darf ich die Torte dann auch versuchen?
3. Vielleicht kann meine Mutter dir ja auch eine Torte schenken?
4. Aber nein, ich zahle sie ihr natürlich zurück.

Der österreichische Dialekt

5. Ein Deutscher fragt eine Österreicherin über die österreichische Politik.
6. Sie beantwortet ihm seine Fragen.
7. Doch leider kennt der Deutsche den österreichischen Dialekt nicht gut.
8. Ein Freund erklärt ihm alles.

Subjekt	Indirektes Objekt	Direktes Objekt
1. _____	_____	_____
2. _____	_____	_____
3. _____	_____	_____
4. _____	_____	_____
5. _____	_____	_____
6. _____	_____	_____
7. _____	_____	_____
8. _____	_____	_____

F. Gespräche. Michael is discussing with his friends which of his belongings he will give to whom for the year while he's studying in England. Complete the sentences using the cues listed before each dialogue.

→ dein Bruder / deine Bücher / du *(2x)*
  GISELA: Was machst du mit ___*deinen Büchern*___ ? Gibst du sie ___*deinem Bruder*___ ?
  MICHAEL: Nein, der hat schon so viele Bücher. Ich kann sie gern ___*dir*___ geben.
          Möchtest du sie?
  GISELA: Toll, ich danke ___*dir*___.

1. ich / meine Schwester / mein Fahrrad / sie

  ALEX: Kannst du _____ in dem Jahr dein

  Fahrrad leihen? Mein Fahrrad ist so alt und klapprig°.   rickety

  MICHAEL: Leider nicht. Das Fahrrad gehört _____ .

  Sie braucht es wieder. Ich muss es _____ zurückgeben.

  ALEX: Oh je, dann muss ich weiter mit _____ fahren.

2. du / ich / sie (2x)

GISELA: Kaufst du in London eigentlich ein Bett und einen Schreibtisch?

MICHAEL: Ich weiß noch nicht. London ist sehr teuer. Ich hoffe, dass

meine Eltern _____ ein bisschen Geld geben.

Ich muss mit _____ sprechen.

GISELA: Sie leihen _____ das Geld doch

sicher°, nicht? Aber wahrscheinlich musst du es   certainly

_____ dann wieder zurückzahlen.

3. ich (2x) / ihr / sie

MICHAEL: Alex und Gisela, braucht ihr Pflanzen? Ich schenke sie

_____.

ALEX: Besser nicht. Bei _____ gefällt es Pflanzen

meistens nicht so gut. Ich gebe _____ immer zu

wenig Wasser.

GISELA: Ich nehme deine Pflanzen gern. Sie gefallen

_____ sehr gut.

4. du / ich / ihr (2x) / wir

GISELA UND ALEX: Michael, du gibst _____ so

viele Dinge°. Wir schreiben _____ dann auch   things

jede Woche einen Brief nach London.

MICHAEL: Das glaube ich _____ nicht. Dann

müsst ihr _____ ja 52 Briefe schreiben! Es ist

schon toll, wenn ich einmal im Monat von _____

höre.

G. Geschenke°. Gisela, Monika, and Stefan are browsing through some catalogs. They are talking about what they could give to whom as birthday presents. In the questions, use the cues provided in the appropriate case. In the answers, replace both objects by pronouns.

presents

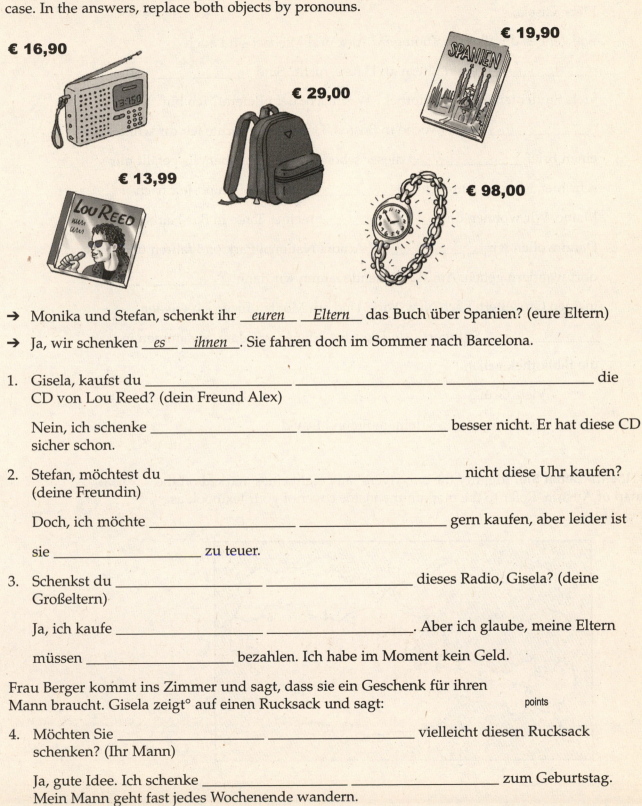

€ 16,90

€ 19,90

€ 29,00

€ 13,99

€ 98,00

➔ Monika und Stefan, schenkt ihr __euren__ __Eltern__ das Buch über Spanien? (eure Eltern)

➔ Ja, wir schenken __es__ __ihnen__. Sie fahren doch im Sommer nach Barcelona.

1. Gisela, kaufst du _____ _____ _____ die CD von Lou Reed? (dein Freund Alex)

   Nein, ich schenke _____ _____ besser nicht. Er hat diese CD sicher schon.

2. Stefan, möchtest du _____ _____ nicht diese Uhr kaufen? (deine Freundin)

   Doch, ich möchte _____ _____ gern kaufen, aber leider ist

   sie _____ zu teuer.

3. Schenkst du _____ _____ dieses Radio, Gisela? (deine Großeltern)

   Ja, ich kaufe _____ _____. Aber ich glaube, meine Eltern

   müssen _____ bezahlen. Ich habe im Moment kein Geld.

Frau Berger kommt ins Zimmer und sagt, dass sie ein Geschenk für ihren Mann braucht. Gisela zeigt° auf einen Rucksack und sagt:

points

4. Möchten Sie _____ _____ vielleicht diesen Rucksack schenken? (Ihr Mann)

   Ja, gute Idee. Ich schenke _____ _____ zum Geburtstag. Mein Mann geht fast jedes Wochenende wandern.

H. Ein Brief. During the semester break, David has returned home to the United States to visit his family. Gisela did not go home to Mainz but has stayed in Tübingen. David has written a letter to Gisela, but is unsure about some of the prepositions. Help him out by supplying the appropriate prepositions.

Prepositions: aus ■ außer ■ bei *(2x)* ■ mit ■ nach ■ seit ■ von ■ zu ■ zum

Liebe Gisela,

wie geht es dir allein in Tübingen? Alex und Michael sind auch

_____[1] ihren Eltern zu Hause, nicht? Sind _____[2] dir

viele Studenten in der Bibliothek? Was macht dein Referat? Ich bin

_____[3] einer Woche in Boston. Und heute möchte ich dir schnell

einen Brief _____[4] dieser schönen Stadt schreiben. Es gefällt mir

sehr hier. Morgen fahre ich _____[5] meinem Freund Jeff nach

Maine. Wir wohnen dort _____[6] meiner Tante in Bar Harbor.

Dann wollen wir _____[7] Acadia National Park *(m.)* fahren und

dort wandern gehen. Am Wochenende fahren wir dann _____[8]

meinen Großeltern nach New York. Und am Montag fliege ich wieder

_____[9] Stuttgart. Am Dienstag können wir dann zusammen in

die Bibliothek gehen.

    Viele Grüße

_____[10] deinem Freund David

I. Identifizieren Sie. Identify the two rivers° and eight cities marked on the map of Austria. Refer to the map on the inside cover of your textbook as necessary.

                                                 Flüsse

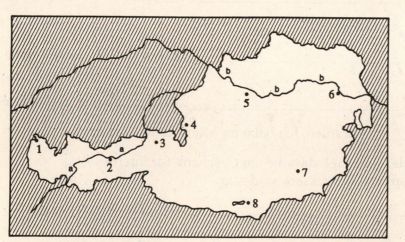

Flüsse   **Städte**

a. _____   1. _____   5. _____

b. _____   2. _____   6. _____

                      3. _____   7. _____

                      4. _____   8. _____

J. Ferien in Österreich. You and your friends are planning to go skiing in St. Anton, a famous ski resort in Austria. You have found a travel brochure in German and are trying to figure out what St. Anton might be like. You won't understand every word, but try to guess the meaning from the words that you do know and from the ones that are similar in English. Answer the questions below using the information from the brochure.

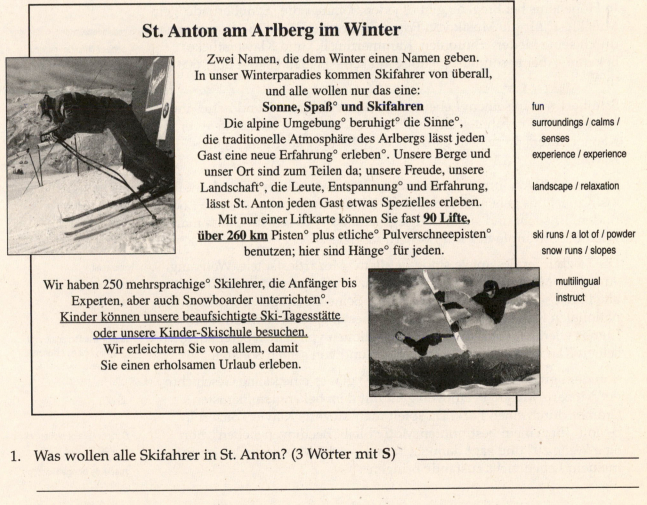

St. Anton am Arlberg im Winter

Zwei Namen, die dem Winter einen Namen geben.
In unser Winterparadies kommen Skifahrer von überall,
und alle wollen nur das eine:
Sonne, Spaß° und Skifahren
Die alpine Umgebung° beruhigt° die Sinne°,
die traditionelle Atmosphäre des Arlbergs lässt jeden
Gast eine neue Erfahrung° erleben°. Unsere Berge und
unser Ort sind zum Teilen da; unsere Freude, unsere
Landschaft°, die Leute, Entspannung° und Erfahrung,
lässt St. Anton jeden Gast etwas Spezielles erleben.
Mit nur einer Liftkarte können Sie fast **90 Lifte,**
über 260 km Pisten° plus etliche° Pulverschneepisten°
benutzen; hier sind Hänge° für jeden.

Wir haben 250 mehrsprachige° Skilehrer, die Anfänger bis
Experten, aber auch Snowboarder unterrichten°.
Kinder können unsere beaufsichtigte Ski-Tagesstätte
oder unsere Kinder-Skischule besuchen.
Wir erleichtern Sie von allem, damit
Sie einen erholsamen Urlaub erleben.

glosses (right margin):
fun
surroundings / calms / senses
experience / experience
landscape / relaxation
ski runs / a lot of / powder snow runs / slopes
multilingual
instruct

1. Was wollen alle Skifahrer in St. Anton? (3 Wörter mit **S**) _____

_____

2. Was macht St. Anton so attraktiv? _____

_____

3. Wie viele Lifte sind dort? _____

4. Wie lang sind die Pisten? _____

5. Wie viele Skilehrer arbeiten in St. Anton? _____

6. Können manche Skilehrer vielleicht auch Englisch? _____

_____

7. Wohin können Kinder gehen, wenn sie Ski laufen lernen wollen? _____

_____

K. Schubert und Mozart. Read the passage and then answer the questions.

Für viele Leute gehören Österreich und Musik zusammen. Im Sommer kann man in Österreich „Musikferien" machen, denn es gibt jeden Sommer über 50 Festspiele°, bekannte° und nicht so bekannte, vom Bodensee im Westen bis zum Neusiedler See im Osten. Es gibt Oper, Operette und Musical, Ballett und Konzerte mit klassischer und moderner Musik.

festivals / well-known

In Hohenems bei Bregenz gibt es jeden Sommer die „Schubertiade", ein Musikfest° für die Musik von Franz Schubert (1797–1828). Schubert ist durch seine Lieder°, Sinfonien, Kammermusik° und Klavierstücke° bekannt. Aber besonders wichtig sind seine Lieder. Es gibt über 600 von ihm.

music festival
songs / chamber music /
piano pieces

Schubert war in seinem Leben° nicht sehr erfolgreich° und hatte° immer wenig Geld. Er wohnte° oft bei Freunden. Hier und da arbeitete° er als Klavierlehrer°. In seinem ganzen Leben hatte er aber kein eigenes° Klavier.

life / successful / had
lived / worked
piano teacher / own

Man erzählt von ihm diese Anekdote: Einmal° will ein Freund mit ihm ins Kaffeehaus gehen, aber Schubert kann keine Strümpfe° ohne Löcher° finden. Er sucht und sucht und sagt endlich°: „Es scheint°, dass man in Wien die Strümpfe nur mit Löchern fabriziert."

one day
stockings / holes
finally / seems

Die Salzburger Festspiele sind vor allem° Mozartfestspiele. Wolfgang Amadeus Mozart (1756–1791) ist in Salzburg geboren°. Er ist für fast° alle Bereiche° der° Musik sehr wichtig. Seine Opern gehören zum internationalen Repertoire. Die großen Orchester spielen seine Sinfonien. Immer wieder° gibt es neue Interpretationen von seinen Serenaden, von seinen Klavier-° und Violinkonzerten° und von seinen Sonaten.

above all
born / almost
areas / of

immer wieder: again and
again / piano **Konzert:**
concerto

Von dem großen Beethoven (1770–1827) gibt es eine kleine Geschichte zu° Mozarts Musik: Beethoven geht mit dem bekannten Pianisten Cramer durch einen Park. Da spielt man Mozarts Klavierkonzert in c-Moll°. Bei einem bestimmten Motiv bleibt Beethoven stehen°, hört eine Weile zu° und sagt dann: „Cramer, solche Musik werde° ich in meinem Leben nicht zustande bringen°."

about

C minor / **bleibt stehen:** stops
/ **hört zu:** listens / will

zustande bringen: accom-
plish

1. Warum kann man in Österreich besonders gut Musikferien machen?

   _____

   _____

2. Was für Musik gibt es bei den Festspielen?

   _____

   _____

3. Welche Musik von Schubert ist besonders bekannt?

   _____

4. Warum kann Schubert keine Strümpfe ohne Löcher finden?

   _____

5. Wo ist Mozart geboren?

   _____

6. Für welche Bereiche der Musik ist Mozart wichtig? Nennen° Sie drei.   name

   _____

   _____

7. Wie findet Beethoven Mozarts Musik?

   _____

   _____

L. *Kulturelle Notizen.* You are planning to visit Germany, Austria, or Switzerland
next year. To prepare for the trip, you are collecting information about cultural differences between these countries and the United States. Provide brief responses in English.

1. Briefly discuss **Jugendherbergen:** where are they located, and who uses them?

   _____

   _____

2. Compare public transportation in German-speaking countries with that in your own country
   (or city): Is it efficient? Well-utilized?

   _____

   _____

3. Name two ways in which Austria is actively involved in world affairs.

_____

_____

4. List four names that are associated with Vienna as an important cultural center.

_____

_____

M. Egon-Schiele Museum. The Austrian expressionist painter Egon Schiele (1890–1918) is one of the most famous artists of the twentieth century. Look at the advertisement for the Egon-Schiele Museum and answer the following questions.

EGON SCHIELE MVSEVM

Geöffnet: **TÄGLICH** - außer Montag: 9-12 und 14-18 Uhr

AN DER DONAULÄNDE°

Von Wien aus in 30 Minuten zu erreichen!   reach

90 Originalwerke und die Dokumentation: "SCHIELE UND SEINE ZEIT."

IM ALTEN STADTGEFÄNGNIS°   open / town jail

TULLN   Danube plain

1. Wo ist das Egon Schiele Museum?

_____

2. Wann ist das Egon Schiele Museum nicht geöffnet?

_____

3. Wie lange fährt man von Wien bis zum Museum?

_____

4. Wie viele Bilder von Schiele gibt es dort?

_____

5. Welchen Titel hat die Dokumentation?

_____

KAPITEL 6   Was hast du vor?

A. Wie war der Samstagabend? Melanie, Uwe, and Alex discuss what they did Saturday evening. Using the cues, give their conversation in the *present perfect tense.*

→ wir / am Samstagabend / Michaels Band / hören
  MELANIE: *Wir haben am Samstagabend Michaels Band gehört.*

1. das Konzert / euch / gefallen / ?

   ALEX: _____

2. ja, / die Band / toll / spielen

   UWE: _____

3. was / du / machen / ?

   MELANIE: _____

4. ich / den ganzen Abend / am Computer / sitzen

   ALEX: _____

5. du / viel / für deine Prüfungen / arbeiten / ?

   UWE: _____

6. ich / im Internet / surfen

   ALEX: Ach nein, leider nicht. _____

B. Was haben Sie als Kind (nicht) gern gemacht? Check off those things that you liked or didn't like to do as a child.

	gern	nicht gern
→ Fisch essen		✔
1. Sport treiben		
2. früh aufstehen		
3. Comics lesen		
4. Rad fahren		
5. zur Schule gehen		

Now form complete sentences in the *present perfect tense.*

➔ *Ich habe nicht gern Fisch gegessen.*

1. _____

2. _____

3. _____

4. _____

5. _____

C. Das hat Daniela heute gemacht. Tell what Daniela did at certain times during the day by using the *present perfect tense.* Use specific times or other time expressions (**morgens, nachmittags, abends, dann, danach°**). Use the   afterwards
pictures as cues.

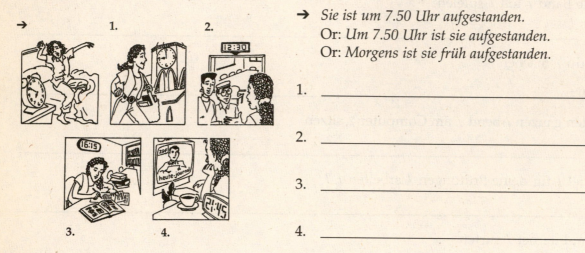

➔   *Sie ist um 7.50 Uhr aufgestanden.*
    Or: *Um 7.50 Uhr ist sie aufgestanden.*
    Or: *Morgens ist sie früh aufgestanden.*

1. _____

2. _____

3. _____

4. _____

D. Das Spiel. Uwe substitutes in a soccer game. Restate each sentence in the *present perfect tense.*

➔ Alex ruft mich um elf an.   *Alex hat mich um elf angerufen.*

1. Ich mache gerade° Pläne für den Nachmittag.   just

_____

2. Das Spiel interessiert mich sehr.

_____

3. Aber ich spiele ziemlich schlecht.

_____

4. Leider fotografieren meine Freunde mein Spiel.

_____

5. Das gefällt mir nicht.

_____

6. Nach dem Spiel feiern wir.

_____

E. In der Mode Halle. There is a special sale in the *Mode° Halle* and you   fashion
and your friend are checking out the bargains. Look at the *Mode Halle*
advertisement and write out the conversation you have with your friend.
You may use the following dialogue as a model or make up one of your
own.

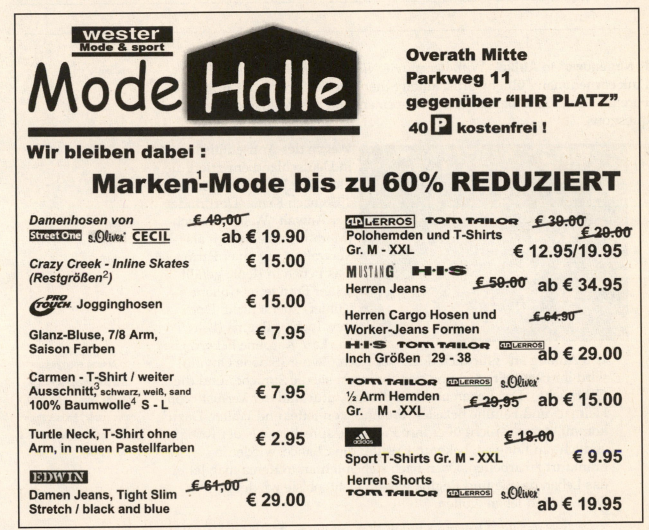

¹ brand   ² not all sizes available (lit: remaining sizes)   ³ neckline   ⁴ cotton

→   BARBARA: Ich brauche eine Jeans.
    HANNA: Hier gibt es Jeans von Edwin – die kosten nur noch € 29,00.
    BARBARA: Das ist aber billig. Was haben die denn vorher° gekostet?   previously
    HANNA: Sie haben € 61,00 gekostet. Und die sind schön.
    BARBARA: Ja, finde ich auch. Ich glaube, ich möchte eine Jeans in schwarz,
                nicht in blau. …

SIE: _____

IHRE FREUNDIN/IHR FREUND: _____

_____

SIE: _____

_____

IHRE FREUNDIN/IHR FREUND: _____

_____

SIE: _____

_____

F. Nirgendwo° in Afrika. With her movie *Nirgendwo in Afrika*, Caroline
Link earned many film awards, among them the 2002 Oscar for Best
Foreign Film. Read the movie announcement and answer the following
questions.

nowhere

Wegen des Antisemitismus
in Deutschland emigriert die
jüdische° Familie Redlich
1938 nach Kenia. Dort findet
der Anwalt° Walter Redlich
(Merab Ninize) Arbeit als
Verwalter° auf einer Farm.
Das Leben in Kenia gefällt
seiner Frau Jettel (Juliane
Köhler) zuerst nicht. Doch
ihre Tochter Regina (Lea
Kurka / Karoline Eckertz) ist
von Anfang an° glücklich dort. Der Koch Owuor (Sidede Onyulo)
wird ihr bester Freund und von ihm lernt sie die Sprache° und die
Gebräuche°. Das Leben in der anderen Kultur und der Verlust° von
Heimat° und Familie belastet° die Ehe° von Jettel und Walter. Dazu°
kommt, dass sie nicht über ihre Probleme sprechen. Als der Krieg°
endlich° zu Ende ist, bekommt Walter die Chance, wieder in
Frankfurt zu arbeiten. Doch nach sieben Jahren in Kenia mag Jettel
das Leben da. Sie und Regina wissen nicht, ob sie wieder in
Deutschland leben wollen.

Jewish

lawyer

manager

von Anfang an: right from
the beginning / language
customs / loss
native country / puts a strain
on / marriage / in addition /
war / finally

Darsteller°: Juliane Köhler, Merab Ninize, Matthias Habich
Regie°: Caroline Link
Filmlänge: 141 Minuten

actors
directed by

1. Wann emigriert die Familie nach Kenia?

_____

2. Wie findet Jettel Redlich das Leben in Afrika?

_____

3. Wie gefällt es der Tochter Regina dort?

_____

4. Welche Probleme haben Walter und Jettel?

_____

5. Warum wissen Jettel und Regina nicht, ob sie wieder in Deutschland leben wollen?

_____

6. Wer hat den Film gemacht?

_____

7. Wie lang ist der Film?

_____

G. Ein Abend bei uns. Monika tells what she, Stefan, and their cousin Susanne did on a Saturday evening. Give her account in the past, using the *present perfect tense.*

➔ Unsere Kusine Susanne besucht uns, weil ihre Eltern in die Schweiz fahren.
   Unsere Kusine Susanne hat uns besucht, weil ihre Eltern in die Schweiz gefahren sind.

1. Weil es regnet, machen wir keine Fahrradtour.

_____

2. Stefan faulenzt den ganzen Samstag, denn er kommt Freitagabend spät nach Hause.

_____

3. Susanne und ich sehen fern, obwohl wir das Programm langweilig finden.

_____

4. Dann bestellen° wir eine Pizza, weil wir zu müde zum Kochen sind.   order

_____

5. Stefan versucht die Pizza nicht, denn er schläft schon.

_____

H. Wie war es bei dir? Choose one of the following days and describe in at least five complete sentences what you did that day.

Days: an Chanukka ■ an deinem Geburtstag ■ am Muttertag ■ am Siversterabend ■ am Valentinstag ■ an Weihnachten

→ *An meinem Geburtstag habe ich morgens lange geschlafen. Um elf Uhr habe ich mit einer Freundin in einem Café gefrühstückt. Danach haben wir für meine Party abends eingekauft und wir haben das Essen vorbereitet. Abends um acht sind die Gäste gekommen. Wir haben gegessen und getrunken und getanzt. Manche Gäste sind bis morgens um drei geblieben.*

_____

_____

_____

_____

_____

I. Freizeit ein Problem? Read the passage and then answer the questions.

„Alle gehen in ihr Zimmer, schließen die Tür und tun eine oder einein-halb Stunden, was sie wollen. Unsere eine Tochter will Musik hören. Unsere andere Tochter will fernsehen. Meine Frau will lesen. Ich will etwas schlafen. So verbringen° wir alle einen sehr schönen Sonntag-nachmittag", erzählt Dr. Feldgen vom Institut für Freizeitforschung° in Hamburg.

Man möchte fragen: „Ja und? Ist das etwas Besonderes?" Nach° Dr. Feldgen, ja. Viele Leute finden nämlich, dass Freizeit ein Problem ist. In den meisten Familien wollen die Menschen vor allem° zwei Dinge°. Sie wollen Kontakt mit anderen, wollen etwas zusammen machen. Sie wollen aber auch allein sein, weg von den anderen. In diesem Dilemma ist Fernsehen oft der einzige° Ausweg°. Man weiß nicht, was man machen soll. So sieht man eben° fern. Wenn der Fernseher kaputt ist, gibt's eine Familienkrise.

Für viele ist Freizeit keine freie Zeit. Am Wochenende machen sie Hausarbeit, waschen das Auto oder arbeiten im Garten. Für diese Aktivitäten gibt man seine freie Zeit auf°. Oder man macht einen großen Plan für die ganze Familie. Dieser Plan soll dann alle in der Familie zufrieden stellen°. Statt° Zufriedenheit° gibt's aber oft Unzufriedenheit, Frustration, Aggression, Stress.

Für viele ist Freitag der schönste° Tag der Woche. Man denkt daran, was man am Wochenende machen kann. Die Wirklichkeit ist dann aber oft gar nicht so schön. Warum? Dr. Feldgen sagt: „Weil wir nicht gelernt haben, was wir brauchen. Wir brauchen freie Zeit für persönliche Wünsche. Wir brauchen freie Zeit für Kontakt mit anderen. Und wir brauchen freie Zeit, nichts zu tun, ohne Langeweile° und ohne Schuldgefühle°."

Glossary (right margin):
- spend
- research on leisure
- according to
- above all / things
- only / way out
- simply
- **gibt auf:** give up
- **zufrieden stellen:** satisfy / instead of / satisfaction
- the best
- boredom
- feelings of guilt

1. Warum ist der Sonntagnachmittag für alle in Dr. Feldgens Familie sehr schön?

   _____

2. Warum ist „ein schöner Sonntagnachmittag" für viele Leute ein Problem?

   _____

3. Was wollen die Menschen in den meisten Familien?

   _____

4. Warum sehen viele Menschen am Wochenende oft fern?

   _____

5. Was machen viele Leute am Wochenende?

   _____

6. Warum ist für viele Freitag der schönste Tag der Woche?

   _____

J. Was machen Sie in Ihrer Freizeit? Write a paragraph of five complete sentences about activities you enjoy doing in your free time. Below are some ideas you may want to use. (You may also want to consult the Supplementary Word Sets in Appendix C of your textbook for additional terminology.)

Time expressions at the beginning of the sentences will make them sound more natural: am Wochenende ■ samstags ■ sonntags ■ morgens ■ nachmittags ■ abends ...

Activities: Karten (Golf, Tennis, Basketball) spielen ■ inlineskaten gehen ■ Fitnesstraining machen ■ schwimmen ■ wandern ■ Freunde besuchen/einladen ■ ins Restaurant (Kino, Theater, Konzert, Museum) gehen ■ in die Kneipe/Disko gehen ■ zum Einkaufszentrum° gehen ■ spät aufstehen ■ faulenzen ...   shopping center

In meiner Freizeit _____

_____

_____

_____

_____

_____

K. *Kulturelle Notizen.* You plan to visit Germany, Austria, or Switzerland next year. To prepare for the trip, you are collecting information about cultural differences between these countries and the United States. Provide brief responses in English.

1. Describe the work week and vacation time of German industrial workers and compare the system with the one in your country.

   _____

   _____

   _____

2. Contrast getting a driver's license in German-speaking countries with the situation in your state or province.

   _____

   _____

   _____

3. Name three things that you've learned about the German movie industry.

   _____

   _____

   _____

SEID BERIESELT,°		inundated
MILLIONEN		
Der Deutschen liebste Freizeit-beschäftigung° ist mit Abstand° die Glotze°		leisure activity / by far / tube
Mache ich regelmäßig:° (Angaben in Prozent)		regularly
Fernsehen	**74,4**	
Radio hören	**59,7**	
Zeitung lesen	**56,3**	
zu Hause gemütlich entspannen°	**47,2**	relax
Zeitschriften/Illustrierte lesen	**39,1**	
kochen	**34,9**	
Sport treiben	**33,2**	

Basis: 20 260 Personen, repräsentativ für die Gesamtbevölkerung
Quelle: TdW Intermedia 2001/2

KAPITEL 7   Andere Länder – andere Sitten

A. Ein paar Tage in München.   Peter is visiting his friend Christine in Munich and he writes a letter to Stefan who is in Mainz at the moment. Read the letter and make up five questions about it.

Hallo Stefan,

vielen Dank für deinen Brief. Schön, dass es dir gut geht. Es macht sicher Spaß°, mal wieder in Mainz und bei deinen Eltern zu sein. Gefällt es Monika auch?

Es ... Spaß: It must be fun

Mir geht es gut. München ist toll und ich glaube, ich bleibe bis Freitag hier. Es gibt so viel, was ich noch sehen möchte. Am Samstag bin ich dann aber pünktlich zu eurem Fest in Mainz. Vielen Dank auch, dass ich bei euch übernachten kann.

Gestern war ich mit Christine im Englischen Garten. Wir sind zuerst mit dem Fahrrad gefahren und haben dann lange in der Sonne gelegen. Es war sehr voll°, aber toll – die Leute spielen Frisbee, machen Picknicks, man kann auch reiten° und auf dem See Boot fahren. Es ist eigentlich wie im Tiergarten in Berlin, aber doch auch anders. Sehr gemütlich und wie Ferien. Einfach typisch bayrisch!

full
ride horseback

Es ist sehr nett mit Christine. Sie war ja letztes Jahr in Amerika und kennt das Leben dort ganz gut. Deshalb sprechen wir natürlich viel über Deutschland und Amerika und was hier und dort anders ist. Das ist interessant und ich denke im Moment auch viel an Washington. Na ja, bald mehr. Ich muss weg – ich will noch ins Deutsche Museum und danach° ein bisschen einkaufen gehen.

afterwards

Dann bis nächsten Samstag zur Party. Viele Grüße, auch an Monika,

von deinem Peter

1. _____

_____

2. _____

_____

3. _____

_____

4. _____

_____

5. _____

_____

B. Eine Wohnung in München. In the magazine *Room* published by the big home furnishings company Ikea, there is a column called "Ich liebe° mein Zuhause°." People talk about their homes with accompanying photos. In this piece, Nick Herrmanns discusses his apartment in Munich. Read the **Steckbrief**° and complete the text below by choosing the appropriate items from the list.

love
home

personal information

STECKBRIEF

NAME Nick Hermanns
ALTER 51
MIETER ODER EIGENTÜMER?[1] Seit fast vier Jahren gemietet[2]
WO? München, Stadtteil Sendling
WIE GROSS? 135 m²[3]
LIEBLINGSZIMMER ‚Das ändert sich[4] täglich mehrmals', sagt Nick Hermanns schmumzelnd[5], ‚wenn ich arbeite, dann ist das Arbeitszimmer mein Lieblingsraum, wenn ich müde bin, das Schlafzimmer und wenn ich mal koche, dann am liebsten[6] in der Küche.' Im kommenden Herbst wird bestimmt wieder das Badezimmer sein Favorit.
FEHLSCHLÄGE[7] ‚Nein, alles gut gegangen', sagt Nick Hermanns, der einige Möbel umgebaut[8] und das komplette Beleuchtungssystem[9] selbst installiert hat. ‚Meine Wohnung hat noch kein Handwerker[10] von innen[11] gesehen.' Selbst ist der Mann.

[1] owner [2] rented [3] square meters [4] **ändert sich:** changes [5] smiling [6] preferably
[7] failures [8] modified [9] lighting system [10] contractor [11] **von innen:** from inside

Wörter: 135 m² groß ■ 51 Jahre alt ■ gemietet ■ München ■ seit fast vier Jahren

Nick Herrmanns ist _____[1]. Er wohnt in einer Wohung in

_____[2]. Die Wohnung gehört ihm nicht, sondern er hat sie

_____[3]. Er wohnt hier schon _____[4]. Die Wohnung

ist _____[5].

Wörter: im Arbeitszimmer ■ installiert ■ die Küche ■ das Schlafzimmer ■ selbst

Welches sein Lieblingszimmer ist, kann Nick Hermanns nicht genau sagen. Wenn er kocht, ist es

_____[6]. Wenn er schlafen will, ist es _____[7]. Und

wenn er arbeitet, ist er am liebsten _____[8]. Nick hat in seiner Wohnung

vieles _____[9] gemacht. Er hat ein paar Möbel umgebaut und alle Lampen

_____[10].

C. Was meinen Sie? Decide whether each sentence is a subjective judgment or generalization, or an objective observation. Write **U** for **Urteil°** or **B** for **Beobachtung°**.

judgment

observation

1. _____ Die Amerikaner sehen den ganzen Tag fern.

2. _____ In Deutschland findet man fast überall Blumen.

3. _____ Die Amerikaner benutzen den Vornamen mehr als die Deutschen.

4. _____ Die Deutschen fahren wie die Wilden.

5. _____ In Amerika kann man das ganze Wochenende einkaufen gehen.

6. _____ Die deutschen Züge sind fast immer pünktlich.

7. _____ Die Deutschen essen zu viel Wurst.

8. _____ Die Amerikaner sind sehr freundlich.

D. Bei Rita. Friends are gathering at Rita's. Describe their activities and locations by supplying appropriate *prepositions*. Contract the two definite articles in parentheses.

Rita steht _____¹ dem Sofa. Paul steht _____²

ihr. Sie sprechen _____³ einen Roman.

　　Drei Freunde sitzen _____⁴ (dem) Tisch. Thomas schreibt

eine Karte _____⁵ seine Freundin. Hans redet

_____⁶ seine Ferien. Anni sitzt _____⁷ ihnen.

　　Nicole kommt gerade° _____⁸ (das) Zimmer.　　　　　just

E. Alexanders Plan. Complete the following passage about Alexander's plan, using the cued *prepositions and articles.*

Alexander arbeitet _____ _____ [1] *(in a)* Café, aber er möchte gern

_____ _____ [2] *(at the)* Universität studieren. Er spricht oft mit

Studenten _____ _____ [3] *(about the)* Universität.

Er will Physik studieren. _____ _____ [4] *(on his)* Schreibtisch zu

Hause liegt ein Buch von Einstein. Darin liest er gern _____ [5] *(in the)* Abend. Und

_____ _____ [6] *(in front of the)* Fenster hat er eine kleine Statue

von dem Physiker Werner Heisenberg gestellt. _____ _____ [7] *(next to*

the) Bücherregal steht sein Computer.

Letzte Woche hat Alexander _____ _____ [8] *(to his)* Eltern

geschrieben. Er möchte wissen, was sie _____ _____ [9] *(of his)*

Plan halten.

F. Nach dem Fest. Stefan and Monika are back in Mainz for the semester break. Last night they had a party at their parents' which has left the house in a mess. Peter, who is staying with them over the weekend, helps them to clean up. Complete their conversation by using **legen/liegen, setzen/sitzen, stellen/stehen, stecken,** or **hängen** where appropriate. (Imperative forms of the verb are indicated by *Imp.;* the present perfect form is indicated by two blanks and *Pres. Perf.*)

1. STEFAN: Das ist nett, dass du uns hilfst, Peter. Dann können wir zusammen die Möbel

    wieder an ihren Platz _____.

2. MONIKA: Ich _____ das große Bild wieder neben das Regal. Ich habe Angst

    gehabt, dass es beim Tanzen kaputtgeht.

3. STEFAN: Es _____ auch überall Zeitungen und Bücher herum. Kannst du die

    Zeitungen bitte auf den Tisch _____ und die Bücher ins Bücherregal

    _____, Monika?

4. PETER: Das ganze Geschirr _____ noch auf dem Esszimmertisch

    _____ *(Pres. Perf.).* Ich _____ es auf den Küchentisch

    _____ *(Pres. Perf.).*

5. MONIKA: Vielen Dank. Wenn du willst, kannst du es in die Spülmaschine einräumen. Judith

    hat ihre CDs vergessen. Sie _____ noch auf dem Regal.

6. STEFAN: _____ *(Imp.)* sie doch in meine Tasche. Ich gehe heute Nachmittag

    zu Judith. Dann nehme ich die CDs für sie mit.

7. MONIKA: Du meine Güte, mein Player _____ ja auf dem Boden. Kannst du

ihn schnell auf den Tisch _____, Peter?

8. STEFAN: Du sollst auch nicht nur auf dem Sofa _____ und reden, Monika!

9. MONIKA: Warum denn nicht? Es sieht hier doch eigentlich wieder ziemlich gut aus. Wenn

wir jetzt noch unsere Mäntel und Jacken in den Schrank _____, ist doch alles

wieder in Ordnung.

G. Die Villa Flora in München. Look at the advertisement for the restaurant Villa Flora in
Munich and then answer the following questions.

ENDLICH: BIERGARTEN-SAISON IN DER VILLA FLORA ERÖFFNET!

In München-Sendling, Hansastraße 44.

Genießen Sie euroasiatische „Lean Cuisine" von unserem Starkoch Frank Heppner!

Im Restaurant Villa Flora wird „Essen gehen" zum Erlebnis.
Wir bieten fantastische Räumlichkeiten,
Multi-Kulti-Küche, einen riesigen Biergarten,
Parkplätze, MVV-Anschluß, Extra-Räume für Tagungen,
einen Kinderspielplatz, Mittags-Specials, Fischspezialitäten
vom Holzkohlengrill und, und, und...

Wir sind täglich von 11.00 Uhr bis 1.00 Uhr
für Sie da. Bei Tagungen selbstverständlich auch schon früher.

VILLA FLORA
MÜNCHEN SENDLING

■ Der extra **Sonntags-Brunch**
Bei schönem Wetter Garten-Brunch.

■ Probieren Sie unser **Sushi**
Extra günstig zur Sushi-Happy-Hour,
Montag bis Freitag von 16.00 bis 19.00 Uhr.

■ Montags **After Work Party**
ab 18.00 Uhr für unglaubliche 6,99 Euro
(Eintritt, ein Getränk und Snacks inklusive)

■ Samstags **Tropischer Fischmarkt** von 08.00 bis 13.00 Uhr
mit erstklassigen Fischen aus Gambia.

Wir reservieren Ihnen gerne einen Platz:
089 - 54 71 75 75
Die Villa Flora von einer ganz anderen Site: www.villa-flora.com

1. Wer kocht in der Villa Flora? _____

2. Denken Sie, dass man auch mit kleinen Kindern gut hierher kommen kann? Warum (nicht)?

_____

3. An welchen Tagen gibt es etwas Besonderes? Und was ist das genau?

    a. Sonntags: _____

    b. _____

    c. _____

4. Wann ist die Sushi-Happy-Hour? _____

5. An welchem Tag möchten Sie die Villa Flora besuchen? Warum? _____

_____

H. Alex und Uwe. Many people who meet Alex and Uwe think that they are very similar
in their interests and attitudes. But Gisela, who knows both of them well, doesn't think so.
Gisela reacts to the following statements by saying that either Alex or Uwe does or does
not do that. Replace the preposition and the noun with a **da-**compound or a *preposition and
personal pronoun*, as appropriate.

➔ Uwe redet gern *über Computer.*   *Alex redet nicht gern darüber.*

➔ Alex redet oft *von seiner Nachbarin Tanja.*   *Uwe redet auch oft von ihr.*

1. Alex hat keine Angst *vor Klausuren.*

_____

2. Uwe schreibt oft *an seine Eltern.*

_____

3. Uwe arbeitet abends immer *an seinem Computer.*

_____

4. Alex hält viel *von seinen Professoren.*

_____

I. Worüber hat Gülfizer gesprochen? A friend of Gülfizer's retells her conversation with
her. The surroundings are noisy and Birgit inquires what Gülfizer has been saying.
Rewrite the prepositional phrase in italics in the following sentences. Form a question by
replacing the preposition and the noun with a **wo-**compound or *preposition and personal
pronoun*, as appropriate.

➔ Gülfizer hat *über ihr neues Auto* gesprochen.   BIRGIT: *Worüber hat sie gesprochen?*

➔ Gülfizer hat *von ihrem Freund* Adem geredet.   BIRGIT: *Von wem hat sie geredet?*

1. Gülfizer denkt meistens *an das Wochenende.*

    BIRGIT: _____

2. Sie kann dann *mit ihrem Freund Adem* Tennis spielen.

    BIRGIT: _____

3. Später haben Gülfizer und Adem *über das Spiel* gesprochen.

   BIRGIT: _____

4. Abends sind sie *mit Gülfizers Eltern* zum Restaurant Rosenau gefahren.

   BIRGIT: _____

J. Viele Fragen über Judith. Yesterday, at Stefan's and Monika's party, Peter met Monika's old friend Judith. He would like to see Judith again and he gets information about her from Monika. Complete the dialogue with **ob, wenn,** or **wann.**

1. PETER: Weißt du, _____ Judith heute Abend mit uns ins Kino

   gehen möchte?

2. MONIKA: Das weiß ich nicht, aber ich kann sie anrufen, _____ du

   willst. Du kannst natürlich auch selbst anrufen und fragen, _____

   sie Zeit hat.

3. PETER: Und was ist, _____ sie schon etwas anderes vorhat?

4. MONIKA: Hmmm, du findest sie wohl° sehr nett, nicht? Weißt du was?   probably

   _____ sie heute Abend keine Zeit hat, frage ich sie, _____ sie

   uns mal in Berlin besuchen möchte. Und _____ sie ja sagt, frage

   ich sie gleich, _____ sie kommen kann. In den Semesterferien

   habe ich zum Beispiel nicht so viel Arbeit und viel Zeit für Besuch.

5. PETER: Weißt du denn schon, _____ du wieder in Berlin bist?

6. MONIKA: Ach, ich denke in ein, zwei Wochen. _____ ich zu lange

   hier in Mainz bei meinen Eltern bin, wird es mir doch ein bisschen

   langweilig.

K. Deutschland ist nicht Amerika. Robert Jones is telling his German professor about his recent trip to Germany. It seems that everything has disappointed him. Read the passage and then answer the questions.

Robert Jones erzählt von seiner Reise nach Deutschland. Er sagt: „Also, wissen Sie, ich bin ja ganz gern in Deutschland gewesen. Aber ich möchte in diesem Land nicht leben. Ich fahre zum Beispiel gern mit dem Auto. Aber das Land ist zu klein. An *einem* Tag bin ich von Hamburg im Norden nach München im Süden gefahren. Nicht ganz 800 Kilometer!

Ich weiß, die Deutschen wandern gern, oder sie gehen spazieren, in den Parks, an den Seen° und auch in den Stadtzentren°. Wirklich! Aber ich arbeite die ganze Woche. Also will ich am Wochenende doch nicht auch noch wandern.

lakes / city centers

Und dann die Restaurants! Das Essen war ja nicht schlecht. Darüber will ich ja nichts sagen. Aber nie° steht kaltes Wasser auf dem Tisch. Und wenn die Ober° kaltes Wasser bringen, ist es ein Miniglas und darin schwimmt dann ein klitzekleines° Eisstück°. Ich will aber trinken und keine Tabletten nehmen. Das deutsche Bier habe ich aber zu schwer und zu bitter und zu warm gefunden. Und der deutsche Wein war mir zu sauer°.

never
waiters
tiny / ice cube

sour

Und dann habe ich immer ‚Herr Schmidt' gesagt und ‚Frau Meyer'. Wie kalt das ist. Und zu mir haben alle Leute ‚Herr Jones' gesagt. Ich habe das furchtbar unpersönlich gefunden. Daher habe ich auch keine Freunde in diesem Land, obwohl ich doch drei Wochen da war. Wenn Sie mich fragen, ob ich eines Tages wieder dahin will, so muss ich sagen, ich weiß es nicht."

1. Warum macht Robert Jones Autofahren in Deutschland keinen Spaß?

   _____

2. Warum will er am Wochenende nicht wandern?

   _____

3. Was hat ihm beim Essen im Restaurant nicht gefallen?

   _____

4. Wie findet er es, wenn er „Herr" und „Frau" benutzen muss und wenn die Leute zu ihm „Herr Jones" sagen?

   _____

5. Warum hat er keine Freunde in Deutschland?

   _____

6. Wie finden Sie Touristen wie Robert Jones?

   _____

Name _____ Datum _____

L. Schreiben Sie. Answer the following questions and give a brief explanation.

1. An wen denken Sie oft? Warum?

   _____

   _____

2. Wovor haben Sie (keine) Angst? Warum (nicht)?

   _____

   _____

3. Auf wen müssen Sie manchmal warten? Warum?

   _____

   _____

4. Wohin gehen Sie gern mit Freunden? Warum?

   _____

   _____

M. *Kulturelle Notizen.* You plan to visit Germany, Austria, or Switzerland next year. To prepare for the trip, you gather information about historical aspects and cultural differences between these countries and your country. Provide brief responses in English.

1. When did Germans begin to immigrate to America? Why did they come? Where did they settle? What has been their numerical impact? Name four states with large German populations.

   _____

   _____

   _____

   _____

2. With whom do German-speaking people use the word **Freund?** Name two or three adjectives that English speakers often use with the noun *friend*.

   _____

   _____

   _____

   _____

3. Name three things you learned about apartments and private homes in Germany.

_____

_____

_____

_____

4. Name two reasons why Munich is popular with visitors, both Germans and tourists.

_____

_____

_____

_____

KAPITEL **8** **Modernes Leben**

A. Job gesucht. Look at the following advertisements by people who are looking for jobs. Then fill out the form with text for your own ad, using the others as models.

Informatik-Studentin

im 8. Semester sucht **Nebenjob[1] in Computerfirma.** Maximal 15 Stunden pro Woche. Neben guten Programmierkenntnissen Berufserfahrung als Controllerin. Fremdsprachen: Englisch und Französisch.
Tel.: (07071) 647 987

Tagesmutter, selbst Mutter und gelernte Erzieherin, hat noch Plätze frei. Für Tageskinder[2] von 1–3 Jahren. Betreuung[3] von 8 bis 15 Uhr.
Tel.: (07071) 998451

Student, 24 Jahre, suche dringend Job für die Semesterferien, wenn möglich in Pizzeria Erfahrung als Pizzabäcker, Hilfskoch[4], Pizzabote[5].
Tel.: (07071) 230778

[1] side job [2] children in daycare [3] care [4] assistant cook [5] pizza deliverer

_____

_____

_____

_____

_____

_____

B. Modernes Leben – moderne Technologie. The chart "Was Internauten wirklich wollen" appeared in the magazine *Focus* and shows what German Internet users do when online. Compare your own activities with theirs. You may use the activities from the list or others that may apply to your own computer use.

WAS INTERNAUTEN WIRKLICH WOLLEN

Online-Anwendungen[1] in Prozent

Anwendung	Prozent
E-Mails	89
zielloses[2] Surfen im Internet	77
Download von Dateien[3]	74
Adressen	71
Reise-Infos (Zug-/Flugpläne usw.)	65
aktuelle[4] Nachrichten[5]	62
Infos über PCs und Software	59
aktuelle Infos aus der Region	58
Newsletter von Organisationen	51
Home-Banking	47
Wetterinformationen	43
Computerspiele	41

[1]uses [2]random [3]files [4]current [5]news

chatten
Informationen fürs Studium
Live-Musik hören
Musik/Videos herunterladen°   download
online shoppen
Produktinformationen

1. Was sind die drei häufigsten° Anwendungen im Internet?   most frequent

   _____

2. Was sind die drei seltensten° Anwendungen der deutschen Internet-   least frequent
   Benutzer°?   users

   _____

3. Welche Aktivitäten vom Schaubild° machen Sie oft?   chart

   _____

   _____

   Nie? _____

4. Benutzen Sie das Internet, wenn Sie Informationen für Ihr Studium
   suchen? Warum (nicht)?

   _____

   _____

C. Suffixe _-heit_ und _-keit_. Write the adjective from which each noun is derived, and then guess the meaning of the noun.

	Adjective	Meaning
1. Mehrheit	_____	_____
2. Genauigkeit	_____	_____
3. Trockenheit	_____	_____
4. Gleichheit	_____	_____
5. Freiheit	_____	_____
6. Lustigkeit	_____	_____
7. Richtigkeit	_____	_____

D. Eine Ferienreise. David and Alex are going mountain biking in Austria. David rents a bike, Alex uses his sister's. Complete the information about their trip by providing the genitive case of the appropriate noun phrase. Use each phrase only once.

ein Freund ■ ihr Freund ■ seine Klausuren ■ seine Schwester

1. Sie hatten die Adresse _____eines Freundes_____ in Salzburg.

2. Alex hatte das Mountainbike _____ mitgenommen.

3. Während der Reise haben sie in der Wohnung _____ gewohnt.

4. Alex musste wegen _____ manchmal abends ein bisschen arbeiten.

der Regen ■ die Stadt ■ das Wetter ■ eine Woche

5. Wegen _____ konnten sie leider nicht jeden Tag Rad fahren gehen.

6. Doch sie haben die Sehenswürdigkeiten° _____ angeschaut.   sights

7. Sie sind statt _____ nur fünf Tage in Österreich geblieben.

8. Doch trotz _____ hat ihnen die Reise gut gefallen.

E. Wer ist das? The following text is about a famous person who lived in Vienna about 100 years ago. Fill in the cues provided in genitive case and name the person.

Wer ist das?

Dieser Wissenschaftler° hat vor etwa 100 Jahren in Wien gelebt. In der   scientist

Geschichte _____¹ (die Stadt) hat er eine große Rolle

gespielt. Der Inhalt° _____² (seine Bücher) beeinflusste die   contents

Welt _____³ (die Medizin) enorm. In seiner Arbeit

beschäftigte° er sich mit der Psyche _____⁴ (der Mensch).   occupied himself

Ein wichtiges Thema war für ihn zum Beispiel die Bedeutung°   meaning

_____⁵ (die Träume°). Der Titel _____⁶   dreams

(ein Buch) von ihm ist „Die Traumdeutung" (*The Interpretation of Dreams*).

   Er war viele Jahre Professor _____⁷ (die

Universität) in Wien. 1938 musste° er wegen _____⁸ (die   had

Nationalsozialisten) Österreich verlassen°. Die letzten zwei Jahre   to leave

_____⁹ (sein Leben) hat er in London gelebt.

Der Name _____¹⁰ (seine Tochter) war Anna. Auch sie war

Wissenschaftlerin. Ihr Spezialgebiet° war die Psyche   specialty

_____¹¹ (das Kind). Mit Hilfe° _____¹² (die   help

Tochter Anna) öffnete° die Stadt Wien ein Museum über den   opened

Wissenschaftler. Der Name _____¹³ (der Wissenschaftler)

ist _____¹⁴.

F. Studium in Deutschland. During the spring break, Gisela and Monika are both home in Mainz. Gisela is telling Monika about the exchange student David Carpenter. Fill in the appropriate *genitive prepositions:* **wegen, trotz, (an)statt, während.**

1. _____ seiner Zeit in Deutschland hat David hier in Tübingen studiert.

2. Das deutsche Uni-System hat ihm gefallen, da man _____ einer Klausur oft nur ein Referat schreiben muss.

3. _____ der vielen Arbeit hat er nur wenige deutsche Studenten kennen gelernt.

4. Am Ende des Semesters hat er _____ einer Reise nach Italien Urlaub in Ungarn gemacht.

5. _____ der Probleme mit der Sprache° hat er in   language
   Budapest Spaß gehabt.

Name _____ Datum _____

G. Ein langer Tag im Einkaufszentrum°. Joan and Diane White from the   shopping center
United States are visiting their friends Monika and Stefan. They all go to a
new shopping center in Berlin. Fill in the blanks with the proper form of
the cued adjectives.

1. Heute besuchen Monika, Stefan, Joan und Diane ein _____

    Einkaufszentrum. (neu)

2. Obwohl sie nur wenig Geld haben, wollen sie doch _____ aber

    _____ Sachen kaufen. (toll, billig)

3. Weil Stefan gern am Abend joggt, kauft er einen _____,

    _____ Jogginganzug. (praktisch, grau)

4. Diane sieht eine _____, _____ Handtasche. (klein, leicht)

    Die muss sie haben.

5. Monika findet eine _____ CD von der _____

    Opernsängerin Maria Callas. (interessant, berühmt)

6. Da Joan eine _____, _____ Frau

    (wählerisch°, jung) mit _____, _____   finicky

    Wünschen ist, kauft sie nichts. (kompliziert, teuer)

7. Am Ende des _____ Tages (lang) gehen alle ins Kino und sehen

    einen _____, _____ Film. (modern, amerikanisch)

H. Was meinen Sie? State your opinion by choosing one or more of the *adjectives* in
parentheses, or provide your own.

1. Ich möchte gern in einer _____ Wohnung wohnen. (groß, klein, gemütlich, alt)

2. Ich will bald ein _____ Auto kaufen. (billig, teuer, blau, weiß)

3. Ich gehe gern zu _____ Partys. (lustig, laut, klein, interessant)

4. Dort treffe ich oft _____ Menschen. (langweilig, berühmt, sympathisch,

    freundlich)

5. In meiner Freizeit sehe ich gern _____ Filme. (amerikanisch, europäisch,

    ernst, lustig)

6. Und ich lese gern _____ Bücher. (deutsch, kurz, lang, modern)

I. Gregs Familie. Greg is participating in an exchange program between an American high school and a German **Gymnasium.** He shows his German host family photos of his family in America. Complete his statements by choosing one of the *attributive adjectives* in parentheses and adjust the indefinite article or the possessive pronoun when necessary.

➜ Das ist mein____ _____ Freund Doug. (neu, gut)
Das ist mein guter Freund Doug.

1. Hier sind mein____ _____ Eltern. (tolerant, freundlich)

2. Ich habe ein____ _____ Schwester. (lustig, sportlich)

3. Das ist mein____ _____ Bruder. (ernst, kompliziert)

4. Wir wohnen in ein____ _____ Haus. (groß, alt)

5. Unser Haus liegt an ein____ _____ See°.   **der See:** lake
(schön, sauber)

6. Mit unser____ _____ Hund gehe ich oft am See spazieren. (klein, schwarz)

Name _____   Datum _____

J. Frauen in Spitzenpositionen°. Read the passage and then answer the questions.

leading positions

Vor kurzer Zeit hat eine deutsche Zeitung eine Studie° über Frauen in Spitzenpositionen in Deutschland geschrieben. Die Studie zeigt, was diese Frauen erfolgreich° gemacht hat und wie ihr Familienleben ist. Man hat nur Frauen in traditionellen Männerberufen wie Professor, Rechtsanwalt°, Direktor eines Krankenhauses und Geschäftseigentümer° interviewt. Diese Frauen haben studiert und verdienen mehr als fünfig-tausend Euro im Jahr. Zu dieser Zeit haben weniger als zehn Prozent der Frauen einen dieser Berufe.

study

successful

lawyer / owner of a business

Die Studie hat gefunden, dass mehr als fünfzig Prozent dieser Frauen nicht verheiratet sind. Frauen mit eigenem Geschäft sind öfter ver-heiratet. Diese Frauen nehmen dann ihr Kind mit zur Arbeit – mit ins Geschäft. Die Mutter eines jungen Mädchens sagt: „Meine kleine Sonja hat oft im Büro auf dem Schreibtisch geschlafen." Für die meisten berufs-tätigen Frauen ist das natürlich unmöglich.

Wenn Frauen verheiratet sind, dann brauchen sie auch viel Energie für die Familie. Eine der Frauen hat gemeint: „Wir haben es im Beruf sehr schwer. Wir haben nicht das, was für den Erfolg° im Beruf sehr wichtig ist: eine Frau."

success

Fast alle Frauen meinen, dass man eine gute Ausbildung° haben muss und auch den Willen° zum Erfolg. Dafür müssen sie oft ihre privaten Interessen aufgeben und auch Pläne für eine eigene Familie. Was ist für diese erfolgreichen Frauen wichtig? Sie suchen weniger das Geld und die Sicherheit, sondern mehr ihre Unabhängigkeit° und eine interes-sante Arbeit.

education
determination

independence

1. Auf welche Fragen will die Studie Antworten finden?

_____

_____

2. Was für Frauen hat man interviewt?

_____

3. Wie viel Prozent Männer gibt es in diesen Berufen?

_____

4. Warum ist es für Frauen mit Kindern leichter, wenn sie ihr eigenes° Geschäft haben?

one's own

_____

5. Was müssen Frauen in Spitzenpositionen oft aufgeben?

_____

6. Was finden sie im Beruf wichtig und was weniger wichtig?

_____

K. Liebes Tagebuch°. Keep a diary for three days. Follow the model below   diary
for the dates, and use the *present perfect tense* in your entries. Use the cues
provided or provide your own activities.

Klausur schreiben ■ Referat vorbereiten ■ in der Bibliothek arbeiten ■
mit anderen Studenten in die Mensa° gehen ■ Hausarbeit tippen° ■   university cafeteria / to type
am Computer arbeiten ■ Wohnung putzen ■ Zimmer aufräumen ■
ausgehen ■ in den Biergarten gehen ■ ins Theater/Kino/Konzert gehen ■
Mountainbike fahren ■ Freunde treffen ■ windsurfen gehen ■ faulenzen ■
fotografieren

➜ *Freitag, den zwölften Februar: Heute habe ich Valerie im Café getroffen. Am Abend
bin ich mit ihr ins Kino gegangen.*

_____, den _____ _____: _____

_____

_____

_____, den _____ _____: _____

_____

_____

_____, den _____ _____: _____

_____

_____

L. Familie in Deutschland heute. The following two graphs from the magazine Focus
show how many people nowadays choose to live alone. Look at the graphs and answer
the following questions with full sentences.

    includes

    unmarried households

    single parents

1. Wie viel Prozent der Deutschen leben alleine?

_____

2. Wie viel Prozent leben in einer traditionellen Familie?

   _____

3. Wie viel Prozent leben ohne Partner, aber mit einem oder mehreren Kindern?

   _____

TOP-TEN DER SINGLE-STÄDTE

Anteil° der Ein-Personen-Haushalte in deutschen
Städten über 500 000 Einwohnern° (in Prozent)

Stadt	Prozent
München	51,8
Hannover	51,2
Frankfurt	50,6
Köln	48,0
Hamburg	47,7
Berlin	47,5
Düsseldorf	47,4
Stuttgart	47,2
Bremen	47,2
Dortmund	39,9

Quelle: Angaben der Städte

portion

inhabitants

4. In welchen drei Städten gibt es die meisten Singles?

   _____

5. In welchen drei Städten wohnen die wenigsten° Singles?   least

   _____

6. Ihrer Meinung nach°, wie muss eine Stadt sein, um interessant für   in your opinion
   Singles zu sein?

   _____

   _____

M. *Kulturelle Notizen.* You plan to travel to Germany next year and you are
preparing for your trip by collecting information about various social and political situations. Provide brief answers in English.

1. Name two benefits established by federal legislation in Germany to aid parents. Do similar
   benefits exist in your country?

   _____

   _____

2. What does German law say about equal rights **(Gleichberechtigung)** in the workplace?

_____

_____

_____

3. Name two working conditions in Germany that make it easier for men and women to participate actively in the life of their family.

_____

_____

_____

KAPITEL 9   Grüezi in der Schweiz

A. Morgens oder abends? Claudia's friends Jasmin and Florian both take courses early in the morning so they are usually getting ready at about the same time. Describe what they are doing in the illustrations and when. You can use *definite* and *indefinite* time.

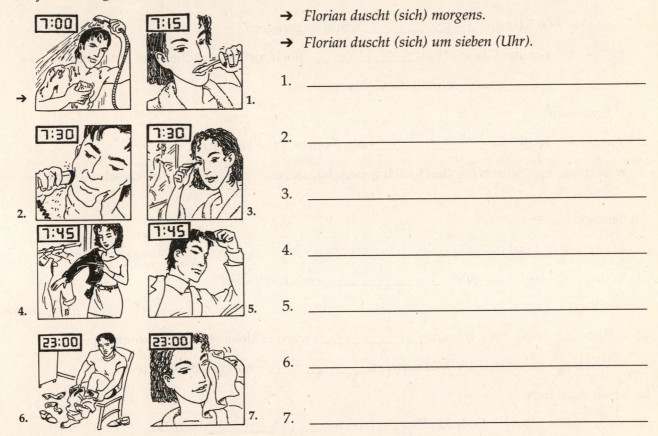

➜ *Florian duscht (sich) morgens.*

➜ *Florian duscht (sich) um sieben (Uhr).*

1. _____

2. _____

3. _____

4. _____

5. _____

6. _____

7. _____

B. Schreiben Sie über Ihr Morgenprogramm. Describe your morning routine. Use *reflexives* where appropriate. Suggested vocabulary:

zuerst	baden	Radio / Kassetten hören
dann	(sich) duschen	Zeitung kaufen / lesen
jetzt	sich waschen	Bett machen
später	sich die Zähne putzen	joggen gehen
nachher	sich anziehen	frühstücken° to eat breakfast
	sich rasieren	Freund / Freundin anrufen
	sich schminken	etwas für die Uni vorbereiten
	sich kämmen	

Ich stehe um _____ Uhr auf. Zuerst _____

_____

_____

_____
_____
_____
_____

C. Kurze Gespräche. In the brief conversations below, complete each sentence with the appropriate *reflexive pronoun*.

Beim Skilaufen

1. a. ALEX: Hat Melanie _____ schon angezogen?

   b. GISELA: Ja, aber Claudia hat _____ noch nicht geduscht. Und ich muss

      _____ noch schnell die Zähne putzen.

Beim Einkaufen

2. a. GISELA: Willst du _____ neue Sportschuhe kaufen?

   b. FREUND/IN: Ja, wir können gleich gehen. Ich ziehe _____ noch schnell eine Jacke an.

An der Uni

3. a. CLAUDIA: Hast du _____ erkältet?

   b. UWE: Ja, leider. Es geht _____ ziemlich schlecht.

Auf der Party

4. a. ALEX UND UWE: Wir fragen _____, warum Melanie nicht gekommen ist.

   b. MICHAEL UND GISELA: Wir können es _____ auch nicht erklären.

In der Sprechstunde°   office hour

5. a. PROFESSOR LANGE: Frau Riedholt, setzen Sie _____ doch. So,

      freuen Sie _____ schon auf das Ende des Semesters?

   b. GISELA: Ja, Professor Lange, ich freue _____ sehr darauf.

D. Zum Studium in Zürich. Tanja has transferred from Tübingen to Zurich to study physics at the famous Eidgenössische° Technische Hochschule° there. Tell about Tanja's first weeks there by writing new sentences. Use the *modal + infinitive*, **zu** + *infinitive*, or **um … zu** + *infinitive* construction, as appropriate. Begin each sentence with the phrase in parentheses.   Swiss Confederation / university

→ Tanja studiert in der Schweiz. (Es ist interessant …)
  Es ist interessant in der Schweiz zu studieren.

1. Tanja studiert an der ETH Physik. (Tanja ist nach Zürich gekommen …)

_____

2. Tanja findet in Zürich ein Zimmer. (Es ist nicht einfach …)

_____

3. Jetzt wohnt sie bei Bekannten ihrer Eltern am Züricher See. (Tanja kann …)

_____

4. Tanja bezahlt dort keine hohe Miete°. (Tanja muss …)   rent

_____

5. Sie kommt schneller zur Uni. (Sie hat sich ein Rad gekauft …)

_____

6. Tanja lernt die Stadt kennen. (Tanja hat leider nicht sehr viel Zeit …)

_____

7. Sie arbeitet viel für ihr Studium. (Sie muss …)

_____

8. Tanja fühlt sich in Zürich richtig wohl. (Doch schon nach ein paar Wochen beginnt Tanja …)

_____

E. Identifizieren Sie. Identify the two rivers and eight cities marked on the map of Switzerland. Refer to the map on the inside cover of your textbook as necessary.

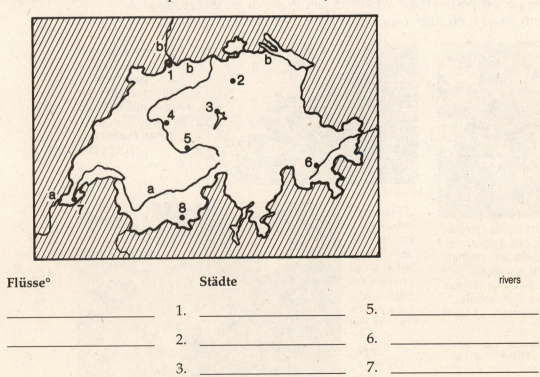

Flüsse°		Städte				rivers
a. _____		1. _____		5. _____		
b. _____		2. _____		6. _____		
		3. _____		7. _____		
		4. _____		8. _____		

F. Meine Freunde in Tübingen. When Gisela is home in Mainz, she tells her parents about her friends in Tübingen. Complete each of her statements with the *comparative* and then the *superlative* of the adjective or adverb.

→ David ist sportlich.
Aber ich bin sportlicher.
Und Alex ist am sportlichsten.

1. Melanies Miete° ist hoch.   rent

   Aber Claudias Miete _____.

   Und Uwes Miete ist _____.

2. Alle arbeiten viel.

   Aber Michael _____.

   Und Claudia _____.

3. Ich höre gern klassische Musik.

   Alex _____ Popmusik.

   Und Michael _____ Rockmusik.

4. David kann gut kochen.

   Aber Uwe _____.

   Und Melanie _____.

G. Worauf freust du dich? The local magazine *Franzz* conducted a survey, asking young people between the ages of 15 and 19 about what they are looking forward to. Read their responses and answer the following questions.

„Ich wechsele[1] den Basketballverein[2] - nach Leverkusen. Vielleicht ist das der Beginn meiner Profi-karriere[3]!"
Lukas Maciejczyk, 15 Jahre

„Ich freue mich total auf meinen 18. Geburtstag und darauf, meinen Führerschein zu machen. Außerdem gibt es dieses Jahr viel zu feiern: Konfirmation* von meinem Bruder zum Beispiel."
Karen Bertram, 17 Jahre

„Dieses Jahr werde ich endlich mit der Schule fertig. Wenn ich mein Abi[4] in der Tasche habe, mache ich erst mal[5] Zivildienst.†"
Jürgen Gloger, 19 Jahre

_____

[1] am changing   [2] basketball team   [3] professional career   [4] = **Abitur**   [5] first of all

* **Konfirmation:** the rite by which Karen's brother is accepted into full membership in the church.
† **Zivildienst:** civilian service, which young German men may choose in place of the required military service.

„Ich mache meinen
Realschulabschluss.[2]
Bin gespannt,[3] was
danach auf mich zu-
kommt[4]."
**Benedikt Kurt, 16
Jahre**

„Die Sommerferien sind für mich
am wichtigsten. Ich hoffe, dass
es diesmal[1] richtig warm wird."
Frauke Mierau, 16 Jahre

[1] this time [2] diploma from the **Realschule** [3] curious
[4] **auf ... kommt**: is in store for me

1. Welche beiden Personen sind bald mit der Schule fertig? Haben beide schon Pläne für die
   Zeit nach der Schule? Welche Pläne?

   _____

   _____

   _____

2. Worauf freut sich Karen?

   _____

3. Wer freut sich auf die Sommerferien? Was hofft sie?

   _____

4. Wem ist der Sport wichtig? Welche Pläne hat er?

   _____

   _____

5. Und worauf freuen Sie sich?

   _____

   _____

H. Die Sage° von Wilhelm Tell. The story of Wilhelm Tell (see page 86) is   legend
one of the most important Swiss legends and probably one of the most frequently performed plays in Switzerland. In order to see it, you need not
travel to Switzerland, you can watch it in New Glarus, Wisconsin, where
each year in August this legend is performed as a tribute to the birth of the
Swiss nation on August 1, 1291.

Was Robin Hood für die Engländer ist, das ist Wilhelm Tell für die Schweizer – ein tapferer° Kämpfer° für die Freiheit und gegen die Ungerechtigkeit°. Lesen Sie bitte die Sage von Wilhelm Tell.

brave / fighter
injustice

Im dreizehnten Jahrhundert haben sich die Schweizer Kantone Schwyz, Uri und Unterwalden zusammengetan, um gegen Österreich zu kämpfen°. Die Schweizer wollten° frei sein und nicht zu Österreich gehören. In drei Kriegen haben sie dann ihre Freiheit gewonnen. Aus dieser Zeit kommt auch die Sage von Wilhelm Tell.

fight / wanted

Zu Tells Zeiten ist Geßler der österreichische Gouverneur in der Schweiz. Um die Treue° der Schweizer zu prüfen°, hängt Geßler einen Hut auf eine Stange° in Altdorf, Kanton Uri. Wer an diesem Hut vorbeigeht°, muss ihn grüßen° und so Respekt für Geßler und Österreich zeigen°. Eines Tages geht Tell mit seinem Sohn an dem Hut vorbei, ohne ihn zu grüßen. Ein Soldat° sieht das und bringt Tell zum Gouverneur. Dieser ist sehr böse und sagt: „Tell, als Strafe° musst du einen Apfel vom Kopf deines Sohnes schießen°." Tell antwortet: „Das mach' ich nicht. Ich schieße nicht." Geßler ist jetzt noch böser: „Tell, ich sage dir, du schießt oder du stirbst° zusammen mit deinem Sohn."

loyalty / test
pole
goes by / greet, salute
show
soldier
punishment
shoot

die

Etwas später legt der Gouverneur selbst dem Jungen den Apfel auf den Kopf. Jetzt kann Tell wirklich nichts mehr machen als schießen. Tell schießt und trifft° den Apfel. Geßler sagt ihm, dass er das gut gemacht hat und dass er gut schießen kann. Geßler will aber auch wissen, warum Tell nicht einen Pfeil°, sondern zwei genommen hat. Tell hat Angst die Wahrheit zu sagen und meint: „Man braucht immer zwei Pfeile, wenn man schießt." Geßler glaubt ihm aber nicht und sagt: „Du brauchst keine Angst zu haben. Dein Leben ist sicher. Sag' mir aber die Wahrheit." Tell antwortet: „Der zweite Pfeil war für dich, wenn ich meinen Sohn getroffen hätte°."

hits

arrow

would have

Als Geßler das hört, wird er zornig° und schreit°: „Dein Leben sollst du behalten°, aber nicht die Freiheit." Dann fesseln° die Soldaten Tell und bringen ihn auf das Schiff des Gouverneurs. Kaum° sind sie auf dem See°, da kommt ein starker Sturm° auf. Alle haben große Angst, weil sie das Schiff nicht mehr steuern° können. Nur Tell kann sie retten°. Die Soldaten binden ihn los und Tell steuert das Schiff sicher ans Land. Als sie ankommen, springt Tell aus dem Schiff, stößt° es wieder auf den See und läuft weg.

enraged / shout
keep / chain
no sooner
lake / storm
steer / save

shoves

Später hört der Sturm auf°, und Geßler und seine Leute kommen auch an Land. Tell steht hinter einem Busch und wartet auf den Gouverneur. Als dieser vorbeireitet°, hört Tell, wie Geßler einige Pläne gegen ihn macht, und er schießt. Mit dem Tod° des Gouverneurs beginnt jetzt der Kampf°, um den Schweizern Freiheit zu bringen. Obwohl diese Geschichte nur eine Sage ist, steht eine Statue von Tell in Altdorf. Für die Schweizer bedeutet° der Name „Tell" auch heute noch Freiheit und Unabhängigkeit°.

hört auf: stops
rides by
death
struggle

means
independence

Name _____ Datum _____

1. Wer ist Wilhelm Tell?

   _____

2. Zu welcher Zeit hat er gelebt?

   _____

3. Wer ist Geßler?

   _____

4. Warum haben die Soldaten Tell zum Gouverneur gebracht?

   _____

5. Was, sagt Geßler, soll Tell machen?

   _____

6. Was will Tell mit dem zweiten Pfeil machen?

   _____

7. Warum haben die Soldaten auf dem See Angst?

   _____

8. Wann beginnt der Kampf um die Freiheit?

   _____

9. Was bedeutet der Name „Tell" für die Schweizer?

   _____

Wilhelm Tell Festival ✚

I. Hallo Wach°! Hallo Wach! Look at the advertisement for Radio Köln and   awake
answer the following questions.

Hallo Wach!

Noch frischer in den Tag!

Wenn Sie morgens
schon mehr wissen
als alle anderen,
dann ist es
Hallo Wach!
auf der 107,1.

Hallo Wach!
ab 6.00 Uhr.

Radio
Köln
107,1

Für die besten Hörer der Stadt!

1. Welche Adjektive im Komparativ finden Sie?

_____

2. Welches Adjektiv im Superlativ finden Sie?

_____

3. Zu welcher Tageszeit° kommt diese Sendung?   time of day

_____

4. Welchen Vorteil° haben die Hörer von „Hallo Wach!"?   advantage

_____

J. Werbung°. Now make up your own commercial or advertisement for a   commercial
newspaper, magazine, or radio/TV station. Use comparative and superlative forms. You can use the ad for „Hallo Wach!" in Exercise I as a model.

K. *Kulturelle Notizen.* You plan to travel to Switzerland next year and you prepare for the trip by taking notes about cultural and political differences between Switzerland and your own country. Provide brief responses in English.

1. Name the four national languages of Switzerland. Name the national language(s) in your country.

    _____

    _____

2. Describe military service in Switzerland. Which aspects are different from those in your country?

    _____

    _____

3. Name one major political similarity and one major political difference between Switzerland and your country.

_____

_____

4. Tell a friend three or four things you find interesting about either Zurich or Basel.

_____

_____

_____

_____

Name _____   Datum _____

KAPITEL 10   Deutschland: 1945 bis heute

A. An der Uni. Describe Peter's experiences as a student at the **Freie Universität** in Berlin by completing the sentences with the *simple past tense* forms of the verbs in parentheses.

1. Während Peter an der FU in Berlin _____, _____ er
   in einem Studentenheim. (studieren / wohnen)

2. Als er wieder nach Hause _____, _____ er seiner Familie,

   wie es in Deutschland an der Uni _____. (kommen / erzählen / sein)

3. Die Universität _____ nichts. (kosten)

4. Viele Studenten _____ Geld vom Staat. (bekommen)

5. Die Studenten _____ nur ein oder zwei Fächer studieren. (müssen)

6. Sie _____ nicht jedes Semester Klausuren. (schreiben)

7. Das _____ Peter sehr. (gefallen)

B. Komödie und Theater am Kurfürstendamm. Look at the program of the "Komödie am Kurfürstendamm" and answer the questions on page 92.

¹ play   ² dream   ³ songs   ⁴ romantic pop

1. Was für Lieder können Sie bei „Männer" hören?

_____

2. Wer singt die Lieder?

_____

3. Was gibt es bei dieser Vorstellung° zu essen?   performance

_____

4. Wovon erzählt das Stück über die Comedian Harmonists?

_____

5. An welchem Abend möchten Sie die „Komödie am Kurfürstendamm" am liebsten besuchen? Warum finden Sie dieses Programm interessant?

_____

_____

_____

C. Eine Reise nach Berlin. Gisela is coming to Berlin for the weekend to visit Monika and to get to know the city. Monika tells her mother on the phone what she is planning for Gisela's visit. (1) In talking to her mother, Monika uses present tense. (2) On Sunday, after Gisela has left, Monika writes her friend about the visit. Complete her letter using the *simple past tense*.

1. Monika erzählt ihrer Mutter von ihren Plänen fürs Wochenende.

Gisela kommt am Freitagabend um 22:30 Uhr an. Ich hole sie am Bahnhof ab. Dann fahren wir zu mir nach Hause und ich zeige Gisela mein Zimmer. Danach gehen wir in die Wunder-Bar – ich habe Gisela schon so viel darüber erzählt. Am Samstag schlafen wir aus° und dann   **schlafen ... aus:** sleep in besuchen wir das Deutsche Historische Museum. Dort ist gerade eine Ausstellung° über die Nachkriegszeit in Deutschland. Da lernen wir   exhibition auch etwas über die Zeit der Berliner Blockade. Abends kochen wir dann zusammen und wir laden Peter und Guido ein. So kann Gisela endlich meine Freunde kennen lernen.

2. Monikas Brief an Sandra:

Liebe Sandra,

wie geht es dir? Mir geht es gut. Am Wochenende war meine Freundin Gisela

in Berlin und hat mich besucht. Gisela _____¹ am

Freitagabend um 22:30 an. Ich _____² sie am Bahnhof ab.

Dann _____³ wir zu mir nach Hause und ich

_____⁴ Gisela mein Zimmer. Danach _____⁵

wir in die Wunder-Bar – ich hatte Gisela schon so viel darüber erzählt. Am

Samstag _____⁶ wir aus und dann _____⁷ wir

Name _____ Datum _____

das Deutsche Historische Museum. Dort ist gerade eine Ausstellung über die

Nachkriegszeit in Deutschland. Da _____ [8] wir auch etwas

über die Zeit der Berliner Blockade. Abends _____ [9] wir dann

zusammen und wir _____ [10] Peter und Guido ein. So

_____ [11] Gisela endlich meine Freunde kennen lernen. Kommst

du auch bald nach Berlin, um mich zu besuchen? Ich würde mich freuen.

Viele Grüße

deine Monika

D. Von Ost- nach Westdeutschland. Nadine Bresan tells about her move from East to West Germany. Complete the paragraphs with the correct *simple past* form of the appropriate verb.

Verbs: müssen ■ finden ■ haben ■ verlieren ■ wollen

Kurz nach der Vereinigung _____ [1] meine Mutter ihren Job

in Leipzig und wir _____ [2] nach Frankfurt am Main

umziehen°, wo sie eine neue Stelle als Chemikerin _____ [3].   move

Ich _____ [4] zwar nicht mitkommen, aber ich

_____ [5] keine andere Möglichkeit.

Verbs: bleiben ■ gehen ■ halten ■ mögen

In Frankfurt _____ [6] ich in die 11. Klasse eines

Gymnasiums und am Anfang _____ [7] ich meine Mitschüler

überhaupt nicht°. Ich _____ [8] sie für arrogant und ober-   not all all

flächlich. Ich war auch überrascht° darüber, wie traditionell das   surprised

Familienleben mancher Mitschüler oft war, denn bei vielen

_____ [9] die Mutter zu Hause.

Verbs: kennen lernen *(fills 2 blanks)* ■ fühlen ■ dürfen ■ gefallen

Die Schule selbst _____ [10] mir aber ganz gut, weil man

offen seine Meinung° sagen _____ [11] und der Unterricht°   opinion / class instruction

auch relativ frei war. Nach ein paar Monaten _____ [12] ich

meine Mitschüler besser _____ [13] und ich

_____¹⁴ mich langsam ganz wohl in Westdeutschland.

Inzwischen° finde ich die Unterschiede zwischen Ost-und Westdeutschen

gar nicht mehr so groß.

in the meantime

E. Eine Reise nach Ostdeutschland. At the beginning of the fall semester Melanie told her friends about the trip Claudia, Alex, and Uwe had taken to East Germany. Tell about their trip by rewriting each sentence in the past perfect.

➔ In den Semesterferien fuhren Claudia, Alex und Uwe nach Dresden.
Melanie sagte, *in den Semesterferien waren Claudia, Alex und Uwe nach Dresden gefahren.*

1. Alex war noch nie in Ostdeutschland.

Sie sagte, _____

_____

2. Claudia hat früher mit ihren Eltern manchmal Verwandte in Weimar besucht.

Sie sagte auch, _____

_____

3. In Dresden übernachteten Claudia, Alex und Uwe in der Jugendherberge.

Melanie sagte, _____

_____

4. Abends hörten sie in der Semperoper die Beethoven-Oper Fidelio.

Sie sagte auch, _____

_____

5. In Leipzig gingen Claudia und Uwe ins Bach-Museum.

Melanie sagte, _____

_____

6. Leider hatte Alex eine Erkältung und er lag einen Tag im Bett.

Sie sagte, _____

_____

F. Überall Fahrräder. Jennifer spent her year abroad in Münster, a university town in Nordrhein-Westfalen. She was surprised to see how popular bicycles were in that area. Combine her statements using **als, wann,** or **wenn,** as appropriate.

eingetragener Verein: registered club

1. Ich war in Münster. Es gab einen Fahrradboom.

   _____

2. Ich weiß nicht. Der Boom hat angefangen.

   _____

3. Die Studenten fuhren fast alle mit dem Rad. Sie mussten in die Stadt.

   _____

4. Niemand° fand es komisch°. Ich fuhr einmal mit dem Rad zum   no one / odd
   Einkaufen.

   _____

5. Ich fuhr immer mit. Meine Freunde machten am Wochenende eine Radtour.

   _____

6. Am Freitag fragte ich sie immer schon. Wir sollten uns am Sonntag treffen.

   _____

7. Und ich war immer traurig. Es regnete und wir konnten keine Radtour machen.

   _____

G. So war es. Ms. Bunge recalls the problems her son encountered in East Berlin before German unification—all for love. Read the passage and then answer the questions.

Als mein Sohn Erik Ingenieurstudent in Berlin war, lernte er eine Frau aus dem Westen kennen. Es war die große Liebe. Die beiden wollten heiraten. Das Problem war nur: Wie konnte mein Sohn legal aus der DDR in den Westen?

Erik war in der FDJ, der Freien Deutschen Jugend, der staatlichen Jugendorganisation, aktiv. Er machte gerade bei einer Firma in Berlin sein Praktikum°, als er beantragte° in den Westen gehen zu dürfen.   internship / applied
Zwei Tage danach wurde er exmatrikuliert° und verlor Arbeit und   expelled

Zimmer. Der Direktor der Ingenieurschule fuhr zu uns. Wir sollten unseren Sohn beeinflussen. Wir konnten es aber nicht. Er wollte zu seiner Inge.

Lange Zeit hörte Erik nun nichts. Er musste also ein neues Zimmer finden. Das war schwer. Eine neue Stelle war gar nicht zu finden. Er fand einige freie Stellen. Aber wenn man hörte, dass er beantragt hatte in den Westen zu gehen, kamen Antworten wie: „Es tut uns Leid, aber die Stelle ist doch nicht frei." Oder: „Wir brauchen doch etwas andere Qualifikationen." In *einer* Firma sagte man ihm ganz offen: „Leute, die in den Westen wollen, können hier nicht einmal° als Hilfsarbeiter° arbeiten."

nicht einmal: not even / unskilled workers

Kein Mensch wusste, wann er eine Antwort erwarten° konnte. Einige Leute hatten nach kurzer Zeit eine Antwort bekommen. Bei anderen wieder war es sehr langsam gegangen. Waren diese Unterschiede nun Teil des politischen Systems, oder war es einfach die Schlamperei° der Bürokratie? Es war schwer zu sagen.

expect

sloppiness

Eines Nachmittags musste es dann plötzlich° sehr schnell gehen. Er musste in drei Stunden reisefertig° sein. Er hatte nicht einmal Zeit zu uns zu fahren.

suddenly
ready to travel

Erst am 9. November 1989° konnten wir unseren Sohn endlich wieder sehen und seine westdeutsche Frau, unsere Schwiegertochter°, endlich kennen lernen.

Berlin wall was opened
daughter-in-law

1. Wo war Erik Bunge zu Hause?

_____

2. Warum konnte er Inge nicht einfach heiraten?

_____

3. Warum sprach der Direktor der Ingenieurschule mit Eriks Eltern?

_____

4. Warum konnte Erik keine Arbeit finden?

_____

5. Wann konnte Erik eine Antwort auf seinen Antrag° erwarten?

application

_____

6. Warum war der 9. November 1989 ein wichtiges Datum° für die Familie Bunge?

date

_____

H. Ein Hundeleben. Tell what is going on in these pictures or make up a story based on the pictures. Use the *simple past tense.* You may use any of the words listed below.

Léon van Roy, © Frick Friedrich

Mutter / Frau	sitzen	zuerst
Vater / Mann	sich setzen	dann
Sohn / Junge / Hund / Sessel	wegschicken°	nachher send away
Buch	lesen	schließlich
Zeitung	stricken°	knit
	mit dem Schwanz wedeln°	**mit ... wedeln:** wag its tail
	schlafen	

_____

_____

_____

_____

_____

_____

_____

_____

I. *Kulturelle Notizen.* You're planning to go to Germany next year and you're preparing for the trip by taking notes about various cultural and political facts related to Germany. Provide brief responses in English.

1. Why is Bertolt Brecht regarded as a prominent figure in 20th-century literature?

   _____

   _____

2. Why and when was the Berlin Wall erected and subsequently demolished?

   _____

   _____

   _____

3. Describe some of the problems Germany faced **Nach der Vereinigung**—after unification.

   _____

   _____

   _____

4. Describe the selection process and function of the **Bundespräsident** and the **Bundeskanzler.**

   _____

   _____

   _____

   _____

5. Name two things about Leipzig and two about Dresden that you find most interesting.

   _____

   _____

   _____

   _____

KAPITEL 11   Wirtschaft und Beruf

A. Eine Frage der Qualität. Dr. Ziegler is trying to sell a previous customer her company's new computer. In a short German paragraph, write a summary of what happened at a recent meeting. Use the questions following the dialogue as a guideline for your paragraph.

FRAU DR. ZIEGLER:	So, Herr Kohler, was halten Sie von unseren Preisen?
HERR KOHLER:	Sie wissen, es ist keine Frage des Preises. Ihre Computer sind nicht gerade billig, aber darüber können wir später reden. Am wichtigsten ist die Frage der Qualität.
FRAU DR. ZIEGLER:	Bei unserem Namen, Herr Kohler? Alle kennen den „Solo".
HERR KOHLER:	Trotzdem°. Die Computer, die wir vor fünf Jahren bei Ihnen gekauft haben, mussten wir ziemlich oft reparieren.
FRAU DR. ZIEGLER:	Leider. Aber jetzt haben wir keine Bildprobleme mehr. Der neue Solo Personal Computer 2008 arbeitet auch schneller. Sie werden also viel Zeit sparen. Außerdem kann man mit unserem Software-Paket ohne Programmierer programmieren. Sie brauchen kein kompliziertes Programm zu schreiben, Sie brauchen nur ein paar Worte zu tippen. Ich bin sicher, Sie werden zufrieden° sein.
HERR KOHLER:	Hm, ja ... Ich rufe Sie am Montag in einer Woche an und sage Ihnen, ob wir uns für den „Solo" interessieren. Dann können wir noch einmal° über die Preise reden, nicht?

Marginal glosses: Nevertheless; satisfied; again

Questions

Was verkauft Frau Dr. Zieglers Firma? Wie sind ihre Produkte?
Was hat Herr Kohler vor fünf Jahren dort gekauft? War er damit zufrieden? Warum (nicht)?
Welche Qualitäten hat der neue Solo Computer 2008?
Kauft Herr Kohler den Computer? Wann will er Frau Dr. Ziegler wieder anrufen? Worüber
  möchte er dann mit ihr sprechen?

_____

_____

_____

_____

_____

B. Was wird Claudia nach ihrem Examen machen? Sometimes, Claudia ponders what she will be doing after she has completed her medical studies. Right now she has certain ideas and intentions for her future. Describe her plans by using the *future tense* in the underlined clauses.

→ Ich suche mir eine Wohnung.
   Ich werde mir eine neue Wohnung suchen.

1. Ich verdiene genug Geld, um mir ein neues Auto zu kaufen.

   _____

2. Dann reise ich für ein paar Monate durch Südamerika.

   _____

3. Vielleicht habe ich dort auch die Möglichkeit, in einem Krankenhaus zu arbeiten.

   _____

4. Wenn ich zurückkomme, studiere ich vielleicht noch ein oder zwei Jahre im Ausland.

   _____

5. Danach suche ich mir eine Stelle in einem Krankenhaus.

   _____

6. Hoffentlich helfe ich in meinem Beruf vielen Menschen.

   _____

C. Und was werden Sie nach Ihrem Examen machen? Write a five-sentence paragraph about some of your plans after graduation. Use the *future tense*.

_____

_____

_____

_____

_____

_____

_____

_____

_____

D. Praktika°. Read what three secondary students have to say about their internship experiences. Then answer the questions that follow.

internships

Ich lese sehr gerne und bin oft in der Buchhandlung oder Bücherei.[1] Das Verkaufen und Lesen der Bücher interessiert mich. Mein Job im Praktikum besteht darin,[2] zu beraten,[3] verkaufen, Bücher zu sortieren oder Pakete[4] zu packen. Ich finde es wichtig, schon vor der zehnten Klasse zu entscheiden,[5] ob ich arbeiten gehen möchte oder lieber studieren. Aber ich denke, ich studiere lieber...
Karolin Jacobs, 16 Jahre

[1] library [2] **besteht darin:** consists of [3] provide help [4] packages [5] decide

Wenn ich später mal einen Nebenjob[1] brauche, ist es sicherlich[2] nicht schlecht, ein Praktikum im Geschäft absolviert[3] zu haben. Vielleicht habe ich dadurch die Möglichkeit, während des Studiums etwas Geld zu verdienen. Hier im Sportgeschäft gefällt es mir sehr gut und es gibt immer etwas zu tun. Ich mache fast die gleiche Arbeit wie die Angestellten auch.
Christoph Pomrehn, 16 Jahre

[1] side job [2] probably [3] completed

Ein Praktikum bedeutet für mich, dass ich das Arbeitsleben kennen lernen kann. So wird für mich deutlicher,[1] in welche Richtung[2] es später mal gehen wird. Es gefällt mir hier im Reisebüro[3] sehr gut. Das Arbeiten am Computer macht Spaß und ich lerne neue Programme kennen. Hier herrscht[4] eine lockere[5] Atmosphäre. Das Praktikum macht mir deutlich, was verkaufen bedeutet.
Sebastian Schmidt, 15 Jahre

[1] clearer [2] direction [3] travel agency [4] exists [5] casual

1. Wo macht Christoph sein Praktikum? Was macht er da?

   _____

   _____

2. Warum findet er es wichtig ein Praktikum zu machen?

   _____

3. Wie gefällt es Sebastian im Reisebüro? Wie ist die Atmosphäre?

   _____

4. Was kann er da lernen?

   _____

5. Wo macht Karolin ihr Praktikum?

   _____

6. Was muss sie dabei alles machen?

   _____

7. Wie sind Karolins Zukunftspläne?

   _____

8. Haben Sie schon einmal ein Praktikum gemacht? Wenn ja, was haben Sie gemacht? Wenn nein, was für ein Praktikum würden Sie gerne machen?

   _____

   _____

   _____

E. Verben, Verben. Give the *present-time subjunctive* forms of the following verb phrases.

➜ ich tue   *ich täte* _____

1. du weißt   _____

2. es gibt   _____

3. er geht   _____

4. sie findet   _____

5. ihr habt   _____

6. sie kommt   _____

7. du bist   _____

F. Dicke Luft° am Arbeitsplatz. Look at the chart on page 103 about the mental and physical problems caused by bad conditions at work. Imagine you are the boss of a company where more than 50% of your employees are complaining about the symptoms on the right side of the chart. What would you do to change the work climate? Write five sentences in the *subjunctive.* You can use the **würde**-construction and the cues listed.

    mit den Angestellten sprechen ■ Aktivitäten für die Freizeit organisieren ■ in der Firma einen Fitnessraum/ein Café einrichten° ■ die Angestellten besser bezahlen ■ andere Mitarbeiter suchen ■ den Arbeitsplatz schöner machen ■ neue Schreibtische/Pflanzen/Lampen/ bessere Computer kaufen ■ mit den Angestellten über ihre Zukunft in der Firma sprechen

(margin notes:) dicke Luft: tense atmosphere

set up

Name _____   Datum _____

find, experience
working conditions

Dicke Luft am Arbeitsplatz

Von je 100 Beschäftigten empfinden das Betriebsklima am Arbeitsplatz als	Schlechtes Betriebsklima führt bei den Betroffenen zu° (Mehrfachnennungen)

those affected
führt zu: leads to

76 — gut bis sehr gut

56 Streßgefühl

52 Nervosität

43 schlechtem Schlaf

bearable

20 — erträglich° bis schlecht

35 Kopfschmerzen

35 Erschöpfungsgefühl°   exhaustion

responses

4 — keine Angaben°

25 Magenschmerzen

10 Appetitlosigkeit

_____

_____

_____

_____

_____

_____

G. Schwierigkeiten°. Michael is trying to schedule a rehearsal with   problems
Sabine, the singer of the band Michael is playing in. Complete each
sentence below to express politeness, using the *present-time subjunctive* of
the cued modal.

➔ MICHAEL: _Könntest_ du um sieben zur Probe kommen? (können)

SABINE: _____ es um sieben sein? (müssen)

MICHAEL: Die Probe _____ vier Stunden dauern. (sollen)

SABINE: _____ ich vielleicht erst um acht kommen? (dürfen)

Ich _____ eigentlich noch meinem Freund bei seinem Referat helfen.

(wollen)

MICHAEL: Sicher _____ du das, aber … (können)

SABINE: Morgen Abend _____ ich dann schon um sieben kommen. (können)

H. Die Welt der Kinder – ein großes Geschäft. Read the passage and then answer the questions. This report is taken from the website of *Deutsche Welle*, which offers news and excerpts from German radio and TV.

Gisela Weinbauer, eine Reporterin aus Düsseldorf, interessiert sich für die Werbung° und ihren Einfluss° auf die deutschen Familien. Sie interviewte einige Personen für ihren Bericht°. Lesen Sie, was diese Leute zu dem Thema „Werbung" zu sagen haben.

advertising / influence

report

Zuerst sprach Gisela Weinbauer mit Frau Greif, die die Werbung kritisierte. Frau Greif sagte, dass sie, als Mutter von drei Kindern, sich wirklich wünschte, es gäbe gar keine Werbung mehr. Zum Geburtstag und zu Weihnachten° kauft sie natürlich Geschenke° für ihre Kinder, aber wegen der ewigen Werbung im Fernsehen ist es schwer „nein" zu sagen, wenn die Kinder zu anderen Zeiten Wünsche haben. Sobald° die Werbung neue Spielsachen° empfiehlt, haben ihre Kinder kein Interesse mehr an den alten Dingen; sofort° wollen sie das Neue haben. Frau Greif meinte auch, dass sie keine Freude mehr daran hat ins Kaufhaus zu gehen, denn es heißt immer nur: „Mami, das möcht' ich gern haben und dieses möcht' ich haben." Da sie aber arbeitslos ist und ihr Mann nicht viel verdient, haben sie wenig Geld. Wenn sie könnte, würde sie lieber das Geld sparen, anstatt so viel für teure Spielsachen zu bezahlen.

Christmas / presents

as soon as

toys

immediately

Als Gisela Weinbauer sich mit Herrn Voss, dem Chef eines Spielzeughauses°, unterhielt, hörte sie, was ein typischer Geschäftsmann zu sagen hat. Für ihn ist die Werbung eben etwas Gutes, ein Boom. Zum Beispiel, wenn die Werbung am Wochenende etwas Neues im Fernsehen zeigt, dann müssen die Kinder das am Montag gleich haben. Das ist ganz selbstverständlich°. Herr Voss war der Meinung°, dass der Lebensstandard der Deutschen sehr hoch ist, sogar einer der höchsten der Welt. Das Resultat ist also, dass die Deutschen Geld haben, um ihren Kindern kaufen zu können, was diese haben möchten. Nicht nur die Eltern kaufen den Kindern sehr viel, sondern auch die Verwandten – Tanten, Onkel und Großeltern – kaufen Spielsachen und geben den Kindern Geld. Vielleicht wäre es besser, wenn sie einen Teil des Geldes sparen würden, aber es gefällt Herrn Voss, dass sie es für Spielsachen ausgeben°. Für die Geschäftsleute ist die Werbung etwas ganz Tolles.

toy store

naturally / war ... Meinung: was of the opinion

spend

[...]

Was das Kind haben will und was das Kind glücklich macht, sagen heute die großen Firmen mit ihrer Werbung. Obwohl Lehrer und Eltern sich Sorgen machen über den negativen Einfluss der Werbung, freut sich die Wirtschaft über die jungen Kunden mit dem vielen Geld.

1. Wofür interessiert sich Gisela Weinbauer?

_____

_____

_____

2. Was ist Frau Greifs Meinung über die Werbung?

_____

_____

_____

3. Warum hat Frau Greif keine Lust mit ihren Kindern einkaufen zu gehen?

_____

_____

4. Was sagt Herr Voss über die Deutschen und ihre Kinder?

_____

_____

_____

5. Was machen die großen Firmen mit ihrer Werbung?

_____

_____

_____

I. Moment mal! What would you do if you were the guest in the cartoon? Write three sentences in the *subjunctive*. You may use any of the words listed below.

»Etwas näher 'ran, bitte!«

der Ober°	sitzen	sich beschweren°	waiter / complain
der Herr	sprechen	verschütten°	spill
das Weinglas/die Weinflasche	einschenken°	schreien°	pour / yell
der Manager	wechseln		
die Tischdecke°			tablecloth
die Zeitung			

_____

_____

_____

_____

J. Wenn ich nur ... Write a ten-sentence essay about what you would do if your life were different. Some suggestions: **Wenn Sie mehr Zeit (Geld, Talent) hätten; wenn Sie weniger Arbeit (Stress, Probleme) hätten; wenn Sie reich (toll aussehend°, berühmt) wären.**

great-looking

Wenn ich (berühmt) wäre, würde ich _____

_____

_____

_____

_____

_____

_____

_____

_____

_____

_____

Wenn ich drei Wünsche freihätte, würde ich mir zuerst Frieden° auf der ganzen Welt wünschen. Das wäre mein größter Traum.° Dann würde ich mir einen kleinen Hund oder eine kleine Katze wünschen. Und als Letztes: viele Wünsche mehr freizuhaben!

peace

dream

Vanessa

Name _____ Datum _____

K. *Kulturelle Notizen.* You plan to travel to Germany next year and you prepare for the trip by collecting information about historical, political, and cultural differences between your country and Germany. Provide brief responses in English.

1. Give one example of social legislation in Germany for which your country has similar legislation. Give two examples of German social legislation for which your country has no legislative equivalents. (You may also refer to your textbook, p. 383.)

   _____

   _____

   _____

2. Explain the term **Mitbestimmung** *(codetermination)*. Does your country have such a policy?

   _____

   _____

   _____

3. State the goals and achievements of the European Union.

   _____

   _____

   _____

4. Describe the apprenticeship system in Germany.

   _____

   _____

   _____

Florian

KAPITEL 12   Die multikulturelle Gesellschaft

A. Etwas Persönliches.   Here is the opportunity to talk about some plans, likes, and dislikes.

1.   Nennen Sie …

  a. zwei Länder, in die Sie gern reisen möchten, oder zwei Kulturen, die Sie gern kennen lernen möchten.

  1. _____   2. _____

  b. zwei Fremdsprachen, die Sie gern fließend° sprechen möchten.   fluently

  1. _____   2. _____

2.   Nennen Sie …

  a. zwei Bands oder Musiker, die Sie gern hören möchten.

  1. _____   2. _____

  b. zwei Filme, die Sie sehen möchten.

  1. _____   2. _____

  c. zwei Bücher, die Sie dieses Jahr gelesen haben.

  1. _____   2. _____

3.   Nennen Sie die Vorlesung, …

  a. die Sie am interessantesten gefunden haben. _____

  b. die Ihnen am wenigsten gefallen hat. _____

  c. die Sie Ihren Freunden empfehlen würden. _____

B. Was ist das? Describe the following items using *relative pronouns*. Use the definitions listed.

Kassetten gehört werden ■ die Bedeutung° von Wörtern erklärt wird ■   meaning
man fliegt ■ Geschirr gespült wird ■ macht Rockmusik ■ man sitzt ■
man kauft Fleisch und Wurst ■ lehrt° an der Uni   teaches

   → Kassettendeck   Ein Kassettendeck ist ein Objekt, mit *dem Kassetten gehört werden.*

1. Ein Professor ist ein Lehrer, _____
_____ .

2. Eine Spülmaschine ist eine Maschine, in _____
_____ .

3. Eine Rockmusikerin ist eine Frau, _____
_____ .

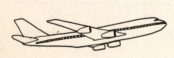

4. Ein Stuhl ist ein Möbelstück, auf _____
_____ .

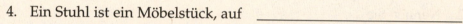

5. Eine Metzgerei ist ein Laden, in _____
_____ .

6. Ein Flugzeug ist ein Verkehrsmittel, mit _____
_____ .

7. Ein Wörterbuch ist ein Buch, in _____
_____ .

C. Deutschland als zweite Heimat. Pedro Olivetti, who came to work in Germany over thirty years ago, talks about his experiences there. Complete the paragraphs with the appropriate relative pronouns.

Ich komme aus Cosenza, einer Stadt in Süditalien, in ___der___ es in den

70er-Jahren für die jungen Leute nur wenig Arbeit gab. Also ging ich nach

Deutschland, um einen Job zu suchen. Die ersten Wochen in Deutschland

sind eine Zeit, an _____¹ ich nicht gern zurückdenke. Ich vermisste°   missed

meine Verwandten, _____² alle in Italien geblieben waren. Außerdem

waren die Deutschen, mit _____³ ich zu tun hatte, ziemlich reserviert.

In der Firma, bei _____⁴ ich zuerst gearbeitet habe, gab es zum Glück

viele ausländische Kollegen.

So waren die Leute, mit _____⁵ ich mich in meiner Freizeit traf,

zum größten Teil Ausländer. Und die Frau, _____⁶ ich bald kennen

lernte, war auch Italienerin. Giovanna und ich heirateten 1975 und wir

bekamen zwei Söhne, _____⁷ heute 25 und 30 sind. Der ältere –

Roberto –, _____⁸ Frau Türkin ist, lebt heute in Berlin. Massimo,

_____⁹ noch nicht verheiratet ist, studiert in Freiburg. Unsere bei-

den Söhne fühlen sich als Deutsche. Für sie ist Deutschland ihre Heimat

und Italien das schöne Land, in _____¹⁰ sie gern ihre Urlaube

verbringen°. Meine Frau, _____¹¹ es in den ersten Jahren in   spend

Deutschland nicht so gut gefiel, möchte auch nicht mehr weg von hier. Für

meine Eltern, _____¹² immer in Cosenza gelebt haben, ist das ein biss-

chen traurig. Sie wären froh, wenn wir auch in Italien leben würden.

Außerdem hätten sie gern Enkelkinder°, _____¹³ richtige Italiener   grandchildren

sind.

D. Kulturelle Unterschiede. Monika has spent one year in the United States. She and Peter are discussing differences they noted between German and American culture. Complete the sentences with a *relative clause,* using the guidelines provided.

→ Monika spricht mit Peter, (sie hat ihn heute Abend in der Studentenkneipe getroffen).
Monika spricht mit Peter, den sie heute Abend in einer Studentenkneipe getroffen hat.

1. Sie sprechen über kulturelle Unterschiede, (sie haben die Unterschiede bemerkt°).   noticed

   _____

2. Die Autofahrer, (die Autofahrer sieht Peter in Deutschland), fahren oft wie die Wilden.

   _____

3. Monika hat in Amerika die öffentlichen Verkehrsmittel, (mit den öffentlichen Verkehrsmitteln kann man überallhin° fahren), vermisst°.   everywhere / missed

   _____

4. Die Züge in Deutschland, (Peter benutzt die Züge oft), sind meistens pünktlich.

   _____

5. Monika fand die Amerikaner, (die Amerikaner lächeln mehr als die Deutschen), manchmal zu freundlich.

   _____

6. Peter mag den amerikanischen Alltag° (der Alltag ist durch die   everyday life
   Freundlichkeit der Leute einfacher), fast lieber.

   _____

E. Von wem wird was in Annikas Familie gemacht? Everyone in Annika's family has chores. You decide what they are. Use *present passive.*

→ Tante – Gartenarbeit machen   *Die Gartenarbeit wird von der Tante gemacht.*

Wer?	Was?	
Vater	Blumen pflanzen	Spülmaschine einräumen
Mutter	Badezimmer putzen	Auto waschen
David	Essen kochen	Tisch decken
Oma	Lebensmittel einkaufen	Garage aufräumen
Opa		
Annika		

1. _____

2. _____

3. _____

4. _____

5. _____

6. _____

F. Ausländer in deutschen Städten. Look at the graph about the percentage of foreigners in German cities. Then answer the following questions.

percentage of foreigners

	Zahl der Ausländer	
Frankfurt	181 200	27,8
Stuttgart	133 800	22,8
München	282 100	22,6
Köln	189 000	18,6
Düsseldorf	94 600	16,6
Hamburg	272 600	16,0
Duisburg	78 900	15,4
Hannover	76 400	14,8
Berlin	435 100	13,1
Dortmund	74 000	12,7
Bremen	66 000	12,2
Essen	56 000	9,4

Welt-Städte — Ausländeranteil in deutschen Städten über 500 000 Einwohner (in Prozent)

F CUSSIERT

Quelle: Angaben der Städte

1. Nennen Sie die drei deutschen Städte mit den meisten Ausländern.

   _____

2. Wie heißen die drei Städte mit den wenigsten Ausländern?

   _____

3. Inwiefern sind die Städte mit vielen Ausländern wohl interessanter? Was meinen Sie?

   _____

   _____

4. Welche Probleme könnten die Städte mit einem hohen Ausländeranteil aber haben?

   _____

   _____

G. Von wem wurde das erfunden° oder geschrieben? Use the cues below and provide the appropriate verb. Use the *simple past passive.*

invented

→ das Telefon – Alexander Graham Bell   *Das Telefon wurde von Alexander Graham Bell erfunden.*

1. *Huckleberry Finn* – Mark Twain _____

   _____

2. das Dynamit – Alfred Nobel _____

   _____

3. die amerikanische Verfassung (*constitution*) – Thomas Jefferson _____

   _____

4. das Musical *West Side Story* – Leonard Bernstein _____

   _____

5. die Buchdruckerkunst (*printing*) – Johann Gutenberg _____

   _____

H. Eine junge Türkin berichtet. Neval is an 18-year-old Turkish woman, who is training to be a practical nurse (**Krankenpflegerin**). She came to Germany with her parents when she was seven years old. In this excerpt from a report she has given, Neval talks about her life in Germany. Answer the questions following her report.

Neval, 18 Jahre:

…

Früher wollte ich zurück [in die Türkei], aber jetzt beginne ich meine Situation zu begreifen°. Früher war ich jünger und habe nicht gesehen, wie es in der Türkei ist. Ich bin hier großgeworden und es würde mir sehr schwer fallen° jetzt in die Türkei zu gehen. Aber ich sage es noch nicht meinen Eltern. Ich glaube, ich würde die Menschen in der Türkei nicht mehr verstehen, weil ich nicht denke wie sie. Ich denke schon ganz anders. Wenn ich in der Türkei bin, dann nur auf Urlaub, und da sehe ich nicht alles. Da bin ich am Strand°, wo es schön und sonnig ist. Ich weiß nicht, wie es sonst ist, wenn kein Urlaub ist. Da wird das Leben hart° sein, wenn man sich behaupten° muss. Hier kenne ich die Regeln°, aber dort weiß ich nichts. Ich fühle mich hier sehr wohl.

Meine Familie will zurück, und bis vor zwei Jahren wollte ich auch zurück. Jetzt nicht mehr. Seit ich die Ausbildung° mache, ist alles ganz anders. Früher habe ich gedacht, ich bin überhaupt nichts°, aber die Ausbildung macht doch sehr viel aus. Als Krankenpflegerin° wird man ganz anders behandelt°, als wenn man nur eine Arbeiterin ist. Es ist ein großer Unterschied zwischen Arbeitern und Angestellten.

Margin glosses:
understand

schwer fallen: find something hard

beach

hard / assert oneself

rules

training

nothing at all

nurse

treated

Mein Vater kann immer noch nicht verstehen, warum ich das mache. Aber er hat es inzwischen akzeptiert. Und mein großer Bruder ist, glaube ich, traurig, dass er damals° keine Ausbildung gemacht hat. Er hätte eine Chance gehabt, aber er wollte nicht. Mein Onkel hat ihm damals eine Ausbildung verschafft°, aber er ist nicht hingegangen. Mein kleiner Bruder macht einen qualifizierten Abschluss°. Er will auch eine Ausbildung machen.

at that time

obtained

school diploma

1. Warum möchte Neval nicht in die Türkei zurückgehen?

   _____

   _____

2. Welche Probleme hätte sie dort vielleicht?

   _____

   _____

3. Kennt sie die Türkei gut?

   _____

   _____

4. Seit wann ist Nevals Leben in Deutschland ganz anders?

   _____

   _____

5. Wie denken ihre Eltern darüber, dass sie eine Ausbildung macht?

   _____

   _____

6. Worüber ist Nevals großer Bruder traurig?

   _____

   _____

7. Welche Pläne hat ihr kleiner Bruder?

   _____

   _____

I. In zwanzig Jahren ... Write a ten-sentence essay about your own *future plans*. What will you be doing in about 20 years from now? Include adverbs like **schon, sicher, wohl.** Suggestions of areas to write about: **Beruf, Wohnung, Reisen, Kinder, Geld, Hobbys, Partnerin/Partner, berühmt sein.**

In zwanzig Jahren werde ich wohl _____

_____

_____

_____

_____

_____

_____

_____

_____

J. *Kulturelle Notizen*. You plan to travel to Germany next year, and you prepare for the trip by collecting information about political aspects of this country. Provide brief responses in English to each of the following questions.

1. Who are the **ausländische Arbeitnehmer** and where do they come from?

   _____

   _____

2. Today, Germany has large numbers of ethnic German resettlers (**Aussiedler**) as well as political asylum seekers (**Asylanten**). Integration of these groups into German society is beset by a number of difficulties. Name two of these problems.

   _____

   _____

3. Look at the following chart and give a brief summary of its content.

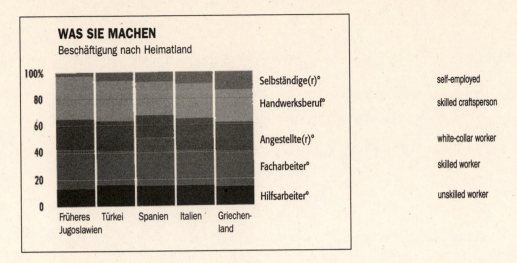

WAS SIE MACHEN
Beschäftigung nach Heimatland

Selbständige(r)°				self-employed
Handwerksberuf°				skilled craftsperson
Angestellte(r)°				white-collar worker
Facharbeiter°				skilled worker
Hilfsarbeiter°				unskilled worker

Früheres Jugoslawien   Türkei   Spanien   Italien   Griechen-land

_____

_____

_____

_____

Viel Spaß und Freude am Geburtstag...

Lab Manual

Name _____ Datum _____

EINFÜHRUNG   Wie heißt du?

In the directions you will hear the following new words:

Übung   exercise
Beispiel   example
Fangen wir an.   Let's begin.

A. Frage und Antwort°. You will hear six questions, each followed by two   question and answer
responses. If both responses are the same, place a check mark in the column
marked **same**. If the responses are different, place a check mark in the column
marked **different**.

	same	different		same	different		same	different
→	____	✓						
1.	____	____	3.	____	____	5.	____	____
2.	____	____	4.	____	____	6.	____	____

B. Welche Nummer? You will hear ten statements about the items pictured below. Put the
number of each statement under the picture to which it refers.

→ _1_   a. _____   b. _____   c. _____

d. _____   e. _____   f. _____   g. _____

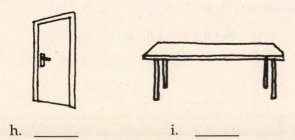

h. _____   i. _____

C. Farben. You will hear eight statements about colors. If a statement is correct, place a check mark in the column marked **richtig**. If the statement is false, place a check mark in the column marked **falsch**.

	richtig *(true)*	falsch *(false)*
→	✓	_____ (der Ozean)

	richtig	falsch			richtig	falsch	
1.	_____	_____	(die Maus)	5.	_____	_____	(die Banane)
2.	_____	_____	(der Asphalt)	6.	_____	_____	(das Gras)
3.	_____	_____	(die Schokolade)	7.	_____	_____	(die Tomate)
4.	_____	_____	(das Gras)	8.	_____	_____	(das Papier)

D. Frage und Antwort. You will hear five questions, each followed by two responses. Place a check mark by the letter of the answer that makes sense. You will hear each set of questions and answers twice.

→ a. _____   b. ✓_____

1. a. _____ b. _____	3. a. _____ b. _____	5. a. _____ b. _____
2. a. _____ b. _____	4. a. _____ b. _____	

E. Diktat°. Write the words you hear spelled.   dictation

→   *Lampe*_____

1. _____	2. _____	3. _____

Copy down the numbers you hear.

1. _____	3. _____	5. _____
2. _____	4. _____	

F. Giselas Telefon. You will hear a conversation between Alex and Gisela. Afterwards you will hear five statements. Place a check mark in the column marked **richtig** if the statement is correct. Place a check mark in the column marked **falsch** if the statement is incorrect. You will hear the conversation twice. You will hear four new expressions:

eigentlich	*actually*	Sag mal.	*Tell me.*
kaputt	*broken*	Wo wohnst du?	*Where do you live?*

	richtig	falsch		richtig	falsch		richtig	falsch
→	✓	_____						
1.	_____	_____	3.	_____	_____	5.	_____	_____
2.	_____	_____	4.	_____	_____			

Name _____ Datum _____

KAPITEL 1   Guten Tag! Wie geht's?

In the directions you will hear the following new words:

Übung   *exercise*
Beispiel   *example*
Fangen wir an.   *Let's begin.*

A. Eine Studentin in Tübingen. Listen to the reading of the *Lesestück* "Eine Studentin in Tübingen."

B. Richtig oder falsch? You will hear eight statements based on the *Lesestück* "Eine Studentin in Tübingen." Check **richtig** if the statement is correct according to the information in the reading passage. Check **falsch** if the statement is incorrect.

	richtig	falsch		richtig	falsch
→		✓			
1.	___	___	5.	___	___
2.	___	___	6.	___	___
3.	___	___	7.	___	___
4.	___	___	8.	___	___

C. Ist das logisch? You will hear seven pairs of questions and responses. Place a check mark in the column marked **logisch** if the response is logical. Place a check mark in the column marked **unlogisch** if the response to the question is not logical.

	logisch	unlogisch		logisch	unlogisch
→	✓				
1.	___	___	5.	___	___
2.	___	___	6.	___	___
3.	___	___	7.	___	___
4.	___	___			

D. Das Gegenteil°. You will hear six questions containing an adjective or an   the opposite
adverb. Complete the answer below by checking the antonym of the adjec-
tive or adverb you hear.

→ Nein, er ist ...   ✓____ a. faul   _____ b. ernst

1. Nein, es geht mir ...   _____ a. schlecht   _____ b. ruhig

2. Nein, sie ist ...   _____ a. krank   _____ b. freundlich

3. Nein, er ist ...   _____ a. lustig   _____ b. müde

4. Nein, es ist ...   _____ a. klein   _____ b. nett

5. Nein, er ist ...   _____ a. gut   _____ b. neu

6. Nein, sie ist ...   _____ a. freundlich   _____ b. kritisch

E. Jürgen. You will hear a brief description of Jürgen and learn what he likes to do.
Afterwards, you will hear eight statements. Place a check mark in the column marked
richtig if the statement is correct. Place a check mark in the column marked **falsch** if the
statement is incorrect. You will hear the description twice.

	richtig	falsch
→ Jürgen ist 22 Jahre alt.	_____	✓____
1. Er ist faul.	_____	_____
2. Er spielt gern Schach.	_____	_____
3. Er treibt nicht gern Sport.	_____	_____
4. Er spielt Fußball.	_____	_____
5. Er spielt Tischtennis.	_____	_____
6. Er geht oft tanzen.	_____	_____
7. Er geht heute Abend ins Kino.	_____	_____
8. Er ist heute müde.	_____	_____

F. Diktat. What are Susi and Oliver doing? Oliver runs into Susi on the street, and they talk about various things. Complete their conversation by supplying the missing words, which you will hear on the recording. You will hear the entire dialogue twice. You will hear a new expression:

mit mir   *with me*

→ Tag, Susi, wie ___*geht's*_____ ?

— Tag Susi, wie geht's?

— Tag, Oliver, danke, _____ _____.

— Du, was _____ du _____ _____?

— Ich _____.

— Hm ... Und _____ _____?

— Nichts _____.

— Spielst du gern _____?

— Ja, _____ gern.

— _____ du mit mir?

— Ja, gern.

G. Übungen zur Aussprache°. Listen and repeat the word pairs. You may   pronunciation
wish to review the pronunciation of long and short **u** and **o** in Appendix E
of your textbook.

long $\bar{u}$	short u	long $\bar{o}$	short o
Mus	muss	Moos	Most
buk	Buckel	bog	Bock
Schuster	Schuss	Schote	Schotte
Stuhle	Stulle	Ofen	offen
tun	Tunnel	Tone	Tonne

Now listen and repeat the sentences, paying special attention to the way you pronounce long and short **u** and **o** in the boldfaced words.

1. Spielt **Monika oft Rockmusik?**
2. Ist heute **Mittwoch oder Donnerstag?**
3. Es ist **Montag.**
4. Geht es Ihnen **gut?**
5. Ja, danke. **Und** Ihnen?

H. Wann gehen wir ins Kino? You will hear a conversation between Gisela and Alex. Afterwards, you will hear four statements. Place a check mark in the column marked **richtig** if the statement is correct. Place a check mark in the column marked **falsch** if the statement is incorrect. You will hear the conversation twice. You will hear four new expressions:

doch	*of course*
immer	*always*
Sag mal.	*Tell me.*
Zeit	*time*

	richtig	**falsch**
→	_____	✓ _____
1.	_____	_____
2.	_____	_____
3.	_____	_____
4.	_____	_____

Name _____ Datum _____

KAPITEL 2   Alles ist relativ

A. Groß oder klein? Alles ist relativ! Listen to the reading of the *Lesestück* "Groß oder klein? Alles ist relativ!"

B. Richtig oder falsch? In your lab manual you will see five questions based on the *Lesestück* "Groß oder klein? Alles ist relativ!" You will hear the questions and three possible answers to each question. Each answer is said twice. Check the letter of each correct answer. A question may have more than one correct answer.

	a	b	c
→ Wie findet David Tübingen?	✓	✓	
1. Wie viele Einwohner hat Deutschland?			
2. Wie groß ist Deutschland?			
3. Wie ist das Klima in Deutschland?			
4. Was für Wetter findet David gut?			

C. Das Wetter. You will hear six short conversational exchanges about the weather. In your lab manual you will see a statement based on each exchange. Check **richtig** if the statement is correct; check **falsch** if it is incorrect. You will hear a new expression:

(schon) wieder   *again*

	richtig	falsch
→ Es regnet heute.		✓
1. Heute ist es kalt.		
2. Heute ist es schön.		
3. Es ist heute kalt.		
4. Morgen ist es bestimmt warm.		
5. Es schneit.		
6. Hoffentlich regnet es morgen wieder.		

D. Welches Wort? You will hear seven words. Check the word in each printed pair that you hear pronounced.

➔   ✓   bleiben   _____ treiben

1. _____ nett   _____ Bett

2. _____ mehr   _____ sehr

3. _____ Schnee   _____ schön

4. _____ morgen   _____ Norden

5. _____ vier   _____ für

6. _____ heiß   _____ weiß

7. _____ scheinen   _____ schneien

E. Entgegnungen°. You will hear four statements about the weather. In your   responses lab manual you will see two possible replies for each statement. Check the letter of the reply that makes sense.

➔   ✓   a. Ja, vielleicht regnet es morgen.

  _____ b. Ja, morgen regnet es bestimmt auch.

1. _____ a. Ja, leider, und gestern war es noch so schön.

  _____ b. Aber morgen regnet es vielleicht.

2. _____ a. Ja, der Wind ist so kalt.

  _____ b. Hoffentlich bleibt es so schön.

3. _____ a. Ja, es bleibt bestimmt so heiß.

  _____ b. Ja, bestimmt, der Wind ist so kalt heute.

4. _____ a. Jetzt bleibt es bestimmt warm.

  _____ b. Aber heute ist es leider sehr heiß.

F. Ein Telefongespräch°. Dieter calls Ingrid on the telephone. Listen to their conversation, then check the correct answers to the questions printed in your lab manual. You will hear the conversation twice. You will hear two new words:

telephone conversation

mit	*with*
oder?	*or will you?*

1. Was macht Ingrid?

   _____ a. Sie spielt Schach.

   _____ b. Sie ist im Bett und hört Musik.

2. Wie war das Wetter gestern?

   _____ a. Nass und kalt.

   _____ b. Schön warm.

3. Warum spielt sie nicht mit Dieter Tennis?

   _____ a. Sie spielt nicht gern Tennis.

   _____ b. Sie ist krank.

4. Wie ist das Wetter heute?

   _____ a. Es ist schönes Wetter.

   _____ b. Es regnet.

5. Was macht Dieter?

   _____ a. Er geht ins Kino.

   _____ b. Er spielt vielleicht mit Barbara Tennis.

G. Übungen zur Aussprache. Listen and repeat the word pairs. You may wish to review the pronunciation of long and short **o** and **ö** in Appendix E of your textbook.

long ē	long ȫ	short e	short ö
Hefe	Höfe	Gent	gönnt
Lehne	Löhne	helle	Hölle
Sehne	Söhne	kennen	können
beten	böten	Beller	Böller
hehle	Höhle	Bäcker	Böcke

long ō	long ȫ	short o	short ö
schon	schön	konnte	könnte
Ofen	Öfen	Frosch	Frösche
losen	lösen	Koch	Köche
hohe	Höhe	Bock	Böcke
tot	töten	Kopf	Köpfe

Now listen and repeat the sentences, paying special attention to the way you pronounce long and short **o** and **ö** in the boldfaced words.

1. Wie ist der **Sommer** in **Österreich?**
2. Im **Sommer** ist es **oft schön.**
3. Deutschland liegt weiter **nördlich** als Amerika.
4. Er **hört** die **Wörter** nicht.

H. Wie ist das Wetter? You will hear a telephone conversation between Gisela and her father in Mainz. Afterwards, you will hear four statements. Place a check mark in the column marked **richtig** if the statement is correct. Place a check mark in the column marked **falsch** if the statement is incorrect. You will hear the conversation twice. You will hear three new words:

dich   *you*
Sag mal.   *Tell me.*
Vati   *Dad*

	richtig	**falsch**
→	_____	✓
1.	_____	_____
2.	_____	_____
3.	_____	_____
4.	_____	_____

KAPITEL 3   Was brauchst du?

A. Einkaufen am Wochenende. Listen to the reading of the *Lesestück* "Einkaufen am Wochenende."

B. Richtig oder falsch? You will hear eight statements based on the *Lesestück* "Einkaufen am Wochenende." Check **richtig** if the statement is correct according to the information in the reading passage. Check **falsch** if the statement is incorrect.

richtig   falsch

1. _____   _____

2. _____   _____

3. _____   _____

4. _____   _____

5. _____   _____

6. _____   _____

7. _____   _____

8. _____   _____

C. Der richtige Laden°. You will hear four short dialogues. For each one, in   the right store
your lab manual you will see the names of two possible shops or stores
where the dialogue might take place. Place a check mark beside the correct
location. You will hear two new words:

Packung   *box*
Paracentamol   *headache medicine*

1. _____ Bäckerei   _____ Buchhandlung

2. _____ Supermarkt   _____ Lebensmittelgeschäft

3. _____ Metzger   _____ Markt

4. _____ Apotheke   _____ Drogerie

D. Entgegnungen°. You will hear six questions or statements. In your lab manual you will see two possible responses to each. Place a check mark beside the response that makes sense. You will hear a new expression:

ein paar   *a few*

1. _____ a. Ja, ich gehe in den Supermarkt.

   _____ b. Ja, ich gehe ins Kino.

2. _____ a. Nein, wir haben noch viel Brot.

   _____ b. Ja, wir brauchen Wurst.

3. _____ a. Gut, ich gehe in den Supermarkt.

   _____ b. Das Brot ist besser bei Müller.

4. _____ a. Ja, geh doch in die Apotheke!

   _____ b. Ich glaube ja.

5. _____ a. Wie viel brauchst du?

   _____ b. Okay, ich gehe in die Buchhandlung.

6. _____ a. Gut, ich kaufe drei Pfund.

   _____ b. Sonst noch etwas?

E. Diktat: Gabis Geburtstag. Complete the following story about Gabi's birthday by supplying the missing words, which you will hear on the recording. You will hear the entire story twice.

Gabi hat heute _____. Drei _____ kommen

zum Kaffee. Angelika geht in _____ _____ und

kauft für Gabi _____ _____ über Frankreich.

Das ist leider nicht ganz _____. Karin hat nicht so viel Geld. Sie geht

auf _____ _____ und kauft schöne

_____. Sie sind ganz _____. Und Susanne kauft

beim _____ viel _____. Jetzt hat auch sie

_____ _____ _____. Aber

bei Gabi ist es sehr _____. Sie _____ Kuchen,

hören Musik und finden _____ wirklich

schön.

F. Übungen zur Aussprache. Listen and repeat the word pairs. You may wish to review the pronunciation of long and short ü and u in Appendix E of your textbook.

long ī	long ǖ	short i	short ü
Biene	Bühne	Kiste	Küste
diene	Düne	Lifte	Lüfte
Kiel	kühl	Kissen	küssen
liegen	lügen	missen	müssen
fielen	fühlen	Binde	Bünde

long ǖ	short ü	long ū	long ǖ	short u	short ü
Füße	Flüsse	Huhn	Hühner	Fluss	Flüsse
Mühle	Müll	Hut	Hüte	Bund	Bünde
Sühne	Sünde	Fuß	Füße	Kuss	Küsse
Blüte	Bütte	Zug	Züge	Luft	Lüfte
Düne	dünne	Blut	Blüte	Kunst	Künste

Now listen and repeat the sentences, paying special attention to the way you pronounce long and short ü and u in the boldfaced words.

1. **Für** ihren Mann kauft sie einen **Butterkuchen.**
2. Der **Student** kann seine **Bücher** nicht finden.
3. **Jürgen sucht** ein **Buch über Musik.**
4. Im **Frühling** sind die **Blumen** auf dem Markt besonders schön.

G. Das neue Zimmer. Melanie and Michael are talking about Melanie's new room. Before listening to their conversation, read the questions in your lab manual. While listening you may wish to take notes. You will hear the conversation twice. Then answer the questions in German. You will hear a new word:

Schreibtisch   *desk*

1. Wie findet Melanie ihr neues Zimmer?

_____

2. Was braucht sie noch?

_____

3. Was hat Michael für Melanie?

_____

4. Wie viel Euro soll sie Michael geben?

_____

KAPITEL 4 Was studierst du?

A. Studieren in Deutschland. Listen to the reading of the *Lesestück* "Studieren in Deutschland."

B. Richtig oder falsch? You will hear eight statements based on the *Lesestück* "Studieren in Deutschland." Check **richtig** if the statement is correct. Check **falsch** if it is incorrect. You will hear a new word:

weil   *because*

	richtig	falsch		richtig	falsch		richtig	falsch
1.	_____	_____	4.	_____	_____	7.	_____	_____
2.	_____	_____	5.	_____	_____	8.	_____	_____
3.	_____	_____	6.	_____	_____			

C. Der richtige Ort°. You will hear six questions concerning the location of   *the right place*
certain activities. For each question you will hear two possible answers.
Check the letter of the correct answer.

1.	a. _____	b. _____	4.	a. _____	b. _____
2.	a. _____	b. _____	5.	a. _____	b. _____
3.	a. _____	b. _____	6.	a. _____	b. _____

D. Die richtige Entgegnung°. You will hear five questions which might   *response*
begin a conversation. In your lab manual are two possible responses to each
question. Check the reply that makes sense.

1. _____ a. Ich kann leider nicht. Ich muss in die Bibliothek.

   _____ b. Ich mache Physik als Hauptfach.

2. _____ a. Mein Referat ist jetzt fertig.

   _____ b. Im Wintersemester mache ich Examen.

3. _____ a. Anglistik und Sport. Und du?

   _____ b. Ich muss in acht Semestern fertig werden.

4. _____ a. Ich muss noch zwei Semester studieren.

   _____ b. Diese Woche muss ich ein Referat schreiben.

5. _____ a. Ja, natürlich, gern.

   _____ b. Ich studiere Musik und Sport.

E. Das richtige Wort. You will hear ten words. Check the word in each printed pair that you hear pronounced.

1. _____ Arbeit _____ Abitur
2. _____ sollen _____ wollen
3. _____ müssen _____ wissen
4. _____ leihen _____ bleiben
5. _____ seit _____ Zeit
6. _____ werden _____ wohnen
7. _____ Klausur _____ Kurs
8. _____ können _____ kennen
9. _____ Fach _____ Fisch
10. _____ zahlen _____ erzählen

F. Eine deutsche Studentin. You will hear a short paragraph about a German student named Dagmar, her studies, and her activities. Listen, then check the correct answers to the questions printed in your lab manual. You will hear the story twice.

1. Was studiert Dagmar?

   _____ a. Sie studiert Physik.

   _____ b. Sie studiert in Marburg.

   _____ c. Sie studiert Germanistik und Geschichte.

2. Warum studiert sie nicht Medizin?

   _____ a. Sie findet es nicht interessant.

   _____ b. Ihre Noten vom Gymnasium waren nicht gut.

   _____ c. Es gibt keinen Numerus clausus in Medizin.

3. Was macht sie dieses Semester?

   _____ a. Sie schreibt viele Klausuren.

   _____ b. Sie leiht Michael ihre Notizen.

   _____ c. Sie schreibt ein Referat.

4. Wo arbeitet Dagmar für die Klausuren?

   _____ a. Im Seminar.

   _____ b. Im Café.

   _____ c. Sie geht in die Bibliothek.

5. Was kann Dagmar nicht oft machen?

   _____ a. In ein Café gehen und ihre Freunde sehen.

   _____ b. Ins Kino gehen.

   _____ c. Einkaufen gehen.

G. Übungen zur Aussprache. Listen and repeat the word pairs. You may wish to review the pronunciation of long and short **a** in Appendix E of your textbook.

long $\bar{a}$	short a	short a	short o
Bahn	Bann	Bann	Bonn
kam	Kamm	Kamm	komm
Staat	Stadt	Matte	Motte
Schlaf	schlaff	knalle	Knolle
lahm	Lamm	falle	volle

Now listen and repeat the sentences, paying special attention to the way you pronounce long and short **a** and short **o** in the boldfaced words.

1. **Komm doch** mit in die **Stadt!**
2. **Was soll** ich **noch machen?**
3. Der **Abend war aber interessant.**
4. Wer **sagt das?**
5. Musst du heute **Nachmittag noch** viel **arbeiten?**
6. Ich **habe noch** eine **Frage** für **Professor Bachmann.**

H. Der Roman. You will hear a conversation between Gisela and Michael. Afterwards, you will hear five statements. Place a check mark in the column marked **richtig** if the statement is correct. Place a check mark in the column marked **falsch** if the statement is incorrect. You will hear the conversation twice. You will hear two new expressions:

echt   *genuine*
Vielen Dank.   *Many thanks.*

	richtig	falsch
→	_____	___✓___
1.	_____	_____
2.	_____	_____
3.	_____	_____
4.	_____	_____
5.	_____	_____

KAPITEL 5   Servus in Österreich

A. Österreich: Ein Porträt. Listen to the reading of the *Lesestück* "Österreich: Ein Porträt."

B. Richtig oder falsch? You will hear eight statements based on the *Lesestück* "Österreich: Ein Porträt." Check **richtig** if the statement is correct. Check **falsch** if it is incorrect.

	richtig	falsch		richtig	falsch		richtig	falsch
1.	_____	_____	4.	_____	_____	7.	_____	_____
2.	_____	_____	5.	_____	_____	8.	_____	_____
3.	_____	_____	6.	_____	_____			

C. Ist das logisch? You will hear eight pairs of questions and responses. If the response is a logical reply to the question, check **logisch**. If the response is not logical, check **unlogisch**.

	logisch	unlogisch		logisch	unlogisch		logisch	unlogisch
1.	_____	_____	4.	_____	_____	7.	_____	_____
2.	_____	_____	5.	_____	_____	8.	_____	_____
3.	_____	_____	6.	_____	_____			

D. Die richtige Wortbedeutung°. You will hear six statements. For each statement, you will see two words printed in your lab manual. Indicate to which of the two words the recorded statement refers.

the correct meaning

→ _____ Flugzeug   ✓ Rad

1. _____ Bern   _____ Wien

2. _____ Ferien   _____ Alpen

3. _____ zu Hause   _____ allein

4. _____ Ski laufen   _____ gehören

5. _____ Brief   _____ Auto

6. _____ fliegen   _____ zu Fuß gehen

E. Ein Interview. A journalist, Frau Berger, is conducting interviews about the traveling habits of Germans. You will hear an interview with Herr Kaiser. Listen, and then check the correct answers to the questions printed in your lab manual. You will hear the interview twice. You will hear two new words:

Reisen   *trips*
reisen   *to travel*

1. Welches Land ist Ferienland Nummer 1 für die Deutschen?

    _____ a. Die Schweiz.

    _____ b. Österreich.

    _____ c. Dänemark.

2. Warum fahren die Deutschen gern nach Österreich?

    _____ a. In Österreich scheint immer die Sonne.

    _____ b. In Österreich ist das Essen teuer.

    _____ c. Österreich ist ein sehr schönes Land.

3. Wie reist man von Deutschland nach Österreich?

    _____ a. Viele Leute fahren mit dem Motorrad nach Österreich.

    _____ b. Man braucht nicht lange zu fahren.

    _____ c. Man kann mit dem Zug oder dem Auto fahren.

4. Was machen die Deutschen, wenn sie nach Österreich fahren?

    _____ a. Sie wandern und schwimmen.

    _____ b. Sie fahren viel mit dem Rad.

    _____ c. Sie spielen Tennis.

5. Mit wem fährt Herr Kaiser in die Ferien?

    _____ a. Mit Freunden.

    _____ b. Mit Deutschen.

    _____ c. Mit Frau Berger.

6. Wo schlafen die Freunde, wenn das Wetter gut ist?

    _____ a. Bei Freunden.

    _____ b. Im Auto.

    _____ c. Sie zelten.

Name _____ Datum _____

F. Übungen zur Aussprache. Listen and repeat the word pairs. You may wish to review the pronunciation of **k, ck, ch,** and **sch,** and the suffix **-ig** in Appendix E of your textbook.

[k]	[x]	[ç]	[š]	[x]	[ç]
Flak	Flach	welche	Welsche	Bach	Bäche
nackt	Nacht	Fächer	fescher	Loch	Löcher
Akt	acht	Wicht	wischt	Bruch	Brüche
buk	Buch	Gicht	Gischt	sprach	spräche
Lack	Lachen	Löcher	Löscher	Buch	Bücher

[iç]	[ig]
Pfennig	Pfennige
König	Könige
schuldig	schuldige
billig	billiger

Now listen and repeat the sentences, paying special attention to the sounds [k], [x], [ç], and [š] in the boldfaced words.

1. Wir **können noch frischen Kuchen** beim **Bäcker kaufen.**
2. Unsere **Nachbarin** Frau **Gärstig kann wirklich keinen** guten **Kaffee kochen.**
3. **Christl spricht** sehr **wenig.**
4. Oft sagt sie die ganze **Woche nichts.**

G. Skilaufen in Österreich. Claudia and Uwe are talking about Claudia's winter vacation. Before listening to their conversation, read the questions in your lab manual. While listening you may wish to take notes. You will hear the conversation twice. Then answer the questions in German.

1. Was macht Claudia in den Winterferien?

_____

2. Mit wem fährt Claudia in die Ferien?

_____

3. Warum macht Claudia einen Skikurs?

_____

4. Warum möchte Claudia nicht mit dem Auto nach Österreich fahren?

_____

KAPITEL 6   Was hast du vor?

A. Freizeitpläne. Listen to the reading of the *Lesestück* "Freizeitpläne."

B. Richtig oder falsch? You will hear ten statements based on the *Lesestück* "Freizeitpläne." Check **richtig** if the statement is correct. Check **falsch** if it is incorrect.

	richtig	falsch
1.	_____	_____
2.	_____	_____
3.	_____	_____
4.	_____	_____
5.	_____	_____
6.	_____	_____
7.	_____	_____
8.	_____	_____
9.	_____	_____
10.	_____	_____

C. Das Gegenteil°. You will hear five questions containing an adjective or   the opposite
an adverb. Complete the answer printed in your lab manual by checking
the antonym of the adjective or adverb you hear.

➜ Nein, er ist …   ✓ a. kalt   _____ b. toll

1. Nein, er hat … Geld.   _____ a. wenig   _____ b. schon

2. Nein, sie war …   _____ a. fertig   _____ b. langweilig

3. Nein, es ist …   _____ a. teuer   _____ b. frisch

4. Nein, ich gehe … nach Hause. _____ a. oft   _____ b. früh

5. Nein, sie ist …   _____ a. gesund   _____ b. möglich

D. Diktat. Tanja and Karla are packing for a trip to Hamburg. Complete their conversation by filling in the blanks with the words you hear on the recording. You will hear the conversation twice. You will hear one new expression:

Was meinst du?   *What do you think?*

TANJA: Glaubst du, wir brauchen sehr warme _____, Karla?

KARLA: Nein, ich glaube nicht. Eine _____ und der

_____ sind bestimmt genug.

TANJA: Gut. Du, _____ du mir deine rote

_____? Die _____ gut

_____ zu meinem schwarzen _____.

KARLA: Ja, ja. Was meinst du – _____ _____

meinen grünen Hut mitnehmen?

TANJA: Nein, bitte nicht!

KARLA: Also gut. Aber den grünen _____ _____

ich.

TANJA: Und deine _____ _____ du auch

mitbringen.

E. Arbeiten am Computer. While having lunch together, Karin and Thomas are talking about what each of them does with the computer. Listen to their conversation, then check the correct answers to the questions printed in your lab manual. You will hear the conversation twice.

1. Wo war Karin gestern Abend?

    _____ a. In der Bibliothek.

    _____ b. Zu Hause.

    _____ c. Bei Freunden.

2. Was hat sie am Computer gemacht?

    _____ a. Sie hat E-Mails geschrieben.

    _____ b. Sie hat ihre Hausarbeit geschrieben.

    _____ c. Sie hat im Internet gesurft.

3. Mag Thomas Computerspiele?

_____ a. Nein, er findet sie langweilig.

_____ b. Ja, er findet sie toll.

_____ c. Ja, er macht ganz gern Computerspiele.

4. Schreibt Karin oft E-Mails?

_____ a. Nein, denn sie schreibt nicht gern.

_____ b. Ja, sehr oft.

_____ c. Ja, denn sie findet Telefonieren zu teuer.

5. Wie findet Thomas das Chatten?

_____ a. Er findet es sehr interessant.

_____ b. Er findet es uninteressant.

_____ c. Er findet es manchmal ganz lustig.

F. Übungen zur Aussprache. Listen and repeat the word pairs. You may wish to review the pronunciation of **s** (before and between vowels), **ß (ss)**, and **z** in Appendix E of your textbook.

[s̩]	[ts]	[s̩]	[s]	[ts]
so	Zoo	reisen	reißen	reizen
sehen	zehn	heiser	heißen	heizen
Seile	Zeile	Geisel	Geiß	Geiz
sog	zog	weisen	weißen	Weizen
Sohn	Zone	leise	beißen	beizen

Now listen and repeat the sentences, paying special attention to the way you pronounce **s, ß (ss)**, and **z** in the boldfaced words.

1. Warum haben **Sie zwei Gläser**, und **Sabine** hat nur ein **Glas**?
2. **Sie müssen** doch **wissen, was Sie essen sollen.**
3. Kann man wirklich **zu** viel **lesen**?
4. Wie **heißt** Ihr **Sohn**, Frau **Seidel**?
5. Wenn ich im **Sommer Zeit** habe, mache ich eine **Reise°** in die **Schweiz**.   trip

G. Im Café an der Uni. Claudia and Alex are meeting at the university café. Listen to their conversation, and then check the correct answers to the questions printed in your lab manual. You will hear the conversation twice. You will hear two new words:

Juraklausur   *law exam*
spontan   *spontaneous*

1. Claudia sieht müde aus, weil …

    _____ a. sie lange gelernt hat.

    _____ b. sie zu viel gelesen hat.

    _____ c. sie zu spät ins Bett gegangen ist.

2. Melanie hat Claudia …

    _____ a. schon vor langer Zeit eingeladen.

    _____ b. gestern Abend ganz spontan eingeladen.

    _____ c. gefragt, ob sie heute Abend zu ihr zum Essen kommen möchte.

3. Melanie …

    _____ a. geht oft mit Claudia ins Kino.

    _____ b. geht immer nach einem guten Essen aus.

    _____ c. kann gut kochen.

4. Alex …

    _____ a. hat lange geschlafen.

    _____ b. hat für eine Juraklausur gelernt.

    _____ c. hat nur vier Stunden für die Klausur gelernt und dann geschlafen.

5. Alex fragt Claudia, ob sie …

    _____ a. heute Abend etwas vorhat.

    _____ b. heute Abend früh ins Bett geht.

    _____ c. etwas essen möchte.

KAPITEL 7 Andere Länder – andere Sitten

A. Ein Austauschstudent in Deutschland. Listen to the reading of the *Lesestück* "Ein Austauschstudent in Deutschland."

B. Richtig oder falsch? You will hear seven statements based on the *Lesestück* "Ein Austauschstudent in Deutschland." Check **richtig** if the statement is correct. Check **falsch** if it is incorrect. You will hear a new word:

Unterschiede   *differences*

	richtig	falsch		richtig	falsch
1.	_____	_____	5.	_____	_____
2.	_____	_____	6.	_____	_____
3.	_____	_____	7.	_____	_____
4.	_____	_____			

C. Ist das logisch? You will hear eight pairs of questions and responses. If the response is a logical reply to the question, check **logisch.** If the response is not logical, check **unlogisch.**

	logisch	unlogisch		logisch	unlogisch
1.	_____	_____	5.	_____	_____
2.	_____	_____	6.	_____	_____
3.	_____	_____	7.	_____	_____
4.	_____	_____	8.	_____	_____

D. Der richtige Ort°. You will hear six questions about locations. Check the   place
letter of the best answer.

1. a. _____ b. _____

2. a. _____ b. _____

3. a. _____ b. _____

4. a. _____ b. _____

5. a. _____ b. _____

6. a. _____ b. _____

E. Erlebnisse° in Deutschland. Thomas, an American student, takes his first °experiences
trip to Germany. He sees many things that are quite different from what he
is used to in the U.S. You will hear some of his impressions. Listen, then
check the correct answers to the questions printed in your lab manual. A
question may have more than one correct answer. You will hear the text
twice. You will hear three new words:

Balkon   *balcony*
Bäume   *trees*
Unterschiede   *differences*

1. Wo wohnt Thomas in Deutschland?

   _____ a. In einem Studentenwohnheim.

   _____ b. Bei einer Gastfamilie.

   _____ c. In München.

2. Was macht Frau Schneider?

   _____ a. Sie geht jeden Tag in die Bibliothek.

   _____ b. Sie arbeitet an den Blumen auf dem Balkon.

   _____ c. Sie arbeitet auf dem Bahnhof.

3. Wie isst man in Deutschland?

   _____ a. Man benutzt Messer und Gabel.

   _____ b. Man hat die Hände unter dem Tisch.

   _____ c. Beim Essen spricht man sehr wenig.

4. Was gibt es im Biergarten?

   _____ a. Es gibt große Gläser.

   _____ b. Es gibt sehr gutes Essen.

   _____ c. Es gibt Blumen und alte Bäume.

5. Was erzählt Thomas über das deutsche Bier?

   _____ a. Es schmeckt ziemlich bitter.

   _____ b. Die Deutschen trinken es sehr gern.

   _____ c. Es ist sehr teuer.

6. Kennt Thomas schon viele Leute?

   _____ a. Nein, er kennt nur Familie Schneider.

   _____ b. Ja, er hat schon viele Leute kennen gelernt.

   _____ c. Nein, er kennt nur Stefan und Karin.

   _____ d. Nein, er kennt nur die Leute im Biergarten.

F. Ein Telefongespräch. Gabi has moved into a new apartment. An old friend telephones her. Listen to their conversation, then check the correct answers to the questions printed in your lab manual. You will hear the conversation twice. You will hear four new expressions:

Arbeitszimmer	*study*
Balkon	*balcony*
ganz schön Geld	*quite a lot of money*
gehen nach Süden	*face the south*

1. Warum ruft Fred bei Gabi an?

   _____ a. Er will sie besuchen.

   _____ b. Er hört, sie hat eine neue Wohnung.

2. Wie viele Zimmer hat Gabis Wohnung?

   _____ a. 3 Zimmer, Küche und Bad.

   _____ b. 6 Zimmer.

3. Was gefällt Gabi sehr an der Wohnung?

   _____ a. Das große Badezimmer.

   _____ b. Der Balkon.

4. Wann kann Fred Gabis Wohnung sehen?

   _____ a. Am Samstag, auf dem Fest.

   _____ b. Heute Abend.

5. Was macht Gabi, wenn am Samstag schönes Wetter ist?

   _____ a. Sie geht Bücherregale kaufen.

   _____ b. Sie macht das Fest auf dem Balkon.

G. Übungen zur Aussprache. Listen and repeat the word pairs. You may wish to review the pronunciation of long and short **i** and **e** in Appendix E of your textbook.

long ī	short i	long ē	short e
bieten	bitten	beten	Betten
vieler	Filter	Fehler	Felle
Wiege	Wicke	Weg	weg
stiehlt	stillt	stehlt	stellt
riet	ritt	Reeder	Retter
ihn	in	fehle	Fälle
		gähnt	Gent

Now listen and repeat the sentences, paying special attention to the way you pronounce long and short **i** and **e** in the boldfaced words.

1. Warum **sind sie nicht hier geblieben**?
2. Er **ist gestern gegen sechs** Uhr gegangen.
3. **Wie findest** du **dieses Winterwetter**?
4. **Diese Männer** haben doch **Recht°**.   Recht haben: are right
5. **Niemand° fliegt** nach **Wien**.   no one
6. **Dieses Beispiel** habe **ich in** der Zeitung **gelesen**.
7. **Jens trinkt immer Milch**.

H. Pläne. When Monika and Peter meet in a café, they discuss plans for the early evening. Before listening to their conversation, read the questions in your lab manual. While listening, you may wish to take notes. You will hear the conversation twice. Then answer the questions in German. You will hear two new expressions:

| (ei)'ne Weile | *a while* |
| zu Besuch | *for a visit* |

1. Was will Peter vielleicht nach der Vorlesung machen?

_____

2. Wohin wollen Monika und Peter heute Abend gehen?

_____

3. Warum will Peter erst° nicht mitgehen?   at first

_____

4. Wann sollen sie bei den Nachbarn sein?

_____

KAPITEL 8 Modernes Leben

A. Zwei Familien. Listen to the reading of the *Lesestück* "Zwei Familien."

B. Richtig oder falsch? You will hear eight statements based on the *Lesestück* "Zwei Familien." Check **richtig** if the statement is correct. Check **falsch** if it is incorrect. You will hear three new words:

Arbeitszeiten   *working hours*
versorgt   *looked after*
freier Architekt   *self-employed architect*

	richtig	falsch
1.	_____	_____
2.	_____	_____
3.	_____	_____
4.	_____	_____
5.	_____	_____
6.	_____	_____
7.	_____	_____
8.	_____	_____

C. Ist das logisch? You will hear six short conversational exchanges. If the response is a logical reply to the question or statement, check **logisch.** If the response is not logical, check **unlogisch.**

	logisch	unlogisch
1.	_____	_____
2.	_____	_____
3.	_____	_____
4.	_____	_____
5.	_____	_____
6.	_____	_____

D. Die gleiche Bedeutung. You will hear six sentences. For each one, you will see a second sentence printed in your lab manual. If the sentence you hear and the printed sentence have the same meaning, check **gleich.** If the meanings are different, check **nicht gleich.**

	gleich	nicht gleich
1. Ich habe das Gefühl, dass du zu wenig Freizeit hast.	_____	_____
2. Frau Zeyse hat ihren Job aufgegeben, als ihre Tochter in den Kindergarten gekommen ist.	_____	_____
3. Frau Meier erzieht ihre Kinder alleine, denn ihr Mann hat keine Zeit.	_____	_____
4. Und, was ist bei euch in letzter Zeit passiert?	_____	_____
5. Herr Taler klagt über seine Kinder.	_____	_____
6. Hier können Sie kommen und gehen, wann Sie wollen.	_____	_____

E. Ein Gespräch. Two former collegues—Isabelle Petzold and Paul Weimer—haven't seen each other since Isabelle has been away from her job for maternity leave. Listen to the following conversation between them. Then check the correct answers to the questions printed in your lab manual. You will hear the dialogue twice. You will hear four new words:

bald	*soon*
Ehemann	*husband*
erwartet	*is expecting*
vermisst	*missed*

1. Was macht Isabelle Petzold im Moment?

   _____ a. Sie ist Hausfrau und Mutter.

   _____ b. Sie arbeitet halbtags in der Bibliothek.

2. Wie findet sie das Leben mit Kindern?

   _____ a. Sie findet es ruhig und gemütlich.

   _____ b. Sie ist manchmal ziemlich gestresst.

3. Wann kann Isabelle wieder in ihrem Beruf arbeiten?

   _____ a. Wenn ihre Mutter die Kinder nimmt.

   _____ b. Wenn ihre Tochter einen Kindergartenplatz hat.

4. Was macht Pauls Frau?

   _____ a. Sie arbeitet nicht.

   _____ b. Sie hat Kinder und arbeitet jetzt wieder halbtags.

5. Was erzählt Paul aus dem Büro?

_____ a. Dass Walter nicht mehr dort arbeitet.

_____ b. Dass Brigitte ein Baby erwartet.

6. Ist Isabelle froh, dass sie bald wieder im Büro arbeitet?

_____ a. Ja, aber sie ist auch ein bisschen nervös.

_____ b. Nein, denn sie mag es nicht, wenn die Kollegen so viel über andere Kollegen sprechen.

F. Übungen zur Aussprache. Listen and repeat the words. You may wish to review the pronunciation of **r** and **l** in Appendix E of your textbook.

[r]	[l]	full [r]	full [r]	full [r]
wird	wild	fragt	ragt	warum
Schmerzen	schmelzen	kriechen	riechen	gierig
Karte	kalte	trugen	rufen	fuhren
Schurz	Schulz	Preis	Reis	Tiere
Worte	wollte	grünen	rühmen	schnüren

Now listen and repeat the sentences, paying special attention to the way you pronounce **r** and **l** in the boldfaced words.

1. Wer hat **Frau Kugel** das **gefragt?**
2. Es hat **Cornelia** nicht **gefallen,** dass wir so **schnell gefahren** sind.
3. Im **Juli wollen** wir im **Schwarzwald wandern** und **zelten.**
4. Im **Frühling fahre** ich mit **Freunden** nach **Österreich.**

G. Ein Jobinterview. Michael is looking for a job during the semester break and he is going for an interview in a bookstore. You will hear the conversation between Frau Berg, the storeowner, and Michael. Afterwards, you will hear six statements. Place a check mark in the column marked **richtig** if the statement is correct. Place a check mark in the column marked **falsch** if the statement is incorrect. You will hear the conversation twice. You will hear three new words:

aufpassen — *watch out*
niemand — *no one*
ohne zu bezahlen — *without paying*

	richtig	falsch		richtig	falsch
→	_____	✓			
1.	_____	_____	4.	_____	_____
2.	_____	_____	5.	_____	_____
3.	_____	_____	6.	_____	_____

KAPITEL 9   Grüezi in der Schweiz

A. Ein Brief aus der Schweiz. Listen to the reading of the *Lesestück* "Ein Brief aus der Schweiz."

B. Richtig oder falsch? You will hear eight statements based on the *Lesestück* "Ein Brief aus der Schweiz." Check **richtig** if the statement is correct. Check **falsch** if it is incorrect. You will hear two new words:

autonom   *autonomous*
Urgroßeltern   *great-grandparents*

	richtig	falsch		richtig	falsch		richtig	falsch
1.	_____	_____	4.	_____	_____	7.	_____	_____
2.	_____	_____	5.	_____	_____	8.	_____	_____
3.	_____	_____	6.	_____	_____			

C. Entgegnungen°. You will hear five statements or questions about being   responses
ill. Check the answer in your lab manual that makes the most sense.

1. _____ a. Du Armer!

   _____ b. Du tust mir Leid.

   _____ c. Nein, ich bin erkältet.

2. _____ a. Ich putze mir morgens die Zähne.

   _____ b. Ich fühle mich schwächer als gestern.

   _____ c. Ich freue mich darauf.

3. _____ a. Du hast Recht, sonst kann ich nächste Woche nicht Ski laufen.

   _____ b. Hoffentlich bekomme ich diesen Herbst keine Erkältung!

   _____ c. Fühlst du dich auch krank?

4. _____ a. Das ist ja toll!

   _____ b. Bist du gestresst?

   _____ c. Geh doch ins Theater!

5. _____ a. Nein, ich glaube nicht.

   _____ b. Morgen gehe ich Ski laufen.

   _____ c. Nein, ich huste nicht.

D. Körperteile. You will hear five sentences describing parts of the body. Check the correct answer.

1. _____ a. Hände   _____ b. Füße
2. _____ a. Ohren   _____ b. Augen
3. _____ a. Hals   _____ b. Nase
4. _____ a. Zähne   _____ b. Beine
5. _____ a. Finger   _____ b. Haare

E. Ein Interview. Herr Gruber, a journalist, is trying to find out what the Swiss think about their standard of living and the European Union. You will hear his interview with an older woman, Frau Beck. Listen, then check the correct answers to the questions printed in your lab manual. A question may have more than one correct answer. You will hear the interview twice. You will hear five new expressions:

Bedeutet das …?	*Does that mean . . . ?*
Europäische Union	*European Union*
fürchten	*to fear*
Gespräch	*conversation*
Unterschied	*difference*

1. Wie findet Frau Beck den Lebensstandard in der Schweiz?

   _____ a. Der Lebensstandard ist relativ hoch.

   _____ b. Die meisten Leute kaufen sich jedes Jahr ein neues Auto.

   _____ c. Vieles ist billiger geworden.

2. Haben die Leute jetzt ein einfacheres Leben?

   _____ a. Ja, viele haben keine Spülmaschine und keinen Fernseher.

   _____ b. Nein, aber sie sind sparsamer° geworden.   more thrifty

   _____ c. Ja, nur wenige können sich ein Auto kaufen.

3. Warum hat Frau Beck kein Auto?

   _____ a. Sie braucht es nicht.

   _____ b. Sie kann es sich nicht kaufen.

   _____ c. Sie fährt immer mit dem Rad oder mit dem Zug.

4. Was denkt Frau Beck über die Europäische Union?

   _____ a. Sie sagt nichts über dieses Thema°.   topic

   _____ b. Sie möchte, dass die Schweiz neutral bleibt.

   _____ c. Sie weiß nicht, was die Europäische Union ist.

5. Fürchtet Frau Beck, dass die Schweiz von der Welt isoliert ist?

_____ a. Ja, sie fürchtet es.

_____ b. Nein, sie glaubt, andere Länder kaufen ihre Qualitätsprodukte.

_____ c. Nein, sie glaubt, dass andere Länder Schweizer Produkte wollen.

6. Was sagt Frau Beck über die Wirtschaft in der Schweiz?

_____ a. Sie hat Angst, dass sie jetzt weniger kaufen kann.

_____ b. Sie hat keine Angst, dass es der Schweiz wirtschaftlich schlechter geht.

_____ c. Sie meint, die Schweiz ist wirtschaftlich stark.

F. Übungen zur Aussprache. Listen and repeat the words. You may wish to review the pronunciation of final **-en, -e,** and **-er** in Appendix E of your textbook.

[ən]	[ə]	[ər]
bitten	bitte	bitter
fahren	fahre	Fahrer
denken	denke	Denker
fehlen	fehle	Fehler
besten	beste	bester

Now listen and repeat the sentences, paying special attention to your pronunciation of final **-en, -e,** and **-er** in the boldfaced words.

1. **Fahren** Sie **bitte** etwas **langsamer!**
2. **Viele Amerikaner fliegen** im **Sommer** nach Europa.
3. **Manche Länder brauchen** mehr **Schulen.**
4. Die **Tage werden kürzer** und **kälter.**
5. **Diese Männer arbeiten** wirklich schwer.
6. **Viele Wörter** sind relativ, zum Beispiel **länger, größer oder jünger.**

G. Bei der Ärztin. Michael isn't feeling well so he has gone to his doctor, Frau Dr. Hauser. Listen to their conversation. Afterwards, you will hear six statements. Place a check mark in the column marked **richtig** if the statement is correct. Place a check mark in the column marked **falsch** if the statement is incorrect. You will hear the conversation twice. You will hear three new expressions:

auf jeden Fall	*in any case*
Ruhe	*quiet*
Was führt Sie zu mir?	*What brings you to me?*

	richtig	falsch		richtig	falsch		richtig	falsch
→	_____	✓						
1.	_____	_____	3.	_____	_____	5.	_____	_____
2.	_____	_____	4.	_____	_____	6.	_____	_____

KAPITEL 10   Deutschland: 1945 bis heute

A. Deutschland: 1945 bis heute. Listen to the reading of the *Lesestück* "Deutschland: 1945 bis heute."

B. Richtig oder falsch? You will hear eight statements based on the *Lesestück* "Deutschland: 1945 bis heute." Check **richtig** if the statement is correct. Check **falsch** if it is incorrect.

	richtig	falsch			richtig	falsch			richtig	falsch
1.	_____	_____		4.	_____	_____		7.	_____	_____
2.	_____	_____		5.	_____	_____		8.	_____	_____
3.	_____	_____		6.	_____	_____				

C. Ist das logisch? You will hear eight short conversational exchanges. If the response is a logical reply, check **logisch**. If the response is not logical, check **unlogisch**.

	logisch	unlogisch			logisch	unlogisch			logisch	unlogisch
1.	_____	_____		4.	_____	_____		7.	_____	_____
2.	_____	_____		5.	_____	_____		8.	_____	_____
3.	_____	_____		6.	_____	_____				

D. Die gleiche Bedeutung. You will hear six sentences. For each one, you will see a second sentence printed in your lab manual. If the sentence you hear and the printed sentence have the same meaning, check **gleich**. If the meanings are different, check **nicht gleich.** You will hear a new word:

wach   *awake*

		gleich	nicht gleich
1.	Das Theater hat schon angefangen.	_____	_____
2.	Du solltest das Musical sehen. Es ist wirklich toll.	_____	_____
3.	Ich habe viel Geld auf der Bank.	_____	_____
4.	Die Kinder schlafen immer noch.	_____	_____
5.	In der DDR war vieles anders als in der Bundesrepublik.	_____	_____
6.	Die Ostdeutschen haben die Mauer gebaut.	_____	_____

E. Ein Gespräch. You will hear a short conversation between Georg and Ursel. Listen, then check the correct answers to the questions printed in your lab manual. You will hear their conversation twice. You will hear the following new word:

Reklame   *publicity*

1. Warum ist Georg so müde?

   _____ a. Er war gestern Abend in der Oper.

   _____ b. Er jobbt auf dem Theaterfestival.

2. Was für eine Arbeit hat Georg?

   _____ a. Er macht Musik.

   _____ b. Er macht Reklame für das Theater.

3. Warum macht Georg diese Arbeit?

   _____ a. Alles, was mit dem Theater zu tun hat, interessiert ihn.

   _____ b. Weil er gut verdient.

4. Was macht Georg meistens mit den Freikarten?

   _____ a. Er benutzt sie selbst.

   _____ b. Er schenkt sie Freunden.

5. Warum geht Ursel mit ins Theater?

   _____ a. Sie hat heute Abend nichts anderes zu tun.

   _____ b. Den *Faust* fand sie sehr interessant, als sie ihn in der Schule las.

6. Wo wollen sie sich treffen?

   _____ a. Sie treffen sich am Theater.

   _____ b. Georg holt Ursel ab.

F. Übungen zur Aussprache. Listen and repeat the word pairs. You may wish to review the pronunciation of **sp** and **st** in Appendix E of your textbook.

[sp]	[šp]	[st]	[št]
lispeln	spielen	Listen	stehlen
knuspern	springen	Hengst	streng
Espen	spenden	Küste	Stücke
Knospe	Sprossen	kosten	stocken
Haspe	Spatz	Last	Stall

Now listen and repeat the sentences, paying special attention to the way you pronounce **sp** and **st** in the boldfaced words.

1. Die **Studentin spricht** die deutsche **Sprache** sehr schön.
2. Schweizerdeutsch **versteht Stefan** nicht.
3. In der **Stadt** müssen Kinder oft auf den **Straßen spielen**.
4. **Sport** treiben macht **Spaß**.
5. Es hat **gestern** am **späten** Nachmittag **stark** geregnet.

G. Ein Dokumentarfilm. Melanie and Michael have just seen a documentary film about German history since the beginning of the Second World War. Now they are talking about the film. Before listening to their conversation, read the questions in your lab manual. While listening you may wish to take notes. You will hear the conversation twice. Then answer the questions in German. You will hear two new expressions:

Hör schon auf! *Just stop!*
täglich *daily*

1. Hat Melanie der Film gefallen?

   _____

   _____

2. Welchen Teil des Filmes fand Michael ein bisschen zu lang?

   _____

   _____

3. Welche Informationen fand Melanie unglaublich?

   _____

   _____

4. Wofür interessiert sich Michael?

   _____

   _____

KAPITEL 11 Wirtschaft und Beruf

A. Die Kündigung, nur noch drei Tage. Listen to the reading of the *Lesestück* "Die Kündigung, nur noch drei Tage."

B. Richtig oder falsch? You will hear eight statements based on the *Lesestück* "Die Kündigung, nur noch drei Tage." Check **richtig** if the statement is correct. Check **falsch** if it is incorrect. You will hear a new word:

jemand   *someone*

	richtig	falsch		richtig	falsch		richtig	falsch
1.	_____	_____	4.	_____	_____	7.	_____	_____
2.	_____	_____	5.	_____	_____	8.	_____	_____
3.	_____	_____	6.	_____	_____			

C. Entgegnungen. You will hear five questions which might begin a conversation. In your lab manual you will see three possible responses to each question. Check the reply that makes sense.

1. _____ a. Tut mir Leid, sie ist heute nicht da.

   _____ b. Ich hoffe, Sie hatten eine gute Reise.

   _____ c. Sie war ein Jahr in den USA.

2. _____ a. Ja, gehen Sie bitte gleich hinein.

   _____ b. Ja, ich habe drei Jahre in Frankreich gearbeitet.

   _____ c. Ja, ich habe einen Termin bei ihm.

3. _____ a. Ja bitte, er erwartet Sie schon.

   _____ b. Ich habe einige Fragen.

   _____ c. Nein, leider nicht.

4. _____ a. Ich möchte bei einer Exportfirma arbeiten.

   _____ b. Ich glaube ja.

   _____ c. Tut mir Leid. Ich habe jetzt keine Zeit.

5. _____ a. Nein, Ihre Preise sind zu hoch.

   _____ b. Oh ja, die Arbeit muss interessant sein.

   _____ c. Nein, sie telefoniert gerade.

D. Die gleiche Bedeutung. You will hear six pairs of sentences. If the meaning of both sentences is the same, check **gleich**. If their meaning is different, check **nicht gleich**.

       gleich   nicht gleich

1. _____   _____

2. _____   _____

3. _____   _____

4. _____   _____

5. _____   _____

6. _____   _____

E. Zwei Gespräche. You will hear two short dialogues. Listen, then read the statements printed in your lab manual. Check **richtig** if the statement is correct, **falsch** if it is incorrect, or **man weiß es nicht** if the information was not in the dialogue. You will hear each dialogue twice.

	richtig	falsch	man weiß es nicht
1. Frau Schulze erwartet Herrn Meier.	_____	_____	_____
2. Frau Schulze kann ihn heute nicht sehen.	_____	_____	_____
3. Die Sekretärin will Frau Schulze fragen, ob sie Zeit hat.	_____	_____	_____
4. Frau Schulze hat jetzt einen Termin.	_____	_____	_____
1. Frau Schulze findet Herrn Meiers Sachen billig.	_____	_____	_____
2. Sie hat aber viele Fragen wegen der Qualität.	_____	_____	_____
3. Frau Schulze ruft Herrn Meier am Montag an.	_____	_____	_____
4. Sie will die Sachen von Herrn Meier kaufen.	_____	_____	_____

F. Übungen zur Aussprache. Listen and repeat the word pairs. You may wish to review the pronunciation of **ei, eu (äu), au,** and **ie** in Appendix E of your textbook.

[ai]	[oi]	[au]	[oi]
nein	neun	Maus	Mäuse
heiser	Häuser	Haus	Häuse
Seile	Säule	Bauch	Bäuche
Eile	Eule	Haufen	häufen
leite	Leute	Laute	Leute

[ī]	[ai]
Miene	meine
Biene	Beine
viele	Feile
diene	deine
Liebe	Leibe

Now listen and repeat the sentences, paying special attention to the pronunciation of **eu (äu), au, ei,** and **ie** in the boldfaced words.

1. Herr **Neumann** ist **heute** nicht **einkaufen** gegangen.
2. Hat **Paula** schon **einen Brief** an **euch geschrieben?**
3. **Eugen** hat **Deutsch studiert.**
4. Abends geht **Klaus** mit **seinen Freunden** in **eine Kneipe.**
5. **Heike läuft** jeden Tag zur **Arbeit.**
6. **Dieter** hat **seit** Ende **Mai sein eigenes Auto.**

G. Eine neue Stelle. Claudia und Uwe are talking about Claudia's cousin, who has just found a new position at Siemens in Munich. Listen to their conversation, and then check the correct answers to the questions printed in your lab manual. You will hear the conversation twice. You will hear two new words:

umziehen	*move to a new residence*
vorher	*previously*

1. Uwe spricht mit Claudia …

    _____ a. über ihre neue Stelle.

    _____ b. über ihre Kusine Andrea.

    _____ c. über das Leben in München.

2. Bevor Andrea die neue Stelle bekam, …

    _____ a. war sie sechs Monate lang arbeitslos gewesen.

    _____ b. hatte sie bei Volkswagen in Wolfsburg gearbeitet.

    _____ c. hatte sie drei Monate lang keine Arbeit gehabt.

3. Als Andrea arbeitslos war, …

    _____ a. ging es ihr sehr gut.

    _____ b. wurde sie von Monat zu Monat nervöser.

    _____ c. war sie froh darüber.

4. Andrea …

    _____ a. ist jetzt schnell nach Wolfsburg gezogen°. *moved*

    _____ b. bleibt noch ein Jahr in Wolfsburg.

    _____ c. sucht jetzt eine eigene Wohnung in München.

Name _____ Datum _____

A. Fremd im eigenen Zuhause. Listen to the reading of the *Lesestück* "Fremd im eigenen Zuhause."

B. Richtig oder falsch? You will hear eight statements based on the *Lesestück* "Fremd im eigenen Zuhause." Check **richtig** if the statement is correct. Check **falsch** if it is incorrect. You will hear two new words:

Koch   *cook*
Kopftuch   *head scarf*

	richtig	falsch			richtig	falsch			richtig	falsch
1.	_____	_____		4.	_____	_____		7.	_____	_____
2.	_____	_____		5.	_____	_____		8.	_____	_____
3.	_____	_____		6.	_____	_____				

C. Ist das logisch? You will hear six short conversational exchanges. If the response is a logical reply, check **logisch.** If the response is not logical, check **unlogisch.** You will hear a new expression:

keinen einzigen   *not a single one*

	logisch	unlogisch			logisch	unlogisch
1.	_____	_____		4.	_____	_____
2.	_____	_____		5.	_____	_____
3.	_____	_____		6.	_____	_____

D. Der richtige Ort. You will hear six questions about locations. Below are two possible answers to each. Place a check mark beside the response that makes sense.

1. _____ a. in der Heimat

   _____ b. in der Industrie

2. _____ a. ins Kino

   _____ b. ins Konzert

3. _____ a. in der Zeitung

   _____ b. in der Literatur

4. _____ a. an der Mauer

   _____ b. in den Bergen

5. _____ a. in ein Lokal

   _____ b. auf eine Demonstration

6. _____ a. in der Bibliothek

   _____ b. auf der Bank

E. Ein Interview. Birgit, a staff member of the local **Jugendzeitung,** is interviewing Ali, a Turk who lives in Germany. Listen to their conversation, then check the correct answers to the questions printed in your lab manual. You will hear the interview twice. You will hear two new words:

eröffnen   *to open*
Viertel   *quarter, district*

1. Wann ist Ali nach Deutschland gekommen?

       _____ a. Als er sehr klein war.

       _____ b. Er ist dort geboren.

2. Warum sind Alis Eltern nach Deutschland gekommen?

       _____ a. Sein Vater fand in der Türkei keine Arbeit.

       _____ b. Aus politischen Gründen.

3. Warum spricht Ali so gut Deutsch?

       _____ a. Er geht auf eine deutsche Schule und hat ein paar deutsche Freunde.

       _____ b. Er spricht mit seinen Eltern oft Deutsch.

4. Was sind Alis Zukunftspläne?

       _____ a. Er will ein türkisches Lokal eröffnen.

       _____ b. Er will Elektroingenieur werden.

5. Wo möchte Ali später mal leben?

       _____ a. Er möchte in der Türkei leben; dort ist seine Heimat.

       _____ b. Er möchte in Deutschland bleiben.

F. Übungen zur Aussprache. Listen and repeat the word pairs. You may wish to review the pronunciation of **d** and **t** in Appendix E of your textbook.

[d]	[t]
hindern	hintern
Sonde	sonnte
Seide	Seite
bieder	Bieter
Mieder	Mieter

Now listen and repeat the sentences, paying special attention to the pronunciation of **d** and **t** in the boldfaced words.

1. **Die Kinder trugen** ihre **beste Kleidung** zum **Fest.**
2. Im **Winter arbeitet Walter** in einem **Hotel.**
3. Sein **Vater hat** viele **Freunde eingeladen.**
4. **Dieters Bruder hat** ein **tolles Kassettendeck.**
5. **Der Bundespräsident redete** über **die** neuen **Länder.**

G. Pläne für Samstag. Monika meets Peter in the student café and they talk about their plans for the weekend. Before listening to their conversation, read the questions in your lab manual. While listening you may wish to take notes. You will hear the conversation twice. Then answer the questions in German. You will hear five new expressions:

ähnlich	*similar*
es hört sich nett an	*it sounds nice*
fröhlich	*merry*
Lieder	*songs*
übrigens	*by the way*

1. Wie ist das Wetter?

   _____

   _____

2. Wohin geht Monika am Samstagnachmittag?

   _____

   _____

3. Wie sind Yilmaz' Verwandte?

   _____

   _____

4. Was wird bei dem Geburtstagspicknick gemacht?

   _____

   _____

5. Mag Peter türkisches Essen?

   _____

   _____

Zwei Kurzgeschichten

■   The following is a reading of the short story "Der Verkäufer und der Elch. Eine Geschichte mit 128 deutschen Wörtern" by Franz Hohler. The text of the short story appears on pages 437–438 of your textbook.

■   The following is a reading of the short story "Schlittenfahren" by Helga Novak. The text of the short story appears on page 439 of your textbook.

Self-Tests

Self-Tests

Einführung

A. How do you ask someone for personal information in German?
1. What is your name?
2. How old are you?
3. What is your address?
4. What is your telephone number?

B. Give the German equivalents of the following courtesy expressions.
1. thank you   2. you're welcome

C. 1. Give the days of the week in German.
2. Ask what day it is.
3. Say it is Thursday.

D. 1. Name five colors in German.
2. Ask what color the wall is.

E. 1. How can you tell what gender a German noun is?
2. Give the gender of the following nouns.
   a. Bleistift   c. Bett   e. Mann
   b. Tür   d. Frau
3. Complete the sentences with the proper definite article.
   a. _____ Kugelschreiber ist neu.
   b. _____ Zimmer ist klein.
   c. _____ Lampe ist alt.
   d. Wie ist _____ Tisch? Groß oder klein?
   e. Wie alt ist _____ Kind?
   f. _____ Uhr ist neu.
4. Say what is in your room. Use the proper indefinite article.
   In meinem Zimmer ist …
   a. _____ Bett.
   b. _____ Lampe.
   c. _____ Bücherregal.
   d. _____ Uhr.
   e. _____ Pflanze.
   f. _____ CD-Player.

F. Complete the answer, using a pronoun that corresponds to the noun in the question.
1. Ist der Junge zwölf? —Nein, _____ ist elf.
2. Ist das Kind drei? —Nein, _____ ist zwei.
3. Ist die Wand grün? —Nein, _____ ist blau.
4. Ist der Rucksack neu? —Nein, _____ ist alt.
5. Heißt die Studentin Anja? —Nein, _____ heißt Christine.
6. Ist das Handy neu? —Nein, _____ ist alt.

Kapitel 1

A. Give three types of answers to the following question:
Gehst du heute Abend ins Kino?
1. Affirmative
2. Negative
3. Maybe

B. 1. How would you greet someone at the following times of day?
   a. in the morning
   b. in the afternoon
   c. in the evening
2. Someone asks how you are. Give one positive and one negative response.
   Wie geht's?

C. 1. Give antonyms for the following words.
   a. faul   c. ernst   e. klein
   b. freundlich d. gut
2. Give two ways to say good-bye in German.

D. 1. Write the German equivalent for each of the following sentences relating to time.
   a. What time is it?
   b. I'm going at one o'clock.
2. Write out the following clock times in German using conversational German (Method 1).
   a. 2:15   b. 3:45   c. 6:30
3. How is official time indicated, for example in train schedules?

E. 1. What are the three words for *you* in German?
2. Which form of *you* do you use in talking to the following people?
   a. a saleswoman   c. a friend
   b. two children   d. your mother
3. Give the German equivalents of the following English pronouns.

a. he   c. we   e. they
b. she   d. I
4. How can you tell whether **sie** means *she* or *they*?
5. Give the German equivalents of:
   a. She plays tennis well.
   b. They play tennis well.

F. 1. What are the German equivalents of the forms of the English verb *to be*?
   a. I am   d. they are
   b. we are   e. you are (*3 forms*)
   c. she is

G. 1. What is the basic form of a German verb?
2. What is the most common ending of the basic verb form?
3. Give the German infinitives for the following verbs:
   a. to believe   b. to hike   c. to work
4. Give the stems of the verbs in 3 above.
5. What do you call the form of the verb that agrees with the subject?
6. What ending does the verb take when used with the following subjects?
   a. du   d. wir   f. sie (*sg.*)
   b. ihr   e. er   g. sie (*pl.*)
   c. ich
7. Complete the following sentences with the proper form of the verb in parentheses.
   a. _____ du heute Volleyball? (spielen)
   b. Ich _____ gern Musik. (hören)
   c. Er _____ viel. (arbeiten)
   d. Gabi _____ gern. (wandern)
   e. Wir _____ gern. (schwimmen)
   f. Das Mädchen _____ Lore. (heißen)
   g. Wie _____ du? (heißen)

H. 1. In German, one form of a verb in the present tense is used to express ideas that require several different forms in English. Give the German equivalents of the following sentences.
   a. You do play well.
   b. Frank is working today.
   c. Ute works a lot.
2. The German present tense also expresses something intended or planned for the future. Give the German equivalents of the following sentences.
   a. I'm going to the movies this afternoon.
   b. What will you do this evening?

I. 1. How do you say you like to do something in German?
2. Say that the following people like to do the things named.

a. Ute spielt Schach.
b. Ich wandere.
c. Wir treiben Sport.

J. 1. Where does **nicht** come in relationship to the following:
   a. predicate adjectives
   b. specific time expressions
   c. most other adverbs, including general time adverbs
   d. dependent infinitives
2. Make the following sentences negative by adding **nicht** in the proper place.
   a. Wir schwimmen gern.
   b. Frank wandert viel.
   c. Ich gehe joggen.
   d. Wir arbeiten morgen.
   e. Heike ist nett.
   f. Mark ist oft krank.

K. 1. What is the first word in an informational question?
2. Where is the verb located? The subject?
3. Name three interrogative words.
4. Ask informational questions using the words in parentheses.
   a. Jürgen spielt gut Fußball. (wer)
   b. Veronika spielt gern Volleyball. (was)
   c. Wir gehen heute Abend ins Kino. (wann)

L. 1. What is the first word in a yes/no question?
2. Convert the following statements into yes/no questions.
   a. Petra spielt oft Fußball.
   b. Kurt arbeitet viel.
   c. Du spielst gut Schach.

M. 1. What words are used to form tag questions in German?
2. Give the German equivalents of the following sentences:
   a. We're playing tennis tomorrow, aren't we?
   b. Paul is tired, isn't he?
   c. You like to dance, don't you? (Use **du**.)

Kapitel 2

A. Give three responses expressing skepticism about the following statement about the weather:
Morgen ist es bestimmt schön.

B. Write out the names of the months in German.

C. 1. What is the gender of the names of most countries in German?
2. Name one feminine country and one plural country in German.

D. Give the feminine and masculine forms of the following nouns.
1. student
2. Swiss (citizen)
3. neighbor

E. Replace the word **heute** with **auch gestern** and rewrite each of the following sentences in the simple past.
1. Ich bin heute müde.
2. Eva ist heute krank.
3. Du bist heute faul.
4. Sie sind heute fleißig.

F. Ask when the birthdays of the following people are:
1. du
2. Frank
3. ihr
4. Ulrike und Kathrin

G. 1. In what position is the finite verb in a German statement?
2. Rewrite the following sentences, beginning with the word(s) in bold type.
   a. Das Wetter war **am Sonntag** nicht gut.
   b. Die Sonne scheint **hoffentlich** morgen.

H. 1. How does English generally signal the grammatical function of nouns in a sentence?
2. What type of signal does German use to indicate the grammatical function of nouns?
3. What case is used for the subject of a sentence and a predicate noun?
4. Which verbs are often followed by predicate nouns?
5. Write out the subjects and any predicate nouns in the following sentences.
   a. Gestern war das Wetter schön.
   b. Frank Schmidt ist Student.
   c. Das Mädchen heißt Cornelia.

I. 1. What is the definite article used with all plural nouns?
2. Give the plural of the following nouns, including the article.
   a. das Fenster   d. die Uhr
   b. der Tisch   e. der Stuhl
   c. das Buch   f. die Studentin

J. 1. Give the two forms of the indefinite article in German.
2. Give the English equivalents.

3. Complete the following sentences with an indefinite article.
   a. Ist das Kind _____ Mädchen oder _____ Junge?
   b. Ist die Frau _____ Nachbarin?
   c. Ist das wirklich _____ Kugelschreiber?

K. 1. What is the negative form of **ein?**
2. What are the English equivalents of the negative form of **ein?**
3. What negative do you use when the noun is preceded by a definite article?
4. Complete the following sentences with **kein** or **nicht,** as appropriate.
   a. Das ist _____ Uhr.
   b. Das ist _____ die Parkstraße.
   c. Warum ist _____ Stuhl hier?

L. 1. Give the German equivalents of the following English possessive adjectives and nouns.
   a. your (*fam. sg.*) radio   d. our country
   b. their basketball   e. my address
   c. her cards
2. Give the German equivalents of the following proper names and nouns.
   a. Klaus's room   b. Tanja's watch

M. 1. Answer the following questions in the affirmative, using personal pronouns.
   a. Ist der Computer neu?
   b. Ist dein Rucksack praktisch?
   c. Ist das Kind drei Jahre alt?
   d. Arbeitet deine Freundin heute Abend?
   e. Tanzen deine Freunde gern?
2. Answer the following questions in the affirmative, using demonstrative pronouns.
   a. Ist Dieters Freund wirklich nett?
   b. Ist Karin oft so lustig?
   c. War der Film sehr gut?
   d. Sind deine Nachbarn oft kritisch?

Kapitel 3

A. Give three responses to the following invitation: **Gehen wir morgen inlineskaten?**
1. Accept the proposal gladly.
2. Reject the proposal with regret.
3. Leave the possibility open.

B. What German word do you use to contradict the assumptions in the following sentences?
1. Monika isst keinen Fisch. _____!
2. Arbeitest du denn nicht? _____!

C. What advice would you give to a friend who said the following:
Ich brauche etwas gegen Kopfschmerzen.

D. Give three foods/beverages a German might have at each of the following meals.
1. Frühstück   3. Abendessen
2. Mittagessen

E. 1. Which noun in a compound determines the gender?
2. Make a compound of the following nouns.
   a. der Tisch + die Lampe
   b. die Kartoffel + der Salat

F. 1. Which forms of the verbs **essen, geben,** and **nehmen** show stem-vowel change?
2. Complete the following sentences with the proper form of the verb in parentheses.
   a. Was _____ du gegen Kopfschmerzen? (nehmen)
   b. Ich _____ Aspirin. (nehmen)
   c. Zum Frühstück _____ Monika immer frische Brötchen. (essen)
   d. Wir _____ oft Eier. (essen)
   e. _____ es hier keinen Kaffee? (geben)
   f. _____ du mir zwei Euro? (geben)

G. 1. When a sentence has both time and place expressions, which comes first in English? In German?
2. Write a sentence from the following cues.
   wann / du / kommen / nach Hause / heute Abend / ?

H. 1. What verb form do you use to tell someone to do something?
2. What is the position of this verb in the sentence?
3. Complete the following commands with the verb form that corresponds to the people indicated.
   a. (Detlev) _____ mir bitte die Butter. (geben)
   b. (Gabi und Stefan) _____ gleich nach Hause. (kommen)
   c. (Herr Huber) _____ bitte hier. (bleiben)

I. 1. Which case is used for:
   a. nouns and pronouns that are subjects?
   b. nouns and pronouns that are direct objects?
2. Complete the following sentences with the possessive adjective that corresponds to the subject pronoun.
   a. Ich brauche _____ Heft wieder.
   b. Inge fragt _____ Freund Michael.

c. Nehmt ihr _____ Bücher?
d. Brauchst du _____ Lampe?
3. A few masculine nouns show a change in the accusative. Give the accusative form of:
   a. der Junge   b. der Nachbar
4. Name the prepositions that take accusative case.
5. Complete the following sentences, using the cues in parentheses.
   a. _____ ist nicht frisch. (der Kuchen)
   b. Warum kaufst du _____? (der Kuchen)
   c. Gisela und Lars kennen _____ gut. (ihre Stadt)
   d. Uwe arbeitet für _____ (sein Professor)
   e. Habt ihr denn _____ mehr? (kein Brot)
   f. Warum kaufst du nur _____? (ein Stuhl)
   g. _____ suchst du? (wer)
   h. Kennst du _____ da? (der Student)
   i. Gibt es hier _____? (kein Supermarkt)
6. Complete the following sentences with demonstrative pronouns.
   a. Der Kaffee ist gut, nicht?
      —Nein, _____ finde ich nicht gut.
   b. Ich brauche Brot.
      —Kauf _____ aber bei Reinhardt!
   c. Wer ist der Herr da?
      —_____ kenne ich nicht.
7. Give the accusative forms of the following pronouns.
   a. Wie findest du _____? (er)
   b. Brauchst du _____? (ich)
   c. Wir kennen _____ nicht. (sie, *pl.*)
   d. Steffi und Daniel finden _____ sehr sympathisch. (du)
   e. Sie brauchen _____ heute nicht. (wir)
   f. Unsere Nachbarn suchen _____. (ihr)

Kapitel 4

A. Give two expressions of regret as a response to the following request:
Sollen wir jetzt einen Kaffee trinken gehen?

B. Give three responses to the following question to indicate you are preparing class work or studying for a test.
Was machst du heute Abend?

C. Tell how many members are in your family and how many relatives you have (for example, **Ich habe zwei Brüder, eine Tante, ...**).

D. Express the following sentences in German.
1. Alex is an American.
2. He is going to be a baker.
3. Andrea is a student.

E. 1. What vowel changes do the verbs **lesen, sehen,** and **werden** have?
2. Give the irregular forms of **werden.**
3. Complete the sentences with the correct form of the verb in parentheses.
   a. Sabine _____ viel. (lesen)
   b. _____ du gern lustige Filme? (sehen)
   c. Erik _____ besser in Mathe. (werden)

F. 1. You have learned two German equivalents for *to know.* For each of the following definitions, write the appropriate German word.
   a. to know a fact
   b. to be acquainted with a person, place, or thing
2. Complete the following sentences with a form of **wissen** or **kennen.**
   a. _____ du den Studenten da?
   b. Ich _____ nicht, wie er heißt.
   c. _____ du, wie alt er ist?

G. 1. What pattern of endings do the words **dieser, jeder, welcher, mancher,** and **solcher** follow?
2. Which **der**-word is used only in the singular? What does it mean?
3. Which two **der**-words are used mostly in the plural? What do they mean?
4. Complete the following sentences with the correct form of the cued **der**-word.
   a. Ist _____ Bücherregal neu? (dieser)
   b. _____ Computer hier ist teuer. (jeder)
   c. _____ Film willst du sehen? (welcher)
   d. _____ Bücher lese ich nicht. (solcher)
   e. _____ Referate waren sehr gut. (mancher)

H. 1. Which kind of verb expresses an attitude about an action rather than the action itself?
2. Give the German infinitives that express the following ideas.
   a. to want to   d. to be allowed to
   b. to be supposed to   e. to be able to
   c. to have to   f. to like

I. 1. German modals are irregular. Which forms lack endings?
2. What other irregularity do most modals show?
3. Give the proper forms of the verbs indicated.
   a. ich _____ (können)
   b. er _____ (dürfen)
   c. du _____ (müssen)
   d. wir _____ (sollen)
   e. Erika _____ (wollen)
   f. Ich _____ es. (mögen)

J. The modal **mögen** and its subjunctive form **möchte** have two different meanings. Give the German equivalents of the following sentences.
1. Do you like Inge?
2. Would you like to work this evening?

K. 1. Modal auxiliaries are generally used with dependent infinitives. Where does the infinitive come in such a sentence?
2. Rewrite the following sentences, using the modal in parentheses.
   a. Arbeitest du heute? (müssen)
   b. Ich mache es nicht. (können)
   c. Petra sagt etwas. (wollen)
3. When is the infinitive often omitted?
4. Give the German equivalent of the following English sentence:
   I have to go home now.

L. 1. Which of the following verbs are separable-prefix verbs?
   a. fernsehen   d. mitbringen
   b. bekommen   e. verdienen
   c. einkaufen
2. In what position is the separable prefix in the present tense and the imperative?
3. Write sentences using the guidelines.
   a. Gerd / mitbringen / einen Freund
   b. du / einkaufen / morgen / ?
   c. ich / müssen / vorbereiten / das Abendessen
   d. du / oft / fernsehen / ?
   e. ich / sollen / meine Notizen / durcharbeiten

Kapitel 5

A. Give three very positive responses to the following sentence:
Mein Auto ist kaputt. Kannst du mich morgen abholen?

B. Name three things you would like to do during the summer vacation.

C. 1. What are two words for *where* in German?
2. Complete the following sentences with **wo** or **wohin.**
   a. _____ wohnt Cornelia?
   b. _____ fährst du in den Ferien?

D. Name in German three forms of private transportation and three forms of public transportation.

E. 1. What vowel change do the verbs **fahren, laufen,** and **schlafen** have?
2. Complete the sentences with the correct form of the verb in parentheses.
   a. Wann _____ Paula nach Hamburg? (fahren)
   b. _____ sie bei Freunden? (schlafen)
   c. Wann _____ Frank nach Hause? (laufen)
   d. _____ du morgen in die Stadt? (fahren)

F. 1. What are the five coordinating conjunctions you have learned?
2. What word means *but* in the sense of *on the contrary?*
3. What word means *but* in the sense of *nevertheless?*
4. Do coordinating conjunctions affect word order?
5. Choose the conjunction that makes sense and use it to combine the sentences.
   a. Gabi bleibt zu Hause. Sie ist krank. (denn, oder)
   b. Holger geht nicht schwimmen. Er spielt Tennis. (aber, sondern)
   c. Er schwimmt nicht gut. Er schwimmt gern. (aber, sondern)

G. 1. Where does the verb go in a dependent clause?
2. If there are both a modal auxiliary and an infinitive, which comes last?
3. If the sentence begins with a dependent clause, does the finite verb of the independent clause come before or after the subject?
4. Combine the following sentences with the conjunction indicated.
   a. Wir können nicht fahren. (weil) Unser Auto ist kaputt.
   b. (wenn) Es regnet morgen. Wir müssen zu Hause bleiben.
5. Rewrite the following direct statements as indirect statements, using **dass.**
   a. Sabine sagt: „Die Nachbarn kaufen oft im Supermarkt ein."
   b. Erik glaubt: „Das Obst ist nicht so frisch."

H. 1. What case is used in German to signal the indirect object?
2. What is the indirect object in the following sentence?
   Gerd schenkt seiner Schwester ein Poster.
3. Give the dative form of the following nouns:
   a. die Frau   d. die Berge
   b. der Mann   e. der Student
   c. das Auto
4. Name the verbs you know that take dative.

5. Which of the following prepositions are followed by dative case?
   aus, durch, für, mit, nach, ohne, seit, von
6. Complete the following sentences with the correct form of the cued words.
   a. Der Vater erzählt _____ eine Geschichte. (die Kinder)
   b. _____ gehören diese Wasserskier? (wer)
   c. Warum glaubst du _____ nicht? (mein Bruder)
   d. Fährst du oft mit _____? (der Zug)
   e. Kaufst du die Uhr für _____? (dein Vater)
   f. Frank wohnt bei _____ (eine Familie)
   g. Erika schenkt ihrer Mutter _____. (ein Kugelschreiber)
   h. Willst du mit _____ fahren? (diese Straßenbahn)
   i. Von _____ Nachbarn (*pl.*) sprecht ihr? (welche)

I. 1. Give the accusative and dative forms of the following pronouns.
   a. ich   c. du   e. sie
   b. er   d. wir   f. Sie
2. Complete the following sentences with the proper form of the cued pronouns.
   a. Ich möchte mit _____ sprechen. (du)
   b. Was fragst du _____? (ich)
   c. Glaubst du _____? (er)
   d. Die CDs gehören _____. (sie, *pl.*)
   e. Soll ich eine Pflanze für _____ kaufen? (sie, *sg.*)
   f. Wann holst du _____ ab? (wir)
   g. Von _____ erzählst du? (wer)

J. Show your understanding of the word order for direct and indirect objects by completing the sentences with the cued words.
1. Kaufst du _____ _____? (dieses Buch / mir)
2. Ich gebe _____ _____. (meinen Eltern / diese Lampe)
3. Der Pulli? Ich schenke _____ _____. (meinem Bruder / ihn)

Kapitel 6

A. Your friend is unhappy with one of your remarks and says: **Sei nicht so kritisch.** Give three possible excuses or apologies.

B. 1. Name three articles of clothing that both men and women wear.
2. Name three articles of women's clothing.

C. 1. The infinitive of a verb may be used as a noun. What gender is such a noun?
2. The English equivalent of such a noun is often a gerund. What ending does an English gerund have?
3. Give the English equivalents of the following sentences, in which one of the infinitives is used as a noun and the other as a dependent infinitive.
   a. Wandern ist gesund.
   b. Musst du heute arbeiten?

D. 1. When is the German present perfect tense used?
2. Why is it often called the "conversational past"?

E. 1. The present perfect tense consists of two parts. What are the two parts of the verb?
2. What verb is used as the auxiliary for most verbs in the present perfect tense?
3. What other verb is used as an auxiliary for some verbs in the present perfect tense?
4. What conditions must be met to use the auxiliary **sein** with a past participle?
5. What two verbs are exceptions to the general rule about verbs requiring **sein?**
6. Supply the auxiliaries.
   a. Er _____ viel gearbeitet.
   b. _____ du spät aufgestanden?
   c. Wir _____ bis elf geblieben.
   d. Ilse und Paul _____ mir geschrieben.
   e. _____ ihr mit dem Zug gefahren?
   f. Ich _____ gut geschlafen.

F. 1. What ending is added to the stem of a regular weak verb like **spielen** to form the past participle?
2. How is the ending different in a verb like **arbeiten,** which has a stem ending in **-t?**
3. How does an irregular weak verb like **bringen** form the past participle differently from regular weak verbs?
4. Give the past participles of the following verbs.
   bringen, kosten, machen, denken, haben, kennen, regnen, wandern, wissen, tanzen

G. 1. What is the ending of the past participle of a strong verb like **sehen?**
2. What other change is characteristic for the past participle of many strong verbs?
3. Give the past participles of the following verbs.
   finden, geben, lesen, nehmen, schlafen, schreiben, trinken, tun

H. 1. What happens to the **ge-**prefix in the past participle of a separable-prefix verb like **einkaufen?**
2. Give the past participles of the following verbs.
   anrufen, einladen, mitbringen

I. 1. How does the past participle of an inseparable-prefix verb like **bekommen** differ from that of most other verbs?
2. What other type of verb adds no **ge-**prefix?
3. Give the present perfect tense of the following sentences.
   a. Ich bezahle das Essen.
   b. Wir erzählen es ihm.
   c. Es gefällt ihm nicht.
   d. Bekommst du es?
   e. Sie studiert in Bonn.
   f. Das Buch interessiert mich nicht.

J. 1. In what position is the past participle in an independent clause?
2. Where do the past participle and the auxiliary verb come in a dependent clause?
3. Rewrite the following sentences in the present perfect tense.
   a. Ich stehe spät auf, denn ich arbeite bis elf.
   b. Frank isst viel, weil das Essen so gut schmeckt.

K. Rewrite the following sentences in the present perfect tense.
1. Wen rufst du an?
2. Bringt ihr das Essen mit?
3. Alles sieht wirklich gut aus.
4. Wir diskutieren viele Probleme.
5. Die Gäste bleiben bis zehn Uhr.
6. Inge kommt nicht.
7. Wir vergessen das nicht.
8. Ich schenke Gerd das Buch, weil es ihm gefällt.
9. Was bekommst du zum Geburtstag?

Kapitel 7

A. Respond to one of the following statements with an expression of agreement and to the other with an expression of disagreement.
1. Klassische Musik ist langweilig.
2. Science-Fiction-Filme sind toll.

B. A friend asks what household chores you do. Give three possible answers.
   Welche Arbeiten machst du zu Hause?

C. Name three pieces of furniture or appliances found in the following rooms.
1. das Wohnzimmer
2. das Schlafzimmer
3. die Küche

D. 1. The words **hin** and **her** can be used alone or in combination with several parts of speech (for example **hierher, hinfahren**) to show direction. Which word indicates direction towards the speaker? Which indicates direction away from the speaker?
2. What position do **hin** and **her** occupy in a sentence when they stand alone?
3. Complete the following sentences with **hin, her, wo, woher,** or **wohin.**
   a. _____ wohnen Sie?
   b. _____ kommen Sie? Aus Österreich?
   c. _____ fahren Sie in den Ferien?
   d. Meine Tante wohnt in Hamburg. Ich fahre jedes Jahr _____.
   e. Kommen Sie mal _____.

E. 1. Indicate which of the following prepositions are always followed by:
   a. the accusative
   b. the dative
   c. either dative or accusative
   an, auf, aus, bei, durch, für, gegen, in, nach, neben, ohne, seit, über, unter, von, vor, zu, zwischen
2. List two contractions for each of the following prepositions:
   a. an   b. in

F. Construct sentences from the guidelines.
1. ich / fahren / in / Stadt
2. wir / gehen / auf / Markt
3. Sabine / studieren / an / Universität Hamburg
4. du / denken / an / dein / Freund / ?
5. warum / Tisch / stehen / zwischen / Stühle / ?
6. Alex / arbeiten / in / ein / Buchhandlung

G. English uses *to put* and *to be* as all-purpose verbs to talk about position. German uses several different verbs. Complete the following sentences with an appropriate verb from the list.
legen, liegen, stellen, stehen, setzen, sitzen, hängen, stecken
1. Lena _____ die Lampe auf den Tisch.
2. Die Lampe _____ auf dem Tisch.
3. Alex _____ die Uhr an die Wand.
4. Lena _____ das Kind auf den Stuhl.
5. Das Kind _____ auf dem Stuhl.
6. Alex _____ das Heft auf den Tisch.

7. Das Heft _____ auf dem Tisch.
8. Er _____ das Buch in den Rucksack.

H. 1. What case must be used for time expressions that indicate a definite time or period of time?
2. What case is used with time expressions beginning with **an, in,** or **vor?**
3. Complete the following sentences with the cued words.
   a. Wir bleiben _____. (ein / Tag)
   b. Bernd hat vor _____ den Führerschein gemacht. (ein / Jahr)
   c. Susi arbeitet _____. (jeder / Abend)
   d. Er kommt in _____ wieder. (eine / Woche)

I. 1. What construction is used in a German statement in place of a preposition + a pronoun that refers to things or ideas?
2. In German questions, what construction is usually used to replace **was** as the object of a preposition?
3. When does **da-** expand to **dar-** and **wo-** expand to **wor-?**
4. Complete the following sentences using a **da**-compound or a preposition and pronoun, as appropriate.
   a. Spricht Anna oft von ihrer Reise?
      —Ja, sie spricht oft _____.
   b. Machst du das für deine Freundin?
      —Ja, ich mache das _____.
5. Complete the sentences using a **wo**-compound or a preposition and interrogative pronoun, as appropriate.
   a. _____ spielst du morgen Tennis?
      —Ich spiele mit Inge.
   b. _____ habt ihr geredet?
      —Wir haben über den Film geredet.

J. 1. What word do indirect informational questions begin with?
2. What conjunction do indirect yes/no questions begin with?
3. Rewrite the following direct questions as indirect questions:
   a. Paul fragt Birgit: „Fährst du morgen zur Uni?"
   b. Birgit fragt Paul: „Wann isst du zu Mittag?"

Kapitel 8

A. The following statement appeared in a recent survey about attitudes toward work:
Bei einem Job ist das Wichtigste ein sicherer Arbeitsplatz.

Give two ways to ask a friend's opinion of this conclusion.

B. Form nouns by adding **-heit** or **-keit** to the following adjectives.
1. krank   2. freundlich   3. frei

C. Add at least two words related to:
1. studieren   2. Sonne   3. backen

D.
1. In the genitive case, what ending is added to masculine (**der-**) and neuter (**das-**) nouns of the following kinds:
   a. one-syllable
   b. two or more syllables
   c. masculine N-nouns
2. Give the genitive of the following nouns.
   a. das Bild   d. ein Haus
   b. dieser Laden   e. ihr Bruder
   c. der Junge
3. What is the genitive form of **wer?**
4. Give the German equivalent of:
   Whose backpack is that?

E.
1. Do feminine (**die-**) nouns and plural nouns add a genitive ending?
2. Give the genitive form of the following:
   a. die Frau   c. diese Kinder
   b. eine Ausländerin d. meine Eltern

F. In German, does the genitive precede or follow the noun it modifies?

G. Give the English equivalents of the following phrases.
1. eines Tages   2. eines Abends

H. Name four prepositions that are followed by the genitive.

I. Complete the following sentences, using the cued words.
1. Wegen _____ kommt er nicht. (das Wetter)
2. Den Studenten gefällt die Vorlesung _____. (der Professor)
3. Kennst du die Adresse _____? (mein Freund Michael)
4. Wir haben während _____ geschlafen. (die Reise)
5. Wie ist die Telefonnummer _____? (deine Freundin)
6. Kennst du die Namen _____? (die Geschäfte)

J. Complete the following sentences, using the cued words.
1. Das ist ein _____ Kind. (nett)

2. Thomas ist ein _____ Student. (gut)
3. Anni ist aber auch _____. (gut)
4. Mark hat ein sehr _____ Fahrrad gekauft. (teuer)
5. Wegen des _____ Wetters bleiben wir zu Hause. (kalt)
6. Ich esse gern Brot mit _____ Butter. (frisch)
7. Ich habe _____ Durst. (groß)
8. _____ Bier schmeckt mir nicht. (warm)
9. Die Sonne ist heute richtig _____. (heiß)
10. Sophie, ist das dein _____ Pulli? (neu)
11. Kennen Sie die Geschichte dieser _____ Häuser? (alt)
12. Das ist keine _____ Idee. (schlecht)

K.
1. How are the ordinal numbers from 2–19 formed in German?
2. Give the German words for:
   a. first   c. fifth
   b. third   d. sixteenth
3. What is added to numbers after 19 to form the ordinals?
4. Give the German words for:
   a. thirty-first   b. hundredth
5. Ordinals take adjective endings. Complete the sentences with the cued ordinals.
   a. Am _____ November habe ich Geburtstag. (7.)
   b. Wir müssen leider ein _____ Auto kaufen. (2.)

L.
1. Ask the date in German.
2. Say it is June first.
3. Write the date, July 6, 2005, as it would appear in a letter heading.

Kapitel 9

A. How would you express sympathetic understanding when your friend says:
Ich habe mir den Arm gebrochen.

B. Name three acts of hygiene that are part of your morning ritual.

C. Complete the German expressions for:
1. *something good*   etwas _____
2. *nothing special*   nichts _____
3. *a good acquaintance* ein guter _____
4. *a German (female)*   eine _____

D. For each subject pronoun below, give the accusative and dative reflexive pronoun.
1. ich   3. sie *(sg. and pl.)*   5. er
2. du   4. wir

E. Some German verbs are called reflexive verbs because reflexive pronouns are regularly used with these verbs. Construct sentences using the following guidelines.
   1. du / sich fühlen / heute / besser/ ?
   2. Cornelia / sich erkälten / gestern

F. When referring to parts of the body, German usage differs from English in some constructions. Complete the following German sentences.
   1. Ich habe mir _____ Hände gewaschen.
   2. Tanja putzt sich _____ Zähne.

G. 1. What word precedes the dependent infinitive with most verbs in German?
   2. When are dependent infinitives *not* preceded by that word?
   3. What is the German construction equivalent to the English *(in order) to* + infinitive?
   4. Complete the following sentences with the cued words.
      a. Es macht Spaß _____. (in den Bergen / wandern)
      b. Ich möchte mir _____. (eine neue CD / kaufen)
      c. Vergiss nicht _____. (Blumen / mitbringen)
      d. Ich beginne _____. (deine Ideen / verstehen)
      e. Ich bleibe heute zu Hause, _____. (um ... zu / machen / meine Arbeit)

H. 1. How are comparative adjectives and adverbs formed in German?
   2. How do some one-syllable adjectives and adverbs change the stem vowel in the comparative?
   3. Complete the following sentences using the comparative form of the cued adjective.
      a. Es ist heute _____ als gestern. (kalt)
      b. Mein neues Auto war _____ als mein altes. (teuer)
      c. Helmut wohnt jetzt in einem _____ Zimmer. (groß, schön)

I. 1. How are superlative adjectives and adverbs formed in German?
   2. What is the ending for the superlative if the base form ends in **-d (wild)**, **-t (leicht)**, or a sibilant **(heiß)**?
   3. How do some one-syllable adjectives and adverbs change the vowel in the superlative?
   4. What form does an adverb or a predicate adjective have in the superlative?

5. Complete the following sentences using the superlative form of the cued adjective or adverb.
   a. Dieser Kassettenrecorder ist _____. (teuer)
   b. Gabi arbeitet _____. (schwer)
   c. Das ist mein _____ Pulli. (schön)
   d. Gestern war der _____ Tag dieses Jahres. (kalt)

J. Give the comparative and superlative forms of:
   1. gern   2. gut   3. viel

Kapitel 10

A. For weeks you have been tired from too little sleep. Your friend suggests a remedy. Give two possible responses showing you are puzzled about how to follow her/his advice. Your friend has said:
Du musst weniger arbeiten. Fünf Stunden am Tag sind genug.

B. Give two logical responses to the question:
Wo warst du gestern Abend?

C. Give one example of
   1. giving an invitation to attend an event
   2. responding to an invitation

D. 1. When is the simple past tense used? What is it often called?
   2. When is the present perfect tense used? What is it often called?
   3. Which verbs occur more frequently in the simple past than in present perfect tense, even in conversation?

E. 1. What tense marker is added to modals in the simple past tense?
   2. What happens to modals with an umlaut in the simple past?
   3. Give the simple past tense forms of the following:
      a. ich darf   c. sie muss
      b. du kannst   d. wir mögen

F. 1. What is the tense marker for weak verbs in the simple past tense?
   2. What is the past tense marker for **regnen, öffnen,** and verbs with stems ending in **-d** or **-t?**
   3. Which forms add no endings in the simple past?
   4. Change each of the following present-tense forms to simple past.

a. ich spiele   c. es regnet
b. Dieter arbeitet   d. wir sagen

G. Irregular weak verbs have a vowel change in the simple past tense, and several of these verbs have consonant changes. Give the simple past form of the following sentences.
1. Ich bringe den Wein.
2. Sie denkt an Gerd.
3. Sie wissen es schon.

H. 1. How do strong verbs show the simple past tense?
2. Which forms add no endings?
3. Give the simple past tense of the following verbs.
   a. er spricht   f. ich bin
   b. sie sieht   g. sie wird
   c. ich gebe   h. sie gehen
   d. wir bleiben   i. ich laufe
   e. er fährt   j. er trägt

I. 1. Where does the prefix of separable-prefix verbs go in the simple past tense?
2. Construct sentences in the simple past, using the guidelines.
   a. Konzert / anfangen / um sieben Uhr
   b. Kerstin / mitbringen / Blumen
   c. ich / aufstehen / immer / früh
   d. wir / einkaufen / in / Stadt

J. 1. When is the past perfect tense used?
2. How is it formed?
3. Give the English equivalents of the following sentences.
   a. Ich habe gut geschlafen, weil ich 20 Kilometer gelaufen war.
   b. Nachdem es den ganzen Tag geregnet hatte, schien die Sonne am Abend.

K. Restate the following sentences in the simple past and present perfect tenses.
1. Stefan schreibt den Brief.
2. Anna geht nach Hause.

L. **Als, wenn,** and **wann** are equivalent to English *when.*
1. Which must be used for *when* to introduce direct or indirect questions?
2. Which must be used for *when* in the sense of *whenever* (that is, for repeated events) in past time?
3. Which must be used for *when* in clauses with events in the present or future?
4. Which must be used for *when* in clauses concerned with a single past event?

5. Complete the following sentences with **als, wenn,** or **wann,** as appropriate.
   a. Wir haben viel Spaß, _____ Schmidts uns besuchen.
   b. Sie kamen mit, _____ wir gestern ins Café gingen.
   c. Immer _____ wir schwimmen wollten, regnete es.
   d. Ich weiß nicht, _____ wir zurück-gekommen sind.

Kapitel 11

A. Your friend tells you of her/his plans for the summer. Give your response in two hypothetical statements. Your friend says:
Im Sommer fahr ich für sechs Wochen nach Italien. Komm doch mit!

B. You have an appointment. Give a possible response from the secretary to your question:
Ist Frau/Herr Neumann zu sprechen?

C. Give the German words for:
1. lawyer (male)
2. computer specialist (female)
3. architect (female)
4. dentist (male)

D. Form adjectives or adverbs from the following nouns by adding **-lich.** Give the English equivalents.
1. Frage   2. Tag

E. 1. Which tense is generally used in German to express future time?
2. Construct a sentence using the guidelines: ich / anrufen / dich / heute Abend (*present tense*)

F. 1. When is the future tense used in German?
2. How is the future tense formed in German?
3. In an independent clause where the future is used, what position is the infinitive in?
4. In a dependent clause where the future is used, what verb form is in the final position?
5. Restate in the future tense.
   a. Sandra hilft uns.
   b. Machst du das wirklich?
   c. Michael sagt, dass er einen neuen Job sucht. (*Do not change* **Michael sagt.**)

G. Express the idea of *assumption* or *probability* in the following sentences.
1. My parents are probably at home.

2. That's probably wrong.

H.
1. Give three uses of the **würde**-construction and the subjunctive of the main verb.
2. Say that Trudi would also like to do the following. Use **würde**.
   Christoph faulenzt viel.
3. Say that you wish the following situation were different. Use **würde**.
   Die Sonne scheint nicht.
   Wenn die Sonne nur ...
4. Restate as a request, using **würde**.
   Bleib noch eine Stunde!

I.
1. What is the subjunctive form of the verb **sein**?
2. What is the subjunctive form of the verb **haben**?
3. Give the present-time subjunctive of the following verb forms.
   a. ich bin   c. wir sind
   b. du hast   d. sie hat

J.
1. How is the present-time subjunctive of modals formed?
2. Give the subjunctive of the following verb forms.
   a. ich muss   b. du kannst

K.
1. How is the present-time subjunctive of strong verbs formed?
2. Give the subjunctive of the following verb forms.
   a. es gibt   c. sie kommen
   b. sie tut es   d. du findest

L.
1. How is the present-time subjunctive of weak verbs formed?
2. Give the subjunctive of the following verb forms.
   a. sie lernt   b. du arbeitest

M.
1. How is the present-time subjunctive of irregular weak verbs formed?
2. Give the subjunctive of the following verb forms.
   a. sie bringt   c. wir wissen
   b. ich denke

N.
1. What are the two clauses in a conditional sentence called?
2. What word begins the condition clause?
3. In what kind of conditional sentence is the indicative used?
4. In what kind of conditional sentence are the **würde**-construction and the subjunctive of the main verb used?

5. Restate as conditions contrary to fact.
   a. Christine kommt sicher, wenn sie Zeit hat.
   b. Wenn ich Geld habe, gehe ich ins Konzert.

O. Construct sentences using the guidelines.
1. ich / tun / das / nicht (*present-time subj.*)
2. du / glauben / mir / nicht (*use* **würde**)
3. wir / können / fahren / morgen (*present-time subj.*)
4. Wenn sie Geld hätte, sie / kaufen / ein neues Auto (*use* **würde**)
5. Ich wollte, du / können / bleiben / länger (*present-time subj.*)

Kapitel 12

A. You have just arrived by train in Hamburg and want first of all to go to the famous gardens **Planten un Blomen.** The person you have asked for directions is very cooperative but speaks too fast and not always distinctly. How would you indicate you don't understand? Give three expressions.

B.
1. What function does a relative pronoun serve?
2. Where does the finite verb come in a relative clause?

C.
1. With what forms are most of the relative pronoun forms identical?
2. Dative plural and genitive forms are exceptions. The genitive forms are **dessen** and **deren.** What is the relative pronoun in dative plural?

D.
1. How do you decide the gender and number of the relative pronoun you use?
2. How do you decide what case of a relative pronoun to use?
3. What case does a relative pronoun have when it follows a preposition?

E. Complete the following sentences with a relative pronoun.
1. Ist das der Mann, _____ so viel arbeitet?
2. Wie heißt die Frau, von _____ du gerade erzählt hast?
3. Wo ist das Restaurant, in _____ wir morgen essen?
4. Wie gefällt dir der Pulli, _____ du zum Geburtstag bekommen hast?
5. Die Freunde, mit _____ wir in den Ferien waren, sind wirklich nette Leute.

184 ■ Deutsch heute / Arbeitsheft

6. Ist das der Mann, _____ das rote Auto gehört?

F. 1. What is the role of the subject of a sentence in active voice?
2. What is the role of the subject in passive voice?

G. 1. How is passive voice formed in German?
2. Construct sentences using the guidelines, and then give the English equivalents.
    a. Haus / verkaufen (*passive, present*)
    b. Geld / gerade investieren (*passive, simple past*)
    c. Stadt / teilen (*passive, simple past*)
    d. Fabrik / modernisieren (*passive, present*)

H. 1. In English, the agent in the passive voice is the object of the preposition *by: The work was done by our neighbors.* How is the agent expressed in German?
2. Complete the following sentences.
    a. Das Museum wurde _____ dem Architekten Sterling gebaut.
    b. Die Arbeit wurde _____ unseren Nachbarn gemacht.

I. 1. What are three uses of **werden?**
2. Identify the use of **werden** and give the English equivalents for the following sentences.
    a. Eine Reise nach Dresden wurde geplant.
    b. Es wird endlich wärmer.
    c. Er wird an uns schreiben.

Self-Tests

Answer Key

Answer Key to Self-Tests

Einführung

A. 1. Wie heißt du [heißen Sie]?
2. Wie alt bist du [sind Sie]?
3. Wie ist deine [Ihre] Adresse?
4. Wie ist deine [Ihre] Telefonnummer?

B. 1. danke   2. bitte

C. 1. Montag, Dienstag, Mittwoch, Donnerstag, Freitag, Samstag [Sonnabend], Sonntag
2. Welcher Tag ist heute?
3. Heute ist Donnerstag.

D. 1. *Answers will vary. Possible answers:* blau, gelb, grau, grün, rot, schwarz, weiß
2. Welche Farbe hat die Wand?

E. 1. By the article and the pronoun that refer to the noun.
2. a. *masculine,* der Bleistift
   b. *feminine,* die Tür
   c. *neuter,* das Bett
   d. *feminine,* die Frau
   e. *masculine,* der Mann
3. a. Der
   b. Das
   c. Die
   d. der
   e. das
   f. Die
4. a. ein   d. eine
   b. eine   e. eine
   c. ein   f. ein

F. 1. er   3. sie   5. sie
2. es   4. er   6. es

Kapitel 1

A. *Answers will vary. Possible answers:*
1. Ja. / Natürlich.
2. Nein. / Natürlich nicht.
3. Ich glaube ja (nicht). / Vielleicht (nicht).

B. 1. a. Guten Morgen!
   b. Guten Tag!
   c. Guten Abend!

2. *Answers will vary. Possible answers:*
Positive: Gut, danke. / Danke, ganz gut.
Negative: Nicht so gut. / Schlecht. / Ich bin krank.

C. 1. a. fleißig   d. schlecht
   b. unfreundlich   e. groß
   c. lustig
2. Auf Wiedersehen; Tschüs

D. 1. a. Wie viel Uhr [Wie spät] ist es?
   b. Ich gehe um ein Uhr [um eins].
2. a. Viertel nach zwei
   b. Viertel vor vier
   c. halb sieben
3. Official time uses a 24-hour clock.

E. 1. du, ihr, Sie
2. a. Sie   c. du
   b. ihr   d. du
3. a. er   c. wir   e. sie
   b. sie   d. ich
4. By the verb: **sie** + singular verb = *she;*
   sie + plural verb = *they*
5. a. Sie spielt gut Tennis.
   b. Sie spielen gut Tennis.

F. 1. a. ich bin   d. sie sind
   b. wir sind   e. du bist; ihr seid; Sie sind
   c. sie ist

G. 1. the infinitive
2. -en
3. a. glauben b. wandern c. arbeiten
4. a. glaub- b. wander- c. arbeit-
5. the finite verb
6. a. -st   d. -en   f. -t
   b. -t   e. -t   g. -en
   c. -e
7. a. Spielst   e. schwimmen
   b. höre   f. heißt
   c. arbeitet   g. heißt
   d. wandert

H. 1. a. Du spielst gut.
   b. Frank arbeitet heute.
   c. Ute arbeitet viel.

2. a. Ich gehe heute Nachmittag ins Kino.
   b. Was machst du [macht ihr/machen Sie] heute Abend?

I. 1. Use **gern** + verb.
   2. a. Ute spielt gern Schach.
      b. Ich wandere gern.
      c. Wir treiben gern Sport.

J. 1. a. before predicate adjectives
      b. after specific time expressions
      c. before most other adverbs, including general time adverbs
      d. before dependent infinitives
   2. a. Wir schwimmen nicht gern.
      b. Frank wandert nicht viel.
      c. Ich gehe nicht joggen.
      d. Wir arbeiten morgen nicht.
      e. Heike ist nicht nett.
      f. Mark ist nicht oft krank.

K. 1. the interrogative expression
   2. The verb comes second, after the interrogative. The subject comes after the verb.
   3. wann, warum, was, wer, wie, wie viel, welch-, was für ein
   4. a. Wer spielt gut Fußball?
      b. Was spielt Veronika gern?
      c. Wann gehen wir ins Kino?

L. 1. the verb
   2. a. Spielt Petra oft Fußball?
      b. Arbeitet Kurt viel?
      c. Spielst du gut Schach?

M. 1. nicht, nicht wahr
   2. a. Wir spielen morgen Tennis, nicht (wahr)?
      b. Paul ist müde, nicht (wahr)?
      c. Du tanzt gern, nicht (wahr)?

Kapitel 2

A. *Answers will vary. Possible answers:*
   Wirklich? / Denkst du? / Vielleicht.

B. Januar, Februar, März, April, Mai, Juni, Juli, August, September, Oktober, November, Dezember

C. 1. neuter (das)
   2. die Schweiz, die Slowakei, die Tschechische Republik, die Türkei; die USA, die Niederlande

D. 1. die Studentin; der Student
   2. die Schweizerin; der Schweizer
   3. die Nachbarin; der Nachbar

E. 1. Ich war auch gestern müde.
   2. Eva war auch gestern krank.
   3. Du warst auch gestern faul.
   4. Sie waren auch gestern fleißig.

F. 1. Wann hast du Geburtstag?
   2. Wann hat Frank Geburtstag?
   3. Wann habt ihr Geburtstag?
   4. Wann haben Ulrike und Kathrin Geburtstag?

G. 1. second position
   2. a. Am Sonntag war das Wetter nicht gut.
      b. Hoffentlich scheint die Sonne morgen.

H. 1. by word order
   2. case
   3. the nominative case
   4. sein; heißen
   5. a. subject = das Wetter
      b. subject = Frank Schmidt; pred. noun = Student
      c. subject = das Mädchen; pred. noun = Cornelia

I. 1. die
   2. a. die Fenster   d. die Uhren
      b. die Tische   e. die Stühle
      c. die Bücher   f. die Studentinnen

J. 1. ein; eine
   2. a, an
   3. a. ein; ein   b. eine   c. ein

K. 1. kein
   2. not a; not any; no
   3. nicht
   4. a. keine   b. nicht   c. kein

L. 1. a. dein Radio
      b. ihr Basketball
      c. ihre Karten
      d. unser Land
      e. meine Adresse
   2. a. Klaus' Zimmer / das Zimmer von Klaus
      b. Tanjas Uhr

M. 1. a. Ja, er ist neu.
      b. Ja, er ist praktisch.
      c. Ja, es ist drei Jahre alt.
      d. Ja, sie arbeitet heute Abend.
      e. Ja, sie tanzen gern.

2. a. Ja, der ist wirklich nett.
   b. Ja, die ist oft so lustig.
   c. Ja, der war sehr gut.
   d. Ja, die sind oft kritisch.

Kapitel 3

A. *Answers will vary. Possible answers:*
   1. Ja, gerne. / Natürlich. / Machen wir.
   2. Das geht leider nicht.
   3. Vielleicht.

B. 1. Doch! 2. Doch!

C. *Answers will vary:* Nimmst du Aspirin? Das habe ich. / Nimm doch Aspirin! / Geh doch in die Apotheke!

D. *Answers may vary.*
   1. Frühstück: Brötchen, Butter, Eier, Kaffee, Tee
   2. Mittagessen: Fisch, Gemüse, Fleisch, Kartoffeln, Salat, Obst, Eis, Pudding
   3. Abendessen: Käse, Brot, Wurst, Würstchen, Bier, Mineralwasser, Tee, Wein

E. 1. the last noun
   2. a. die Tischlampe   b. der Kartoffelsalat

F. 1. **du-** and **er/es/sie**-forms
   2. a. nimmst   c. isst   e. Gibt
      b. nehme   d. essen   f. Gibst

G. 1. Time follows place in English. Time precedes place in German.
   2. Wann kommst du heute Abend nach Hause?

H. 1. the imperative
   2. first position
   3. a. Gib   b. Kommt   c. Bleiben Sie

I. 1. a. nominative case   b. accusative case
   2. a. mein   c. eure
      b. ihren   d. deine
   3. a. den Jungen   b. den Nachbarn
   4. durch, für, gegen, ohne, um
   5. a. Der Kuchen   f. einen Stuhl
      b. den Kuchen   g. Wen
      c. ihre Stadt   h. den Studenten
      d. seinen Professor   i. keinen
      e. kein Brot   Supermarkt
   6. a. den   b. das   c. Den
   7. a. ihn   c. sie   e. uns
      b. mich   d. dich   f. euch

Kapitel 4

A. *Answers will vary. Possible answers:*
   Es geht leider nicht. / Leider kann ich jetzt nicht. / Ich kann leider nicht. / Nein, es tut mir Leid. / Nein, leider nicht.

B. *Answers will vary. Possible answers:*
   Ich bereite mein Referat vor. / Ich schreibe meine Seminararbeit. / Ich mache Deutsch. / Ich lese einen Artikel über ... / Ich arbeite für die Klausur.

C. *Answers will vary.* Ich habe einen Bruder, eine Schwester, vier Tanten, usw.

D. 1. Alex ist Amerikaner.
   2. Er wird Bäcker.
   3. Andrea ist Studentin.

E. 1. **lesen** and **sehen** change **e** to **ie; werden** changes **e** to **i**
   2. du wirst, er/es/sie wird
   3. a. liest   b. Siehst   c. wird

F. 1. a. wissen   b. kennen
   2. a. Kennst   b. weiß   c. Weißt

G. 1. the same as the definite articles
   2. **jeder;** it means *each, every*
   3. **manche, solche; manche** means *some,* **solche** means *such*
   4. a. dieses   d. Solche
      b. Jeder   e. Manche
      c. Welchen

H. 1. modal auxiliary
   2. a. wollen   d. dürfen
      b. sollen   e. können
      c. müssen   f. mögen

I. 1. **ich-** and **er/es/sie**-forms
   2. a stem-vowel change
   3. a. kann   d. sollen
      b. darf   e. will
      c. musst   f. mag

J. 1. Magst du [Mögen Sie] Inge?
   2. Möchtest du [Möchten Sie] heute Abend arbeiten?

K. 1. in last position
   2. a. Musst du heute arbeiten?
      b. Ich kann es nicht machen.
      c. Petra will etwas sagen.
   3. If a verb of motion or the idea of *to do* is clear from the context.

4. Ich muss jetzt nach Hause.

L. 1. The separable-prefix verbs are **fernsehen, einkaufen, mitbringen.**
2. in last position
3. a. Gerd bringt einen Freund mit.
   b. Kaufst du morgen ein?
   c. Ich muss das Abendessen vorbereiten.
   d. Siehst du oft fern?
   e. Ich soll meine Notizen durcharbeiten.

Kapitel 5

A. *Answers will vary. Possible answers:*
Ja sicher. / Klar. / Kein Problem. / Ja, klar. / Ja, natürlich.

B. *Answers will vary:* Ich möchte wandern, viel schwimmen, Tennis spielen, schlafen, usw.

C. 1. wo; wohin
   2. a. Wo   b. Wohin

D. *Private:* das Auto/der Wagen, das Fahrrad/das Rad, das Flugzeug, das Motorrad
   Public: der Bus, das Flugzeug, das Schiff, die Straßenbahn, die U-Bahn, der Zug

E. 1. **a** to **ä** for **du-** and **er/es/sie**-forms
   2. a. fährt   c. läuft
      b. Schläft   d. Fährst

F. 1. aber, denn, oder, sondern, und
   2. sondern
   3. aber
   4. no
   5. a. Gabi bleibt zu Hause, denn sie ist krank.
      b. Holger geht nicht schwimmen, sondern er spielt Tennis.
      c. Er schwimmt nicht gut, aber er schwimmt gern.

G. 1. in last position
   2. modal auxiliary comes last
   3. The finite verb comes before the subject.
   4. a. Wir können nicht fahren, weil unser Auto kaputt ist.
      b. Wenn es morgen regnet, müssen wir zu Hause bleiben.
   5. a. Sabine sagt, dass die Nachbarn oft im Supermarkt einkaufen.
      b. Erik glaubt, dass das Obst nicht so frisch ist.

H. 1. dative
   2. seiner Schwester

3. a. der Frau   d. den Bergen
   b. dem Mann   e. dem Studenten
   c. dem Auto
4. gefallen, gehören, glauben
5. aus, mit, nach, seit, von
6. a. den Kindern
   b. Wem
   c. meinem Bruder
   d. dem Zug
   e. deinen Vater
   f. einer Familie
   g. einen Kugelschreiber
   h. dieser Straßenbahn
   i. welchen

I. 1.   *acc.*   *dat.*
      a. mich   mir
      b. ihn   ihm
      c. dich   dir
      d. uns   uns
      e. sie   ihr
      f. Sie   Ihnen
   2. a. dir   d. ihnen   f. uns
      b. mich   e. sie   g. wem
      c. ihm

J. 1. mir dieses Buch
   2. meinen Eltern diese Lampe
   3. ihn meinem Bruder

Kapitel 6

A. *Answers will vary. Possible answers:*
Entschuldigung. / Verzeihung. / Es tut mir Leid, aber … / Das wollte ich nicht. / Das habe ich nicht so gemeint.

B. 1. der Handschuh, der Hut, der Pulli, der Stiefel, der Regenmantel, der Schuh, der Sportschuh, das Hemd, das T-Shirt, die Hose, die Jacke, die Jeans, die Shorts, die Socke, die Mütze
   2. der Rock, das Kleid, die Bluse, die Strumpfhose

C. 1. neuter
   2. -ing
   3. a. Hiking is healthy.
      b. Do you have to work today?

D. 1. To refer to past actions or states.
   2. It is used especially in conversation.

E. 1. an auxiliary and the past participle of the verb
   2. haben

3. sein
4. The verb must (1) be intransitive and (2) indicate change of condition or motion to or from a place.
5. bleiben; sein
6. a. hat   c. sind   e. Seid
   b. Bist   d. haben   f. habe

F. 1. -t
2. adds **-et** instead of **-t**
3. There is a stem-vowel change and sometimes a consonant change: **gebracht**
4. gebracht, gekostet, gemacht, gedacht, gehabt, gekannt, geregnet, gewandert, gewusst, getanzt

G. 1. -en
2. Many past participles have a stem-vowel change; some also have consonant changes.
3. gefunden, gegeben, gelesen, genommen, geschlafen, geschrieben, getrunken, getan

H. 1. The prefix **ge-** comes between the prefix and the stem of the past participle: **eingekauft.**
2. angerufen, eingeladen, mitgebracht

I. 1. It adds no **ge-**prefix.
2. verbs ending in **-ieren**
3. a. Ich habe das Essen bezahlt.
   b. Wir haben es ihm erzählt.
   c. Es hat ihm nicht gefallen.
   d. Hast du es bekommen?
   e. Sie hat in Bonn studiert.
   f. Das Buch hat mich nicht interessiert.

J. 1. in final position
2. The auxiliary follows the past participle and is in final position.
3. a. Ich bin spät aufgestanden, denn ich habe bis elf gearbeitet.
   b. Frank hat viel gegessen, weil das Essen so gut geschmeckt hat.

K. 1. Wen hast du angerufen?
2. Habt ihr das Essen mitgebracht?
3. Alles hat wirklich gut ausgesehen.
4. Wir haben viele Probleme diskutiert.
5. Die Gäste sind bis zehn Uhr geblieben.
6. Inge ist nicht gekommen.
7. Wir haben das nicht vergessen.
8. Ich habe Gerd das Buch geschenkt, weil es ihm gefallen hat.
9. Was hast du zum Geburtstag bekommen?

Kapitel 7

A. *Answers will vary. Possible answers:*
Agreement: Richtig. / Du hast Recht. / Das finde ich auch.
Disagreement: Wirklich? / Meinst du? / Das finde ich gar nicht. / Ich sehe das ganz anders.

B. *Answers will vary. Possible answers:*
Ich mache die Wohnung sauber. / Ich wische Staub. / Ich wasche die Wäsche. / Ich sauge Staub. / Ich putze das Bad.

C. *Answers will vary. Possible answers:*
Wohnzimmer: das Sofa, der Couchtisch, der Sessel, der Schreibtisch, der Teppich, der Fernseher, der Videorecorder, der DVD-Player
Schlafzimmer: das Bett, die Kommode, der Spiegel, der Nachttisch, die Lampe
Küche: der Herd, der Kühlschrank, die Spülmaschine, der Tisch, der Stuhl

D. 1. **Her** indicates direction towards the speaker; **hin** indicates direction away from the speaker.
2. last position
3. a. Wo   c. Wohin   e. her
   b. Woher   d. hin

E. 1. a. *accusative:* durch, für, gegen, ohne
   b. *dative:* aus, bei, nach, seit, von, zu
   c. *two-way prepositions:* an, auf, in, neben, über, unter, vor, zwischen
2. a. ans, am   b. ins, im

F. 1. Ich fahre in die Stadt.
2. Wir gehen auf den Markt.
3. Sabine studiert an der Universität Hamburg.
4. Denkst du an deinen Freund?
5. Warum steht der Tisch zwischen den Stühlen?
6. Alex arbeitet in einer Buchhandlung.

G. 1. stellt   5. sitzt
2. steht   6. legt
3. hängt   7. liegt
4. setzt   8. steckt

H. 1. accusative
2. dative
3. a. einen Tag   c. jeden Abend
   b. einem Jahr   d. einer Woche

I. 1. **da**-compound   2. **wo**-compound
    3. When the preposition begins with a vowel.
    4. a. davon   b. für sie
    5. a. Mit wem   b. Worüber

J. 1. with the question word
    2. with **ob**
    3. a. Paul fragt Birgit, ob sie morgen zur Uni fährt.
       b. Birgit fragt Paul, wann er zu Mittag isst.

Kapitel 8

A. *Answers will vary. Possible answers:*
Was meinst du? / Was glaubst du? / Wie siehst du das? / Was hältst du davon?

B. 1. die Krankheit   3. die Freiheit
    2. die Freundlichkeit

C. *Answers will vary. Possible answers:*
    1. Studium, Student, Studentin, Studentenheim
    2. sonnig, die Sonnenbrille, Sonntag, Sonnabend
    3. Bäcker, Bäckerin, Bäckerei

D. 1. a. -es   b. -s   c. -(e)n
    2. a. des Bildes   d. eines Hauses
       b. dieses Ladens   e. ihres Bruders
       c. des Jungen
    3. wessen
    4. Wessen Rucksack ist das?

E. 1. no
    2. a. der Frau   c. dieser Kinder
       b. einer Ausländerin   d. meiner Eltern

F. The genitive follows the noun it modifies.

G. 1. one day; some day   2. one evening

H. (an)statt, trotz, während, wegen

I. 1. des Wetters   4. der Reise
    2. des Professors   5. deiner Freundin
    3. meines Freundes   6. der Geschäfte
      Michael

J. 1. nettes   5. kalten   9. heiß
    2. guter   6. frischer   10. neuer
    3. gut   7. großen   11. alten
    4. teures   8. Warmes   12. schlechte

K. 1. By adding -t to the numbers
    2. a. erst-   c. fünft-
       b. dritt-   d. sechzehnt-
    3. -st is added.
    4. a. einunddreißigst-   b. hundertst-
    5. a. siebten   b. zweites

L. 1. Der Wievielte ist heute? / Den Wievielten haben wir heute?
    2. Heute ist der erste Juni. / Heute haben wir den ersten Juni.
    3. den 6. Juli 2005 / 6.7.05

Kapitel 9

A. *Answers will vary. Possible answers:*
Du Armer/Du Arme! / Das ist ja dumm. / Das tut mir aber Leid für dich. / Dass dir das passieren muss!

B. *Possible answers:*
Ich dusche (mich). / Ich bade. / Ich putze mir die Zähne. / Ich rasiere mich. / Ich kämme mich. / Ich wasche mir Gesicht und Hände.

C. 1. etwas Gutes
    2. nichts Besonderes
    3. ein guter Bekannter
    4. eine Deutsche

D. 1. mich, mir   4. uns, uns
    2. dich, dir   5. sich, sich
    3. sich, sich

E. 1. Fühlst du dich heute besser?
    2. Cornelia hat sich gestern erkältet.

F. 1. die   2. die

G. 1. zu
    2. when used with modals
    3. **um ... zu** + infinitive
    4. a. Es macht Spaß *in den Bergen zu wandern.*
       b. Ich möchte mir *eine neue CD kaufen.*
       c. Vergiss nicht *Blumen mitzubringen.*
       d. Ich beginne *deine Ideen zu verstehen.*
       e. Ich bleibe heute zu Hause, *um meine Arbeit zu machen.*

H. 1. -er is added to the base form.
    2. The vowel **a, o,** or **u** adds umlaut.
    3. a. kälter   c. größeren, schöneren
       b. teurer

I. 1. **-st** is added to the base form.
2. **-est**
3. The vowel **a**, **o**, or **u** adds umlaut.
4. am + (e)sten
5. a. am teuersten   c. schönster
     b. am schwersten   d. kälteste

J. 1. lieber, am liebsten
2. besser, am besten
3. mehr, am meisten

Kapitel 10

A. *Answers will vary. Possible answers:*
Ich weiß wirklich nicht, wie ich das machen soll. / Ich will ja, aber es geht nicht. / Es geht nicht. / Ich kann nicht.

B. *Answers will vary. Possible answers:*
Ich war im Theater [Kino, Konzert]. / Ich war in der Kneipe [Disco, Bibliothek]. / Ich war zu Hause.

C. 1. Hast [Hättest] du Lust ins Kino [Theater, Konzert] zu gehen? / Möchtest du ins Kino [Theater, Konzert] gehen?
2. *Answers will vary. Possible answers:*
Ja, gern. / Wenn du mich einlädst, schon. / Nein, ich habe keine Lust. / Nein, ich habe keine Zeit.

D. 1. to narrate a series of connected events in the past; often called narrative past
2. in a two-way exchange to talk about events in the past; often called conversational past
3. modals, **sein, haben**

E. 1. **-te**
2. They lose the umlaut.
3. a. ich durfte   c. sie musste
     b. du konntest   d. wir mochten

F. 1. **-te**   2. **-ete**
3. **ich-** and **er/es/sie**-forms
4. a. ich spielte   c. es regnete
     b. Dieter arbeitete   d. wir sagten

G. 1. Ich brachte den Wein.
2. Sie dachte an Gerd.
3. Sie wussten es schon.

H. 1. They undergo a stem change.
2. **ich-** and **er/es/sie**-forms

3. a. er sprach e. er fuhr   h. sie gingen
    b. sie sah   f. ich war   i. ich lief
    c. ich gab g. sie wurde j. er trug
    d. wir blieben

I. 1. in final position
2. a. Das Konzert fing um sieben Uhr an.
    b. Kerstin brachte Blumen mit.
    c. Ich stand immer früh auf.
    d. Wir kauften in der Stadt ein.

J. 1. It is used to report an event or action that took place before another event or action in the past.
2. It consists of the simple past of the auxiliaries **haben** or **sein** and the past participle of the verb.
3. a. I slept well because I had run 20 kilometers.
    b. After it had rained all day the sun shone [shined] in the evening.

K. 1. Stefan schrieb den Brief. Stefan hat den Brief geschrieben.
2. Anna ging nach Hause. Anna ist nach Hause gegangen.

L. 1. wann
2. wenn
3. wenn
4. als
5. a. wenn   c. wenn
    b. als   d. wann

Kapitel 11

A. *Answers will vary. Possible answers:*
Das wäre schön. / Wenn ich nur genug Geld hätte! / Wenn ich nur Zeit hätte. / Das würde ich gern machen. / Das würde Spaß machen. / Dazu hätte ich große (keine) Lust.

B. *Answers will vary. Possible answers:*
Es tut mir Leid. Sie/Er ist im Moment beschäftigt [nicht zu sprechen]. Sie/Er telefoniert gerade. / Sie/Er hat einen Termin. / Gehen Sie bitte gleich hinein. Sie/Er erwartet Sie.

C. 1. der Rechtsanwalt   3. die Architektin
2. die Informatikerin   4. der Zahnarzt

D. 1. **fraglich** = questionable
2. **täglich** = daily

E. 1. present tense
2. Ich rufe dich heute Abend an.

F. 1. When it is not clear from the context that the event will occur in the future, or to express an assumption.
2. a form of **werden** plus an infinitive
3. final position
4. the auxiliary (**werden**), just after the infinitive
5. a. Sandra wird uns helfen.
  b. Wirst du das wirklich machen?
  c. Michael sagt, dass er einen neuen Job suchen wird.

G. 1. Meine Eltern werden wohl [schon/sicher] zu Hause sein.
2. Das wird wohl [schon/sicher] falsch sein.

H. 1. hypothetical statements (conditions contrary to fact), wishes, polite requests
2. Trudi würde auch gern faulenzen.
3. Wenn die Sonne nur scheinen würde.
4. Würdest du noch eine Stunde bleiben?

I. 1. wäre
2. hätte
3. a. ich wäre   c. wir wären
  b. du hättest   d. sie hätte

J. 1. The subjunctive of modals is identical to the simple past, except that where there is an umlaut in the infinitive there is also an umlaut in the subjunctive (**wollen** and **sollen** do not have an umlaut).
2. a. ich müsste   b. du könntest

K. 1. Add subjunctive endings to the simple past stem. (An umlaut is added to the vowels **a, o,** or **u.**)
2. a. es gäbe   c. sie kämen
  b. sie täte es   d. du fändest

L. 1. The subjunctive is identical to the simple past forms.
2. a. sie lernte   b. du arbeitetest

M. 1. An umlaut is added to the simple past stem.
2. a. sie brächte   c. wir wüssten
  b. ich dächte

N. 1. the condition (**wenn**-clause) and the conclusion
2. wenn
3. conditions of fact
4. conditions contrary to fact

5. a. Christine würde sicher mitkommen, wenn sie Zeit hätte. *or* Christine käme sicher mit, wenn sie Zeit hätte.
  b. Wenn ich Geld hätte, würde ich ins Konzert gehen. *or* Wenn ich Geld hätte, ginge ich ins Konzert.

O. 1. Ich täte das nicht.
2. Du würdest mir nicht glauben.
3. Wir könnten morgen fahren.
4. ... würde sie ein neues Auto kaufen.
5. ... du könntest länger bleiben.

Kapitel 12

A. *Answers will vary. Possible answers:*
Entschuldigung, was haben Sie gesagt? / Ich verstehe Sie leider nicht. / Ich habe Sie leider nicht verstanden. / Könnten Sie das bitte wiederholen? / Würden Sie bitte langsamer sprechen? / Ich kenne das Wort ... nicht.

B. 1. It introduces a relative clause. It refers back to a noun or pronoun in the preceding clause.
2. in last position (The auxiliary follows the infinitive or the past participle.)

C. 1. Most forms are identical with the definite article forms.
2. denen

D. 1. It depends on the gender and number of the noun to which it refers, its antecedent.
2. It depends on the relative pronoun's grammatical function in the clause (subject, direct object, etc.).
3. It depends on what case that preposition takes.

E. 1. der   4. den
2. der   5. denen
3. dem   6. dem

F. 1. The subject is the agent and performs the action expressed by the verb.
2. The subject is acted upon by an expressed or unexpressed agent.

G. 1. a form of the auxiliary **werden** + past participle of the main verb
2. a. Das Haus wird verkauft.
  The house is (being) sold.
  b. Das Geld wurde gerade investiert.
  The money was just (being) invested.

c. Die Stadt wurde geteilt.
   The city was (being) divided.
d. Die Fabrik wird modernisiert.
   The factory is (being) modernized.

H. 1. It is the object of the preposition **von.**
   2. a. von   b. von

I. 1. (1) main verb *(to grow, get, become)* in the
            active voice
         (2) auxiliary verb in the future tense (a
             form of **werden** + dependent infinitive)
         (3) auxiliary verb in the passive voice (a
             form of **werden** + past participle)

2. a. A trip to Dresden was/was being
       planned. *(passive voice, simple past tense)*
   b. It's finally getting warmer. *(active
       voice—main verb, present tense)*
   c. He'll write to us. *(active voice—auxiliary
       verb, future tense)*

Video Workbook

Unterwegs!

SZENE 1   Willkommen in Tübingen

A. Vorschau (Preview).

1. The setting of the video *Unterwegs!* is Tübingen, a small city of 83,000 located on the Neckar River in the southwest part of Germany, on the northern edge of the Black Forest **(Schwarzwald)**. Tübingen is known for its excellent university of 25,000 students. As you watch the brief opening section that precedes *Szene 1*, note the things that are different from those where you live.
   List five of the differences you perceive.

   _____

   _____

   _____

   _____

2. In *Szene 1* Sabine is meeting her cousin Lisa, whom she hasn't seen in five years. As you watch the video, look for answers to the following questions.

   • How does Lisa travel to Tübingen? Would you be likely to use this form of transportation where you live?

   • Why is Lisa coming to Tübingen? (Remember what Tübingen is famous for.)

   • Who is Julian? Why does he keep looking at Lisa as Sabine describes the cousin she remembers from five years ago?

   • How does Lisa greet Sabine? Julian? Are these forms of greeting common among people you know?

   • Do the clothes the young people wear strike you as different or similar to those of young people you know?

B. Besondere Ausdrücke. Here are some words and idiomatic expressions that you will hear in *Szene 1* of the video. Read through the list to get acquainted with the expressions and listen for them as you view the video. Memorize the ones that you think would be most useful to you. The items are listed in order of appearance.

Es tut mir Leid.	*I'm sorry.*
Entschuldige bitte.	*Excuse me.*
Warum?	*Why?*
Wie sieht sie aus?	*What does she look like?*
kurze lockige Haare	*short curly hair*
trägt eine Brille	*wears glasses*

mollig	*plump*
schlank	*slender*
sicher	*sure, certain*
Darf ich vorstellen?	*May I introduce?*
einen Kaffee trinken gehen	*to go for coffee*
in den Wagen reintun	*to put into the car*
Das wäre sehr nett.	*That would be very nice.*

C. Ich hab's gesehen (I saw it). Watch the video segment with the sound off. Write in the letter of the person (or persons) that corresponds to the article of clothing or physical characteristic. For the meanings of words you do not understand, you may consult the glossary at the end of the video workbook section of the *Arbeitsheft* or the German–English Vocabulary at the end of your textbook.

> **a. Sabine**   **b. Lisa**   **c. Julian**

1. _____ gelbes Hemd
2. _____ braune Haare
3. _____ klein
4. _____ weiße Strickjacke°
5. _____ groß

6. _____ blonde Haare
7. _____ blaue Jacke
8. _____ graue Hose
9. _____ Jeans   cardigan
10. _____ blaue Hose

D. Schauen Sie genau (Look carefully). Watch *Szene 1* again with the sound off and look for information to help you complete the statements below. Circle the best choice based on what you see.

1. Sabine wartet vor _____.

    a. dem Bahnhof   b. der Universität   c. dem Flughafen

2. Julian kommt _____.

    a. auf einem Fahrrad   b. mit dem Bus   c. mit dem Auto

3. Lisa trägt _____.

    a. eine Büchertasche   b. eine Tasche   c. einen Rucksack

4. Lisa _____.

    a. küsst Sabine   b. gibt Sabine die Hand   c. küsst Julian

5. Julian nimmt von Lisa _____.

    a. die Jacke   b. den Rucksack   c. die Tasche

E. Hören Sie zu (Listen). Read the following list of German remarks. You will find the meaning of unfamiliar words in the glossary at the end of the workbook or of your textbook. Then view *Szene 1*. Mark each question, statement, or fragment you hear.

1. _____ Ah, hallo Julian!

2. _____ Es tut mir Leid.

3. _____ Wie heißt denn deine Kusine?

4. _____ Und woher kommt sie?

5. _____ Sie ist sehr klein.

6. _____ ... und sie sind hellbraun oder blond ...

7. _____ Sie ist sehr freundlich.

8. _____ Ja, aber natürlich.

9. _____ Tag, Sabine.

10. _____ Das ist meine Kusine Lisa.

11. _____ Sollen wir einen Kaffee trinken gehen?

12. _____ Das wäre sehr nett.

13. _____ Gut, dann, geh'n wir zum Auto!

F. Stimmt's? (Is that right?) Read through the following statements. Then watch *Szene 1* again. Put a check mark before the statements that are true according to the video.

1. _____ Es ist 11 Uhr.

2. _____ Sabine wartet vor der Universität.

3. _____ Julian ist Sabines Freund.

4. _____ Lisa kommt aus Hamburg.

5. _____ Sabine hat ein Bild von Lisa.

6. _____ Lisa ist nicht sehr groß.

7. _____ Lisa trägt eine Brille.

8. _____ Lisa sieht anders aus als vor fünf Jahren.

9. _____ Julian legt Lisas Tasche in den Wagen.

10. _____ Sabine, Lisa und Julian gehen einen Kaffee trinken.

G. Zusammenfassung (Summary). Put a check mark under the person(s) with whom you associate the words in the list below. Note that some of the adjectives relate to your feeling about the persons.

	Sabine	Lisa	Julian	
Kusinen	_____	_____	_____	
Hamburg	_____	_____	_____	
Tübingen	_____	_____	_____	
Auto	_____	_____	_____	
Tasche	_____	_____	_____	
Jeans	_____	_____	_____	
Strickjacke°	_____	_____	_____	cardigan
Jacke	_____	_____	_____	
lange Haare	_____	_____	_____	
kurze Haare	_____	_____	_____	
hellbraune oder blonde Haare	_____	_____	_____	
brünett	_____	_____	_____	
groß	_____	_____	_____	
klein	_____	_____	_____	
jung	_____	_____	_____	
schlank	_____	_____	_____	
fleißig	_____	_____	_____	
ernst	_____	_____	_____	

SZENE 2 Meine Familie

A. Vorschau. In this video segment Sabine, Lisa, and Julian are having something to drink at an outdoor café. To bring Sabine up to date on her family, Lisa shows photographs of her sister's wedding.

- What do you see in this scene that is different from your experience where you live?
- What do you learn about Lisa's family?
- What do you learn about Sabine's parents?
- What are Lisa's interests?
- What do you learn about Julian?

B. Besondere Ausdrücke. Here are some words and idiomatic expressions that you will hear in this segment of the video. Read through the list to get acquainted with the expressions and listen for them as you view the video. Memorize the ones that you think would be most useful to you. The items are listed in order of appearance.

seit fünf Jahren	*for five years*
lange her	*a long time ago*
dabei	*here (with me)*
zeige sie uns	*show them to us*
geschieden	*divorced*
hat ... geheiratet	*got married*
die gleiche Augenfarbe	*the same eye color*
wegen der Hochzeit	*because of the wedding*
auf Reisen	*on a trip*
ich interessiere mich für	*I'm interested in*
Naturwissenschaften	*natural sciences*
wir engagieren uns	*we're involved (in)*
Umweltschutz	*protection of the environment*
Medienwissenschaften	*media studies*
eingeschrieben	*enrolled*
Brechen wir auf.	*Let's leave.*

C. Landeskunde.

- **Outdoor cafés.** The setting of this segment is an outdoor café. Outdoor cafés are very popular in Germany.

- Heidelberg is also located on the Neckar, about 120 kilometers north of Tübingen. Its university, the oldest in Germany (1386), is famous throughout the world.

- **das Gymnasium.** Lisa is apparently attending a **Gymnasium,** a college preparatory high school. She is enrolled in a **Biologie-leistungskurs,** an advanced course in biology. To get into a university students must take a certain number of advanced courses and then pass the **Abitur.** The **Abitur** is a series of oral and written examinations that cover major subject areas which the student has taken at the **Gymnasium.** The scores along with her grades in courses often determine when, where, and what the student will be eligible to study.

- **Schultaschen.** Note that school children carry books and materials in a book bag **(die Schultasche)** that is usually worn on their backs.

- **das Haar/die Haare.** Note that you will hear the German word for hair used in either the singular **(schwarzes Haar)** or the plural **(dunkle Haare).** Both forms are used.

D. Ich hab's gesehen. Watch the video segment with the sound off. Check off the objects and people you see.

1. _____ die Blumen

2. _____ die Straße

3. _____ das Auto

4. _____ das Fenster

5. _____ die Kinder

6. _____ eine Frau mit Rucksack

7. _____ der Jogger

8. _____ das Fahrrad

9. _____ das Café

10. _____ das Telefon

11. _____ der Kaffee

12. _____ der Tisch

13. _____ der Stuhl

14. _____ die Uhr

15. _____ das Zimmer

Name _____   Datum _____

E. Schauen Sie genau. Watch *Szene 2* again with the sound off and watch for information to help you answer the questions. Circle the choices that you think are best based on what you see.

1. Wo sind Sabine, Lisa und Julian?

   a. Sie sitzen am Tisch.   b. Sie stehen an der Tür.   c. Sie gehen im Park.

2. Wie ist das Wetter?

   a. Es regnet.   b. Es ist warm.   c. Es ist sehr heiß.

3. Was trinkt Sabine?

   a. Milch   b. Cola   c. Kaffee

4. Wie viele Fotos zeigt Lisa?

   a. zwei   b. drei   c. vier

5. Wie viele Personen sitzen an anderen Tischen?

   a. sechs   b. zwei   c. keine

F. Hören Sie zu. Read the following list of German remarks. Then view *Szene 2* with the sound on. Mark each question, statement, or fragment you hear.

1. _____ Unsere Väter sind Brüder.

2. _____ Ja, es ist sehr lange her.

3. _____ Ich habe viele Bilder dabei.

4. _____ Ah, wer ist das?

5. _____ Meine Eltern sind geschieden.

6. _____ Ah, er ist auch groß und schlank.

7. _____ Das ist meine Freundin.

8. _____ Sie hat an diesem Tag geheiratet.

9. _____ Sie trägt noch immer gerne Hüte.

10. _____ Immer noch schwarzes Haar?

11. _____ Sag mal, was machst du eigentlich so gerne?

12. _____ Ich spiel' Basketball.

13. _____ Ich fotografiere gerne.

14. _____ Ich komme aus Stuttgart.

15. _____ Wie spät ist es denn?

G. Stimmt's? Read through the following statements. Then watch *Szene 2* again. Put a check mark before the statements that are true according to the video.

1. _____ Lisas Eltern sind geschieden.

2. _____ Lisas Vater hat nochmal geheiratet.

3. _____ Lisas Vater ist klein und schlank.

4. _____ Der Mann von Lisas Schwester trägt eine Brille.

5. _____ Lisas Schwester hat blaue Augen.

6. _____ Lisas Mutter trägt gern Hüte.

7. _____ Sabines Eltern sind bei ihrem Opa in Heidelberg.

8. _____ Lisa interessiert sich für die Natur.

9. _____ Lisa spielt Klavier.

10. _____ Julian studiert Medizin.

H. Zusammenfassung. Put a check mark under the person(s) to whom the comments apply.

	Sabine	Lisa	Julian
die Eltern sind auf Reisen	_____	_____	_____
hat eine Stiefmutter	_____	_____	_____
spielt Klavier	_____	_____	_____
der Opa lebt in Heidelberg	_____	_____	_____
hat ein Zimmer	_____	_____	_____
studiert an der Uni	_____	_____	_____
singt gern	_____	_____	_____
lebt in Tübingen	_____	_____	_____
kommt nicht aus Tübingen	_____	_____	_____

SZENE 3   Ich möchte gern ...

A. Vorschau. In this video segment Sabine, Lisa, and Julian go food shopping.

- Where do the young people shop?
- How do the streets and buildings differ from those where you live?
- Note the constant use of **bitte** and **danke.** Are the English counterparts typical where you live?
- What does Sabine say when she takes leave of the vendor? Is the English counterpart typical where you live?
- What does Julian suggest to entertain Lisa? What does Sabine suggest? Why? What would Lisa like to do?

B. Besondere Ausdrücke. Here are some words and idiomatic expressions that you will hear in this segment of the video. Read through the list to get acquainted with the expressions and listen for them as you view the video. Memorize the ones that you think would be most useful to you. The items are listed in order of appearance.

Guck mal.	*Look.*
lecker	*tasty*
lieber	*rather (I prefer)*
Magst du?	*Do you like?*
hätte ich gern	*I would like*
So, das wär's dann schon.	*That's all.*
Auf Wiederschauen.	*an alternate word for* Auf Wiedersehen
hast du Lust	*do you feel like*
lass uns	*let's*
am liebsten	*prefer most of all*
eine Klausur	*a test*
Machen wir es so!	*Let's do that.*
treffen wir uns	*let's meet*

C. Landeskunde.

- **Fachwerk** (*half-timbered*). Note the number of half-timbered houses surrounding the square in which the market is held. This type of architecture is quite common in many old city centers in Germany.

- **Colloquial German.** The fruit vendor speaks a German that is influenced by the Swabian dialect he probably speaks at home. He says: **Jetzt kriaget Se a Kilo oder a Pfund? (Jetzt kriegen Sie ein Kilo oder ein Pfund?** *Do you want a kilo or a pound?).*

- **Bitte/danke.** Notice how often you hear **bitte** and **danke.** A request in German usually includes the word **bitte** and an acknowledgment with **danke**, in addition to **danke** as thanks.

- Notice that Sabine does not touch the fruit and vegetables. The vendor tells her it is a nice head of lettuce and picks one out for her.

- **Tourist sights in Tübingen.** Sabine thinks Lisa should see:

  a. **Der Hölderlinturm,** the tower that the German poet Friedrich Hölderlin (1770–1843) lived in for the last 36 years of his life while he was mentally ill.

  b. **Das Schloss** (*palace*). The **Schloss** in Tübingen was built during the Renaissance. There are hundreds of **Schlösser** and **Burgen** (*castles*) in Germany, many of them tourist attractions.

D. Ich hab's gesehen. Watch the video segment with the sound off. Check off the foods and things you see.

1. _____ Häuser

2. _____ Straßenlaterne

3. _____ Fenster

4. _____ Markt

5. _____ Nektarinen

6. _____ Fisch

7. _____ Brot

8. _____ Tomaten

9. _____ Kartoffeln

10. _____ Kamera

11. _____ Blumen

12. _____ Äpfel

13. _____ Bananen

14. _____ Eier

15. _____ Käse

16. _____ Salat

E. Schauen Sie genau. View *Szene 3* again with the sound off and watch for information to help you complete the statements below. Circle the choices that you think are best, based on what you see. More than one response may be possible. Remember that the meanings of unfamiliar words can be found in the glossary at the end of the video workbook section of the *Arbeitsheft*.

1. Der Obsthändler trägt _____.

   a. einen blauen Mantel   b. eine Brille   c. eine Mütze

2. Der Obsthändler ist _____.

   a. freundlich   b. lustig   c. ruhig

3. Der Gemüsehändler hat _____.

   a. eine Mütze   b. eine Brille   c. graue Haare

4. Sabine kauft _____.

   a. Obst   b. Gemüse   c. Blumen

5. Lisa _____.

   a. trägt die Einkaufstasche   b. trinkt eine Cola   c. isst von dem Obst

6. _____ bezahlt alles.

   a. Sabine   b. Lisa   c. Julian

7. _____ geht weg und kommt später zurück.

   a. Sabine   b. Lisa   c. Julian

8. Die drei jungen Leute stehen vor einem Plakat. Das Plakat annonciert _____.

   a. ein Rockkonzert   b. einen französischen Film   c. ein Afro-Brazil Konzert

F. Hören Sie zu. Read the following list of German remarks. Then view *Szene 3* with the sound on. Mark each question, statement, or fragment you hear.

1. _____ ein bisschen Obst

2. _____ Das sieht aber gut aus.

3. _____ Wir brauchen auch noch Käse.

4. _____ Ich habe kein Geld.

5. _____ Und 500 Gramm Erdbeeren, bitte.

6. _____ Ja, wie viel macht das?

7. _____ Schöner Kopfsalat.

8. _____ Was kostet das alles?

9. _____ Lass uns ins Kino gehen.

10. _____ Wozu hast du Lust?

11. _____ Wir gehen morgen in die Altstadt.

G. Stimmt's? Read through the following statements. Then watch *Szene 3* again. Put a check mark before the statements that are true according to the video.

1. _____ Lisa möchte Kirschen haben.

2. _____ Sabine kauft Erdbeeren und Kirschen.

3. _____ Julian geht Käse kaufen.

4. _____ Lisa isst am liebsten Gouda Käse.

5. _____ Sabine kauft drei Pfund Äpfel.

6. _____ Sabine kauft keinen Salat.

7. _____ Julian möchte ins Kino gehen.

8. _____ Lisa möchte ins Konzert gehen.

9. _____ Morgen schreibt Sabine eine Klausur.

10. _____ Abends gehen alle drei ins Restaurant.

H. Zusammenfassung. Check off the items Sabine buys.

_____ Äpfel   _____ Karotten (Mohrrüben)

_____ Aprikosen   _____ Kartoffeln

_____ Brot   _____ Käse

_____ Butter   _____ Kirschen

_____ Erdbeeren   _____ Kopfsalat

_____ Fisch   _____ Nektarinen

_____ Gurken   _____ Tomaten

I. Sie sind dran (It's your turn). Write three short sentences in German describing objects, actions, or impressions in this scene. Use your imagination.

_____

_____

_____

SZENE 4   Denk dran!

A. Vorschau. In this video segment Lisa is preparing to meet Julian in town. While there she plans to do some shopping. Sabine tells Lisa where she should go and what she should do. She also tells Lisa what personal items she should take along.

- Note the outside and inside of Sabine's house.
- Sabine again suggests that Lisa should visit certain sights in Tübingen. What impression do you have of Lisa's reactions to these suggestions?
- Why isn't Sabine going with Lisa on her trip to town? Who is Lisa's guide?
- What was Sabine about to forget to take along? Why does Lisa enjoy pointing out this oversight?

B. Besondere Ausdrücke. Here are some words and idiomatic expressions that you will hear in this segment of the video. Read through the list to get acquainted with the expressions and listen for them as you view the video. Memorize the ones that you think would be most useful to you. The items are listed in order of appearance.

die Weste	*vest*
auf jeden Fall	*in any case*
das Geschenk	*gift*
die Sachen (*pl.*)	*clothing*
die Hose	*slacks*
mache dir ja keine Sorgen	*don't worry*
hinführen	*to take there*
schaut euch ... an	*look at*
entlang	*along*
das lohnt sich	*it's worthwhile*
sicher	*sure, certain*
vergiss nicht	*don't forget*
überzeugt	*convinced*
der Geldbeutel	*wallet*
benötigt man	*one needs*

C. Landeskunde.

- The majority of Germans live in apartments. However Sabine's family lives in an older home in a residential neighborhood. Note the balcony (**der Balkon**) on the second floor. Germans like to be outside and therefore many German homes and apartments have balconies.
- The **Stiftskirche** (Collegiate Church of St. George) was built in the 15th century and is one of the sights to see in Tübingen.

D. Ich hab's gesehen. Watch the video segment with the sound off. Write the names of the objects for which you have learned the German word. Include the gender.

_____   _____   _____

_____   _____   _____

_____   _____   _____

E. Schauen Sie genau. Watch *Szene 4* again with the sound off and look for information to help you complete the statements below. Circle the choices that you think are best, based on what you see. More than one response may be possible.

1. Sabines Familie wohnt in einem _____ Haus.

   a. sehr alten   b. großen   c. sehr kleinen

2. Um das Haus gibt es _____.

   a. viele Pflanzen   b. viele Blumen   c. einen Garten

3. Auf dem Balkon sind _____.

   a. Blumen   b. ein Tisch   c. Stühle

4. Lisas Zimmer hat _____.

   a. einen Tisch   b. ein Bett   c. Bilder an der Wand

5. Lisa und Sabine bereiten sich vor _____.

   a. ins Bett zu gehen b. auszugehen   c. Jogging zu gehen

6. Lisa sitzt _____.

   a. auf dem Bett   b. auf einem Stuhl   c. am Tisch

7. Lisa _____ Sabine ihre Jacke.

   a. gibt   b. zeigt   c. leiht

Name _____   Datum _____

F. Hören Sie zu. Read the following list of German remarks. Then view *Szene 4* with the sound on. Mark each question, statement, or fragment you hear.

1. _____ Die hat nächste Woche nämlich Geburtstag.

2. _____ Da gibt's eine kleine Boutique.

3. _____ Es gibt einen kleinen Buchladen ...

4. _____ Ich kann das Buch nicht finden.

5. _____ Leider muss ich die Klausur schreiben ...

6. _____ Julian weiß, wo alles ist.

7. _____ Wir gehen in das Stadtmuseum.

8. _____ Hast du den Fotoapparat?

9. _____ ... und draußen ist es kalt.

10. _____ Wann kommt Julian?

11. _____ ... ich brauch' nur mein Buch.

12. _____ Danke schön.

G. Wie heißt das auf Deutsch? As Sabine names the items Lisa should take along, Lisa shows them. View *Szene 4* again with the sound on and match the items listed on the right with the German names on the left.

1. _____ die Haarbürste   a. *camera*

2. _____ der Fotoapparat   b. *sunglasses*

3. _____ der Regenschirm   c. *bunch of keys*

4. _____ die Sonnenbrille   d. *checks and ATM card*

5. _____ der Schlüsselbund   e. *hairbrush*

6. _____ die Schecks und Scheckkarte   f. *jeans jacket*

7. _____ das Portemonnaie   g. *umbrella*

8. _____ die Jacke   h. *wallet*

H. Stimmt's? As Lisa is preparing to go downtown, Sabine offers advice about what she should see and do. Read through the following statements. Then watch *Szene 4* again and check the statements that reflect Sabine's suggestions.

1. _____ Lisa soll in die Stadt gehen. Sie soll in Richtung Stiftskirche gehen. Dort ist eine kleine Boutique.

2. _____ Lisa soll sich eine Jacke kaufen.

3. _____ Lisa soll ein Buch für ihre Mutter kaufen.

4. _____ Lisa soll nicht nur in den Cafés sitzen.

5. _____ Lisa soll auf den Hölderlinturm 'raufgehen.

6. _____ Sie soll nicht in das Stadtmuseum gehen.

7. _____ Sie soll auch am Neckar spazieren gehen.

I. Zusammenfassung. Check off the places or events that one can visit or go to in Tübingen.

1. _____ die Boutiquen   9. _____ der Neckar

2. _____ der Marktplatz   10. _____ ein Buchladen

3. _____ die Stiftskirche   11. _____ die Altstadt

4. _____ die Jazzkeller   12. _____ die Uni

5. _____ die Cafés   13. _____ der Zoo

6. _____ die Oper   14. _____ ein Konzert

7. _____ der Hölderlinturm   15. _____ ein Kino

8. _____ das Stadtmuseum

J. Sie sind dran. Sabine tells Lisa what she ought to do. Judging by her responses and body language, tell what you think Lisa would not want to do and what she would like to do. Use your imagination. Write four short German sentences.

Lisa will nicht ... Lisa möchte lieber ...

_____

_____

_____

_____

Name _____ Datum _____

SZENE 5 Freundschaften

A. Vorschau. In this video segment Sabine tells Lisa how she met Julian.

- Sabine and Lisa walk to the bus stop. What is the German word for *bus stop*?

- How did Julian and Sabine meet?

- What does Lisa imply about the relationship between Sabine and Julian?

- Sabine says Julian is **zu chaotisch,** that is, too loose or disorganized. What example of this trait was apparent in *Szene 1* at the train station?

- When Sabine tells about meeting Julian, she relates events in the past. Two of the common signals for conversational past tense in German is a form of **haben** and the verb beginning with **ge-: es hat geregnet** = *it rained* or *it has rained.*

B. Besondere Ausdrücke. Here are some words and idiomatic expressions that you will hear in this segment of the video. Read through the list to get acquainted with the expressions and listen for them as you view the video. Memorize the ones that you think would be most useful to you. The items are listed in order of appearance.

bewölkt	*cloudy*
Wie habt ihr euch kennen gelernt?	*How did you meet?*
haben ... eine Radtour gemacht	*went on a bike tour*
damalig	*at that time*
surfen	*to go windsurfing*
ins Gespräch gekommen	*started to talk, got into a conversation*
nichts noch	*nothing further*
lose Freunde	*just friends, nothing more*
soweit	*as far*
chaotisch	*loose, disorganized*
Studentenwohnheim	*dormitory*
um die Ecke	*around the corner*

C. Landeskunde.

- Sabine and Lisa wait at the bus stop **(die Haltestelle)** for the bus. Although only a small city of 83,000, Tübingen has regular bus service. Buses and sometimes streetcars are found in most cities, while larger cities like Berlin and Munich also have subway systems. Payment for public transportation is usually based on the honor system. One buys the ticket from a machine **(der Fahrschein-automat)**. After entering a public transportation vehicle, the passenger is then expected to insert the ticket into a machine **(der Entwerter)** which stamps the date and time on the ticket. Those who try to ride for free **(schwarzfahren)** run the risk of being caught during random inspections, resulting in rather large fines.

- The following places play a part in the bike tour Sabine and Julian made. Locate them on the map in your textbook:

  die Ostsee, Baltic Sea ■ **Rostock,** a city on the Baltic ■ **Insel Rügen,** the island of Rügen in the Baltic

D. Ich hab's gesehen. Watch the video segment with the sound off. Check off the things and people you see.

1. _____ ein Auto

2. _____ Schulkinder

3. _____ eine Joggerin

4. _____ ein Recycling-Container

5. _____ eine Haustür

6. _____ eine Pflanze

7. _____ eine Straßenbahn

8. _____ eine Haltestelle

9. _____ ein Bus

10. _____ ein Studentenwohnheim

11. _____ ein Fahrrad

12. _____ ein Motorrad

E. Schauen Sie genau. Watch *Szene 5* again with the sound off. Check the statements that you think are true, based on what you see.

1. _____ Es ist sehr kalt.

2. _____ Die Sonne scheint.

3. _____ Lisa hat ihren Regenschirm mit.

4. _____ Sabine und Lisa gehen zu Fuß zur Haltestelle.

5. _____ Auf der Straße gibt es viele Autos und Fahrräder.

6. _____ Ein Mann läuft über die Straße.

7. _____ Ein junger Mann wartet schon an der Haltestelle.

8. _____ Der Bus kommt und Lisa und Sabine steigen ein°.   get in

9. _____ Ein paar Fahrräder stehen vor Julians Studentenwohnheim.

10. _____ Julian sitzt schon im Auto und wartet auf die jungen Frauen.

Name _____ Datum _____

F. Hören Sie zu. Read the following list of German remarks. Then view *Szene 5* with the sound on. Mark each question, statement, or fragment you hear.

1. _____ ... die Sonne scheint ...

2. _____ ... seit wann kennst du Julian ...

3. _____ ... seit zwei Jahren ...

4. _____ ... mit dem Zug ...

5. _____ ... surfen gehen ....

6. _____ Ich finde ihn sehr nett.

7. _____ ... chaotisch ...

8. _____ ... soweit ich weiß ...

9. _____ ... recht sympathisch ...

10. _____ ... um die Ecke ...

G. Stimmt's? Sabine tells how she met Julian and about her relationship with him. Read through the following statements. Then watch *Szene 5* again and check the statements that reflect what you find out from Sabine.

1. _____ Sabine kennt Julian seit elf Monaten.

2. _____ Julian und Sabine haben zusammen eine Fahrradtour an der Ostsee gemacht.

3. _____ Sie sind mit dem Zug bis nach Rostock gefahren.

4. _____ Sie waren drei Tage auf der Insel Rügen.

5. _____ Julians damalige Freundin war auch da.

6. _____ Die jungen Leute gehen fast jeden Tag schwimmen.

7. _____ Sabine möchte surfen lernen.

8. _____ Sabine findet Julian sehr sympathisch, aber er ist ihr zu chaotisch.

9. _____ Julian und seine damalige Freundin machen nichts mehr zusammen.

10. _____ Lisa findet Julian sehr nett und recht sympathisch.

H. Sie sind dran. Choose Activity 1 or 2.

1. Write:
   a. two sentences about what Sabine and Julian like to do on vacation;
   b. two sentences about Sabine's feelings for Julian. Use your imagination.

   _____

   _____

   _____

   _____

2. Role-play. Below are four questions that could be part of a conversation between Sabine and Lisa. Make up responses that reflect what you have learned in *Szene 5* or use your imagination.

   LISA: Wie ist das Wetter heute?

   SABINE: _____

   SABINE: Willst du surfen gehen?

   LISA: _____

   LISA: Sabine, magst du Julian sehr?

   SABINE: _____

   LISA: Ist Julian dein fester Freund°?   **fester Freund:** boyfriend

   SABINE: _____

SZENE 6 Bei Julian

A. Vorschau. In this video segment Sabine and Lisa pick up Julian at his dormitory and he shows them his room.

- Where did Julian eat his breakfast?
- What word does Sabine use to describe Julian's room? When did she use this word previously?
- Why is the setting of the movie Lisa mentions of special interest to Sabine and Julian?
- What do the computer, the stereo set, and the CD in Julian's room have in common?
- How did Julian get the stain on Sabine's book?
- Does the condition of her book surprise her?
- How will Julian correct the problem?

B. Besondere Ausdrücke. Here are some words and idiomatic expressions that you will hear in this segment of the video. Read through the list to get acquainted with the expressions and listen for them as you view the video. Memorize the ones that you think would be most useful to you. The items are listed in order of appearance.

eine Tasse Kaffee anbieten	*to offer a cup of coffee*
wir haben schon gefrühstückt	*we've already had breakfast*
stimmt nicht	*that's not true*
rat mal	*just guess*
echt?	*really?*
anfange	*begin*
egal	*doesn't matter*
Anlage	*stereo set*
irgendwas	*anything (at all)*
Der Kuss	*The Kiss*
Muss ich mir überlegen.	*I'll have to think about it.*
ist passiert	*happened*
ich schlage vor	*I suggest*
es eilt nicht	*there's no hurry*
Ich muss mich umziehen	*I have to change my clothes*

C. Landeskunde.

- Julian was lucky to find a room in a dormitory. At most universities there are not enough rooms for all the students who want them. These students must then rent a room from a family or rent an apartment with other students (die Wohngemeinschaft). Dorms are particularly popular with students in their early semesters. Students in later semesters often prefer the WG (Wohngemeinschaft) or apartments, which are, however, expensive and hard to find.

- Julian's dormitory is typical in that the toilets (die Toiletten) and showers (die Dusche) are down the hall, but his room has a wash-basin (das Waschbecken).

D. Ich hab's gesehen. Watch the video segment with the sound off and write in German the names of the things you see. Include the gender if you know it.

_____   _____   _____

_____   _____   _____

_____   _____   _____

E. Schauen Sie genau. Watch *Szene 6* again with the sound off and look for information to help you complete the statements below. Circle the choices that you think are best, based on what you see. More than one response may be possible.

1. Als Sabine und Lisa Julian besuchen, ist er _____.

   a. in seinem Zimmer   b. in der Küche   c. bei Freunden

2. In Julians Zimmer sieht man Kleidungsstücke _____.

   a. auf dem Computer   b. auf dem Bett   c. an der Tür

3. An der Wand hängen _____.

   a. Poster   b. Bilder   c. zwei Uhren

4. Die Gruppe auf der CD heißt _____.

   a. Take Two   b. Tab Two   c. Two Together

5. Julian nimmt ein Buch _____.

   a. aus dem Bücherregal   b. vom Tisch   c. vom Fernseher

Name _____ Datum _____

F. Hören Sie zu. Read the following list of German remarks. Then view *Szene 6* with the sound on. Mark each question, statement or fragment you hear.

1. _____ Noch beim Frühstücken?

2. _____ ... eine Tasse Kaffee ...

3. _____ ... kommt mal mit.

4. _____ Stimmt nicht, ...

5. _____ ... ein Bild von mir ...

6. _____ Keine Ahnung.

7. _____ ... wenn ich anfange zu studieren ...

8. _____ Die sind ganz toll.

9. _____ ... eine CD geliehen ...

10. _____ ... gehört dir irgendwas ...

11. _____ ... Vor ungefähr einem halben Jahr ...

12. _____ Was hat es gekostet?

13. _____ Vielleicht finden wir ihn ja?

14. _____ ... es eilt nicht ...

15. _____ ... warten auf dich ...

G. Stimmt's? When Sabine and Lisa get a look at Julian's room, it confirms Sabine's opinion that Julian is rather disorganized. Read through the following statements. Then watch *Szene 6* again and check the statements that you think are true.

1. _____ Sabine sagt, dass Julians Zimmer chaotisch ist.

2. _____ Julian lernt Türkisch.

3. _____ Auf dem Poster ist der Titel eines Filmes und dieser Film spielt in Tübingen.

4. _____ Der Computer gehört Julians Vater.

5. _____ Die Stereoanlage gehört Julians ehemaliger Freundin.

6. _____ Alle Bücher im Bücherregal gehören Julian.

7. _____ Julian hat ein Buch von Sabine geliehen.

8. _____ Sabine sagt, Julian muss ihr ein neues Buch kaufen.

9. _____ Die tolle CD von Tab Two gehört Julian.

10. _____ Sabine muss zur Universität.

H. Sie sind dran. Do either Activity 1 or 2 in writing. Be as complete as possible in your writing.

1. Was hat Julian alles geliehen?

    a. Von seinem Bruder hat er _____.

    b. Von seiner ehemaligen Freundin hat er _____.

    c. Von einem guten Freund hat er _____.

    d. Von Sabine hat er _____.

2. Role-play. Below are four questions that could be part of a conversation between Sabine, Lisa, and Julian. Make up responses that reflect what you have learned in *Szene 6* or use your imagination.

JULIAN: Wie gefällt dir mein Zimmer, Sabine?

SABINE: _____

JULIAN: Weißt du, wo der Film spielt, Lisa?

LISA: _____

SABINE: Hast du auch einen Computer, Lisa?

LISA: _____

JULIAN: Kennst du die Gruppe Tab Two, Lisa? Wie findest du sie?

LISA: _____

SZENE 7   In der Altstadt

A. Vorschau. In this video segment Julian is showing Lisa the **Altstadt** and the parts of the university in this section of town. They start their tour on a wall looking out over the town.

- What buildings does Lisa see in Tübingen?
- Where are the various departments (**Fakultäten**) that Julian mentions located?
- What choices of entertainment is Lisa presented with?
- What does Lisa buy for her mother?
- Why is Julian's friend Sia a good choice for someone to tell Lisa about studying medicine at Tübingen?

B. Besondere Ausdrücke. Here are some words and idiomatic expressions that you will hear in this segment of the video. Read through the list to get acquainted with the expressions and listen for them as you view the video. Memorize the ones that you think would be most useful to you. The items are listed in order of appearance.

da drüben	*over there*
das Gebäude	*the building*
die Fakultäten	*departments (of university)*
trampen	*to hitchhike*
Daumen raus.	*Thumb out.*
hässlich	*ugly*
Kann man nichts machen.	*Can't be helped.*
Lass uns mal 'reingehen.	*Let's go in.*
Da freue ich mich drauf.	*I'm looking forward to it.*
Freut mich.	*Glad to meet you.*
Prima.	*Great. Excellent.*
Ciao.	*So long.*

C. Landeskunde.

- In her visit to Tübingen, Lisa gets a view of a medium-sized city whose roots go back hundreds of years (the university was founded in 1477). Note the old buildings with high gables, the half-timbered houses (**Fachwerkhäuser**), the fountains (**Brunnen**), narrow streets, and the old town hall (**das Rathaus**) with its green roofs (**grüne Dächer**).
- The old universities in Germany did not have campuses. The buildings were located throughout the old town. In the downtown area the university has a new building, **der Brecht-Bau**, where Sabine and Julian have classes. On the hill beyond the town are the natural science departments (**Fakultäten für Naturwissenschaften**).

- You will hear two literary references.
  a. *Faust,* a drama playing in the **Zimmertheater,** is by Germany's most famous literary figure, Johann Wolfgang von Goethe (1749–1832).
  b. Uwe Johnson (1934–1984) is a well-known modern writer. His novels deal with the division of Germany between 1949–1989 and with conflicts between East and West.

D. Ich hab's gesehen. Watch the video segment with the sound off. Check off the things and people you see.

1. _____ Schulkinder
2. _____ alte Häuser
3. _____ Fahrräder
4. _____ Supermarkt
5. _____ Theater
6. _____ Straßenmusiker
7. _____ Metzgerei
8. _____ Schuhgeschäft
9. _____ Hüte
10. _____ Straßencafé
11. _____ Buchladen

E. Schauen Sie genau. Look at *Szene* 7 again with the sound off and watch for information to help you complete the statements below. Circle the best choices based on what you see. More than one response may be possible.

1. Straßenmusiker spielen und Lisa und Julian _____.

   a. hören ruhig zu   b. gehen an ihnen vorbei   c. tanzen zusammen

2. Sie gehen durch _____.

   a. die Fußgängerzone   b. den Park   c. ein Kaufhaus

3. Sie bleiben vor _____ stehen.

   a. einem Schuhgeschäft   b. einer Bäckerei   c. einer Drogerie

4. _____ setzt sich einen großen Hut auf.

   a. Sabine   b. Lisa   c. Julian

5. Im Buchladen hat _____ ein Buch gekauft.

   a. Sabine   b. Lisa   c. Julian

6. Auf der Straße treffen Julian und Lisa _____.

   a. eine junge Frau   b. einen jungen Mann   c. zwei junge Frauen

Name _____   Datum _____

F. Hören Sie zu. Read the following list of German remarks. Then view *Szene 7* with the sound on. Mark each question, statement, or fragment you hear.

1. _____ Ach was …

2. _____ zum Beispiel

3. _____ Kann man nichts machen.

4. _____ Wie hat es dir in der Bibliothek gefallen?

5. _____ Ich habe ein Problem.

6. _____ deine Vorlesungen

7. _____ Ich lade dich ein.

8. _____ berühmt

9. _____ Viel später.

10. _____ tolle Konzerte

11. _____ Du studierst doch Medizin.

12. _____ zu Hause

13. _____ Ganz schön früh.

G. Stimmt's? Read through the following statements. Then watch *Szene 7* again and check the statements that you think are true.

1. _____ Die Fakultäten für Chemie und Physik sind in Gebäuden auf dem Berg.

2. _____ Zu der Fakultät für Medizin fahren viele Studenten mit dem Bus.

3. _____ Julian studiert in einem modernen braunen Gebäude.

4. _____ Die Bibliothek hat Lisa gar nicht gefallen.

5. _____ Der Jazzkeller ist ziemlich berühmt.

6. _____ Lisa kauft ihrer Mutter einen Hut zum Geburtstag.

7. _____ Im Buchladen hat Julian einen neuen Krimi gekauft.

8. _____ Julian kennt Sia aus dem Jazzkeller.

9. _____ Sia kann Lisa etwas über das Medizinstudium an der Universität erzählen.

10. _____ Julian hat vergessen das Buch für Sabine zu kaufen.

H. Sie sind dran. Do one of the activities in German. Be as complete as possible in your writing.

1. List two or more of the expressions used by Julian, Lisa, or Sia to convey the following:

    a. Agreement _____

    _____

    b. Enthusiasm _____

    _____

    c. A greeting _____

    _____

    d. A farewell _____

    _____

2. Role-play. Below are four sentences that could be part of a conversation between the persons named. Make up responses that reflect what you have learned in *Szene 7* or use your imagination.

    JULIAN: Wie hat es dir in der Bibliothek gefallen?

    LISA: _____

    JULIAN: Hörst du gern Jazz?

    LISA: _____

    JULIAN: Das ist ein schöner Bildband von Tübingen.

    LISA: Ja. Ich _____.

    JULIAN: Sia, Lisa möchte Medizin studieren.

    SIA: _____

SZENE 8 An der Uni

A. Vorschau. In this video segment Lisa goes with Sia to her anatomy class.

- Note what Sia still needs to do to finish her medical studies.

- Lisa still needs to finish her **Abitur** before she can go to the university. Note what her concerns are about being able to study medicine.

- What other career is Lisa interested in?

- How does Lisa plan to get back to Sabine's home?

B. Besondere Ausdrücke. Here are some words and idiomatic expressions that you will hear in this segment of the video. Read through the list to get acquainted with the expressions and listen for them as you view the video. Memorize the ones that you think would be most useful to you. The items are listed in order of appearance.

einmal die Woche	once a week
das Labor	lab
wir sollten uns ... beeilen	we should hurry
ich freue mich darauf	I'm looking forward to it
beliebt	popular
die Sprechstunde	office hour
Schlange stehen	to stand in line
büffeln	to cram (for a course or test)
der Versuch	attempt; experiment
Es hört sich gut an.	It sounds good.
die Umwelt	environment
die Verabredung	appointment
die Bushaltestelle	bus stop

C. Landeskunde.

- **Der Schnarrenberg** is the name of the hill on which the Tübingen University clinics and natural science buildings are located. **Die Morgenstelle** is the name of the building in which Sia has physics and chemistry.

- In the U.S. students usually go to medical school only after getting a B.S. or B.A. In Germany students go directly into medical studies after the **Gymnasium.** Sia tells Lisa about some of her courses and what she needs to do in order to complete her medical studies. The requirements Sia mentions are listed here: **der Präparationskurs** – slide preparation (histology); **der Sezierkurs** – anatomy course; (**die Leiche** – cadaver; **die Organe** – organs; **die Wirbelsäule** – spine); **die Laborübungen** – lab experiments; **das Praktikum** – practical experience; **das Physikum** – preliminary medical examination.

- Lisa mentions her concern and hope that she will do very well on her **Abitur.** Only then will she have a chance to be accepted for an opening **(der Studienplatz)** to study medicine, since such openings are limited at the universities **(der Numerus clausus).** Even then there aren't enough openings at German universities for all the eligible students.

D. Ich hab's gesehen. Watch *Szene 8* with the sound off. Write in German the names of the things you see in the categories listed below. The number in parentheses indicates how many things you should list.

Verkehrsmittel (1)   _____

Menschen (3)   _____   _____

      _____

draußen vor dem Hörsaal (3)   _____   _____

      _____

Kleidungsstücke (4)   _____   _____

      _____   _____

E. Schauen Sie genau. Look at *Szene 8* again with the sound off and watch for information to help you complete the statements below. Circle the best choices based on what you see. More than one response may be possible.

1. Lisa fährt mit dem _____ auf den Berg.

   a. Fahrrad   b. Taxi   c. Bus

2. Oben auf dem Berg sind _____.

   a. die Kliniken   b. die Bibliothek   c. die Fakultäten für moderne Sprachen

3. Lisa und Sia gehen zusammen _____.

   a. ins Labor   b. in den Hörsaal   c. ins Seminar

4. Der Professor hält eine Vorlesung über _____.

   a. Anatomie   b. Chemie   c. Mathematik

5. Lisa und Sia _____ draußen vor dem Hörsaal.

   a. sprechen   b. sitzen   c. stehen

F. Hören Sie zu. Read the following list of German remarks. Then view *Szene 8* with the sound on. Mark each question, statement, or fragment you hear.

1. _____ Vorlesung

2. _____ das ist klar

3. _____ Es ist schon acht.

4. _____ eine gute Idee

5. _____ da hab ich Mathematik

6. _____ eine schwere Klausur

7. _____ Kinderärztin

8. _____ ich habe zwei Brüder

9. _____ möchte … gerne Medizin studieren

10. _____ Gut, dann dank' ich dir.

11. _____ Auf Wiedersehen.

G. Stimmt's? Read through the following statements. Then watch *Szene 8* again and check the statements that you think are true.

1. _____ Sia hat einmal die Woche Anatomievorlesung.

2. _____ Sie arbeitet auch im Labor.

3. _____ Die Anatomievorlesung ist kurz nach acht.

4. _____ Es sind nur ein paar Studenten im Hörsaal.

5. _____ Die Studenten mögen den Professor nicht.

6. _____ Für das Medizinstudium braucht man 12 bis 13 Semester.

7. _____ Sia hat drei Geschwister.

8. _____ Sia möchte Kinderärztin werden.

9. _____ Lisa weiß schon, dass sie Medizin an der Universität Tübingen studieren kann.

10. _____ Vielleicht studiert sie aber Biologie.

H. Sie sind dran. Write one of the two activities in German. Be as complete as possible in your writing.

1. Describe four people in this segment (size, age, clothing, etc.).

→ *Ein junger Mann trägt ein blaues Hemd.*
  Sia ist eine freundliche junge Frau.

a. _____

b. _____

c. _____

d. _____

2. Role-play. Sabine asks Lisa about her day with Sia. Pretend you are Lisa and reply. Write four German sentences.

SABINE: Du, Lisa, wie war es heute? Erzähl mal.

LISA: _____

   _____

   _____

   _____

SZENE 9   Im Beruf

A. Vorschau. In this video segment Lisa, Sabine, and her parents, Gudrun and Werner, are having late evening refreshments.

- Note what Sabine's father says about starting out as an actor.
- Note what Sabine's mother says about starting out as a speech therapy teacher for children.
- What considerations does Sabine consider important in any future career she chooses?
- What are Lisa's professional interests?
- What advice does Sabine get about what to say and how to act at her job interview at the tourist office (**das Fremdenverkehrsbüro)?**

B. Besondere Ausdrücke. Here are some words and idiomatic expressions that you will hear in this segment of the video. Read through the list to get acquainted with the expressions and listen for them as you view the video. Memorize the ones that you think would be most useful to you. The items are listed in order of appearance.

bedient euch	*help yourselves*
Ich bin satt.	*I've had enough.*
Mach dir keine Sorgen.	*Don't worry (about it).*
der Bereich	*area (of interest)*
viele Menschen kennen lernen	*to meet lots of people*
könnt ihr euch das vorstellen	*can you imagine that*
vor allen Dingen	*above all*
der Umweltschutz	*protection of the environment*
das Ozonloch	*hole in the ozone*
das Vorstellungsgespräch	*job interview*
aufgewachsen	*grown up*
Austauschschüler	*exchange student (secondary school)*
Wir drücken dir die Daumen.	*We'll cross our fingers for you.*
nach oben	*(to go) upstairs*
Zum Wohl!	*To your health! (as a toast)*
Prosit (Prost)!	*Cheers! (as a toast)*

C. Landeskunde.

- One of the aspects that contributes to Germany's reputation for quality products and its strong economy is its apprenticeship system. Sabine's father completed a commercial apprenticeship **(die kaufmännische Lehre),** one of the 357 possible apprenticeships open to young people. However, he wanted to be an actor **(der Schauspieler)** so he then attended acting school **(die Schauspielschule)** for three years to earn his diploma.

- After finishing her work at a teachers' college (**die Pädagogische Hochschule**) and her internship (**das Praktikum**), Sabine's mother got a teaching position at the same school she is still at. She did advanced work for four semesters so she could become a speech therapist for speech-impaired children (**sprachbehinderte Kinder**).

D. Ich hab's gesehen. Watch *Szene 9* with the sound off. Write in German the names of the pieces of furniture and the things on the table you see. In addition, include several verbs describing actions taking place in this room.

E. Schauen Sie genau. Look at *Szene 9* again with the sound off and check the statements that you think are true, based on what you see.

1. _____ Ein paar Flaschen stehen auf dem Couchtisch.

2. _____ Sabines Vater trinkt Kaffee.

3. _____ Lisa sitzt neben Sabines Mutter.

4. _____ Sabines Mutter trägt ein blaues Kleid.

5. _____ Sabines Vater trägt ein blaues Hemd.

6. _____ Sabines Vater hat braune Haare.

7. _____ Alle sind sehr lustig.

8. _____ Am Ende der Szene stößt° man an.   drink a toast

F. Hören Sie zu. Read the following list of German remarks. Then view *Szene 9* with the sound on. Mark each question, statement, or fragment you hear.

1. _____ nett und sympathisch   8. _____ in Belgien wohnen

2. _____ hat sehr viel Spaß gemacht   9. _____ Da warten die Leute drauf.

3. _____ keine Ahnung   10. _____ keine Angst

4. _____ zu Hause arbeiten   11. _____ du ... ziehst dich gut an

5. _____ Wir kennen die Geschichte.   12. _____ Sag den Leuten

6. _____ am liebsten   13. _____ Hoffentlich bekomme ich den Job.

7. _____ viel Geld verdienen   14. _____ Danke schön.

G. Stimmt's? Read through the following statements. Then watch *Szene 9* again and check the statements that you think are true.

1. _____ Sabines Mutter sagt, sie sollten etwas essen.

2. _____ Lisa hat gestern einen schönen Tag gehabt.

3. _____ Sabines Vater hat Shakespeare auf der Uni studiert.

4. _____ Sabines Mutter ist Lehrerin.

5. _____ Sabine möchte einen Beruf, in dem sie viel mit Menschen zusammen ist.

6. _____ Sabine sagt, der Beruf ist alles – Geld ist nicht so wichtig.

7. _____ Lisa möchte einen Beruf, in dem sie etwas für die Menschen tun kann.

8. _____ Sabine hat morgen im Fremdenverkehrsbüro ein Vorstellungsgespräch.

9. _____ Sabine weiß schon, was sie dem Chef erzählen will.

10. _____ Sabine war im Sportverein aktiv.

11. _____ Sabine kennt Tübingen sehr gut.

12. _____ Lisa sagt, sie ist müde und möchte schlafen gehen.

H. Sie sind dran. Choose one of the people in this segment and write four short German sentences about that person.

_____

_____

_____

_____

Name _____ Datum _____

SZENE 10 Beim Vorstellungsgespräch

A. Vorschau. In this video segment Sabine interviews for a summer job at the local tourist information office.

- What impression do you get of the director (**der Leiter**) of the tourist information office (**das Fremdenverkehrsbüro**)?
- Note the experience that helps qualify Sabine for work in the tourist information office.
- What would be Sabine's duties in her summer job?

B. Besondere Ausdrücke. Here are some words and idiomatic expressions that you will hear in this segment of the video. Read through the list to get acquainted with the expressions and listen for them as you view the video. Memorize the ones that you think would be most useful to you. The items are listed in order of appearance.

Reisende	*travelers*
einerseits	*on the one hand*
vornehme Hotels	*first-class hotels*
andererseits	*on the other hand*
Rucksacktouren	*backpacking trips*
Erlebnisse	*experiences*
Bräuche und Sitten	*customs and manners*
Fremdsprachenkenntnisse	*knowledge of foreign languages*
fließend	*fluently*
(die) Büroarbeit	*office work*
(die) Theke	*counter*
viel Betrieb	*lots of activity*
herumgeführt	*showed around*
die Mitarbeiter	*fellow employees*
vorstellen	*to introduce*
ob's klappt	*whether it'll work out*
(das) Gehalt	*salary*
(die) Anzeige	*advertisement*

C. Landeskunde.

- Because of its long history and practice of preserving cultural monuments and buildings, Germany attracts many tourists. Every town has a **Fremdenverkehrsbüro** that is generous in providing information on what to do and see and where to stay. Most tourist information offices have websites on the Internet and one can receive information and brochures through e-mail or by writing to them.

- Sabine studied both English and French in school. Students at the **Gymnasium** must study two foreign languages for a total of thirteen years. The minimum length of time for the first foreign language is seven years and for the second five years. After that students can choose which language they wish to continue.

D. Ich hab's gesehen. Watch *Szene 10* with the sound off. Write in German the names of the objects and clothing you see.

_____   _____   _____

_____   _____   _____

_____   _____   _____

E. Schauen Sie genau. Look at *Szene 10* again with the sound off and watch for information to help you complete the statements below. Circle the best choices based on what you see. More than one response may be possible.

1. Auf dem Tisch liegt der Lebenslauf° von Sabine. Auf dem Lebenslauf   résumé

   _____.

   a. ist ein Bild von Sabine   b. ist kein Bild   c. sind zwei Fotos von Sabine

2. Sabine trägt _____.

   a. einen braunen Rock   b. eine graue Jacke   c. eine weiße Bluse

3. Der Leiter des Büros trägt eine _____ Krawatte.

   a. grüne   b. blaue   c. rote

4. Auf dem Tisch stehen _____.

   a. Flaschen   b. Gläser   c. Tassen

5. Der Leiter des Fremdenverkehrsbüros sitzt _____ dem Tisch.

   a. hinter   b. auf   c. neben

6. An der Wand hängt _____.

   a. eine große Uhr   b. ein großes Poster   c. ein Foto von Tübingen

7. Der Leiter ist _____.

   a. traurig   b. nett   c. unfreundlich

Name _____   Datum _____

F. Hören Sie zu. Read the following list of German remarks. Then view *Szene 10* with the sound on. Mark each question, statement, or fragment you hear.

1. _____ warum interessieren Sie sich   8. _____ habe nichts gegessen

2. _____ würde ich mich freuen   9. _____ und kann auch Italienisch

3. _____ Was für Reisen   10. _____ sehr viele Amerikaner

4. _____ mit dem Zug gefahren   11. _____ am Telefon

5. _____ Jugendherbergen   12. _____ es gibt auch viele Studenten

6. _____ eines Tages   13. _____ weil ich aus Tübingen komme

7. _____ im Ausland   14. _____ Das stand in der Anzeige.

G. Stimmt's? Below is a list of possible qualifications for working in the tourist information office. Read through the list. Then watch *Szene 10* again and check those qualifications and experiences which apply to Sabine.

1. _____ Sie reist gern.

2. _____ Sie lernt gerne andere Menschen kennen.

3. _____ Sie hat Rucksacktouren gemacht.

4. _____ Sie hat in einem Restaurant in Italien gearbeitet.

5. _____ In Italien hat sie gelernt andere Kulturen zu respektieren und verstehen.

6. _____ Sie spricht sehr gut Spanisch.

7. _____ Sie kann auch sehr gut Englisch und Französisch.

8. _____ Sie kennt sich in Tübingen sehr gut aus.

9. _____ Sie hat vielen Engländern die Stadt Tübingen gezeigt.

10. _____ Sie macht Büroarbeit gern.

H. Sie sind dran. In German, describe the director of the tourist information office (physical appearance, clothing). Then state whether you would like to work for him and give the reason(s).

1. Aussehen:

    _____

    _____

2. Warum ich (nicht) für den Leiter des Fremdenverkehrsbüros arbeiten möchte:

    _____

    _____

SZENE 11 Ich würde gern ...

A. Vorschau. In this video segment Sabine tells Lisa what her summer job at the tourist information office would involve and gives some historical facts about Tübingen. Then they both talk about what they would do if they had time and money.

- What are the reasons Sabine gives for wanting to work at the tourist information office?
- What historical information does Sabine provide about Tübingen?
- Why would Sabine like to visit Australia?
- Why would Lisa like to visit Norway?

B. Besondere Ausdrücke. Here are some words and idiomatic expressions that you will hear in this segment of the video. Read through the list to get acquainted with the expressions and listen for them as you view the video. Memorize the ones that you think would be most useful to you. The items are listed in order of appearance.

aufgeregt	*excited*
im Grunde	*basically*
gegründet	*founded, established*
(das) Dorf	*village*
(der) Turm	*tower*
(der) Blick	*view*
(der) Dichter	*poet*
(der) Philosoph	*philosopher*
(der) Bürger	*citizen*
(der) Handwerker	*craftsman*
(der) Bauer	*farmer*
erfahren	*to find out*
spannend	*exciting*
zusammenpacken	*to pack (put) together*

C. Landeskunde. Sabine gives Lisa the following information about Tübingen:

- The town was founded 1500 years ago by **Alemannen,** a German tribe.
- A fortress **(die Burg)** was built in the 11th century by Count Tübingen **(Graf von Tübingen).**
- The university was established in 1477.
- The church, **das Evangelische Stift,** was built in 1530.
- The poet **(der Dichter)** Friedrich Hölderlin (1770–1843) lived in Tübingen.

- Two well-known philosophers **(der Philosoph)** studied at the university: Georg Wilhelm Friedrich Hegel (1770–1831) and Friedrich Wilhelm Joseph von Schelling (1775–1854).
- The town consists of two main sections:
  a. The upper part **(die Oberstadt)**, where professional people **(akademische Bürger)**, noble families **(adelige Familien)**, and a few craftsmen **(der Handwerker)** lived.
  b. The lower part **(die Unterstadt)**, where craftsmen, wine growers **(der Weinbauer)**, and regular farmers **(der Bauer)** lived.

D. Ich hab's gesehen. Read through the following list of things you might expect to see in a city like Tübingen. Then watch *Szene 11* with the sound off. Check the things and people you do see.

Gesehen habe ich ...

1. _____ einen Fluss°
2. _____ ein Boot°
3. _____ hohe alte Häuser
4. _____ den Marktplatz
5. _____ Fachwerkhäuser°

6. _____ eine Mauer   river
7. _____ eine Kirche   boat
8. _____ einen Bus
9. _____ einen Rucksack
10. _____ ein Fahrrad   half-timbered houses

E. Schauen Sie genau. Look at *Szene 11* again with the sound off. Check the statements that you think are true, based on what you see.

1. _____ Ein Kind trägt eine Baseballmütze.

2. _____ Eine Frau hält ein Kind an der Hand.

3. _____ Ein junger Mann hat den Arm um seine Freundin gelegt.

4. _____ Kinder spielen Fußball.

5. _____ Ein Mann trägt einen roten Pullover.

6. _____ Sabine und Lisa gehen durch die Fußgängerzone.

7. _____ Lisa trägt eine rote Bluse.

8. _____ Sabine zeigt mit der Hand auf etwas.

9. _____ Lisa und Sabine sitzen nebeneinander auf einer Bank°.   bench

10. _____ Sie stehen auf und gehen einkaufen.

F. Hören Sie zu. Read the following list of German remarks. Then view *Szene 11* with the sound on. Mark each question, statement, or fragment you hear.

1. _____ Aber ich glaub' es ging ganz gut.

2. _____ Das würde mir gut gefallen.

3. _____ einen wunderschönen Blick über die ganze Stadt

4. _____ Das ist schwer zu glauben.

5. _____ Was haben denn die anderen Leute gemacht?

6. _____ das muss sehr interessant gewesen sein

7. _____ Die meisten Leute haben gefaulenzt.

8. _____ Die kann man auch anschauen.

9. _____ es gibt keine Nacht mehr

10. _____ im Süden ist es wärmer

11. _____ Sollen wir gehen?

G. Wer hat es gesagt? Read through the list of sentences that are either said by Sabine or Lisa or reflect their views. Watch *Szene 11* again and write in the appropriate letter.

a. Sabine   b. Lisa

1. _____ Die Arbeit im Fremdenverkehrsamt würde mir Spaß machen.

2. _____ Ich käme in Kontakt mit vielen verschiedenen Menschen.

3. _____ Ich würde am liebsten in Tübingen bleiben.

4. _____ Ich finde die alten Häuser sehr schön.

5. _____ Ich möchte den Touristen Tübingen zeigen.

6. _____ Ich war gestern oben auf dem Turm.

7. _____ Wenn ich Geld hätte, würde ich nach Australien fliegen.

8. _____ Ich hätte gern vor hundert Jahren in Tübingen gelebt.

9. _____ Ich würde am liebsten nach Norwegen fahren.

10. _____ Ich wäre am liebsten wieder selber Touristin.

11. _____ Im Norden ist die Natur nicht so zerstört wie irgendwoanders.

12. _____ Am Nordkap° ist es sehr lange hell.   North Cape

H. Sie sind dran. Both Sabine and Lisa tell what they would do if they had time and money. Choose the "dream" of one of them and tell in 3–4 German sentences why you would like to share her dream or why you would not.

Wenn sie Zeit und Geld hätte, würde …

1. Sabine nach Australien fliegen, Sydney anschauen und ein paar Wochen mit den Aborigines zusammenleben.

2. Lisa nach Norwegen fahren, die schöne Natur und die Fjorde anschauen und ans Nordkap fahren, wo es im Sommer keine Nacht gibt.

_____

_____

_____

_____

SZENE 12 Und was sind die Aussichten°? prospects

A. Vorschau. In this video segment Sabine, Lisa, und Julian have a last conversation before Lisa takes the train back to Hamburg.

- How does Lisa hope to combine her future medical degree with her environmental concerns?
- What is Sabine's career goal?
- What would Julian like to do after finishing his university degree?
- What advantages do the young people find in the European Union?

B. Besondere Ausdrücke. Here are some words and idiomatic expressions that you will hear in this segment of the video. Read through the list to get acquainted with the expressions and listen for them as you view the video. Memorize the ones that you think would be most useful to you. The items are listed in order of appearance.

herumgeführt	*led around*
Hast du dich entschlossen?	*Have you decided?*
Umweltverschmutzung	*environmental pollution*
die Auswirkung	*effect*
die Gesundheit	*health*
nötig	*necessary*
der Umweltschutz	*environmental protection*
Vorteile	*advantages*
die Karriere	*career*
Geldwechseln	*changing money*
der Abschied	*departure*

C. Landeskunde.

- Germany, with the largest population of any member of the European Union and its strong economy, is an important and committed member of the European Union. Sabine, Lisa, and Julian express their enthusiasm for the EU. They like the EU's commitment to improving the environment and the fact that one can travel without border restrictions and live and work in any of the EU countries. They are looking forward to the **Euro,** the single European currency. Note that they refer to the currency as **Ecu,** which was the provisional name preceding the final choice of **Euro.**

- Even though East Germany, **die neuen Bundesländer** (the new states), and West Germany, **die alten Bundesländer** (the old states), have been united since October 3, 1990, many discrepancies and misunderstandings have not been overcome. One serious problem in the new states is the catastrophic extent of environmental pollution. To help solve the problem, once she has her medical degree, Lisa would like to live in the new states and research the connection between pollution and the health of the citizens. Julian expresses the hope that technological progress can be made that is environmentally friendly. In this way, he believes, new jobs can be created, especially in the new states where in some regions unemployment has been twice as high as in the old states.

D. Ich hab's gesehen. Watch *Szene 12* with the sound off. Write in German the verbs that describe what the people are doing.

_____   _____   _____

_____   _____   _____

E. Schauen Sie genau. Look at *Szene 12* again with the sound off and watch for information to help you complete the statements below. Circle the best choices based on what you see. More than one response may be possible.

1. Der Titel einer Zeitschrift ist _____.

    a. *Finanz und Wirtschaft*   b. *Computer*   c. *Informatik*

2. Sabine, Lisa und Julian sind draußen _____.

    a. am Bahnhof   b. in einem Café   c. im Park

3. Sie sitzen _____.

    a. an einem Tisch   b. unter einem Schirm   c. neben einer Mauer

4. Die drei jungen Leute _____.

    a. essen etwas   b. reden zusammen   c. trinken etwas

5. Ein Mann hinter ihnen _____ etwas.

    a. isst   b. trinkt   c. liest

6. _____ schaut auf die Armbanduhr.

    a. Julian   b. Lisa   c. Sabine

7. Lisa fährt mit dem _____.

    a. Zug   b. Bus   c. Auto

F. Hören Sie zu. Read the following list of German remarks. Then view *Szene 12* with the sound on. Mark each question, statement, or fragment you hear.

1. _____ nett von dir

2. _____ Das habe ich gerne gemacht.

3. _____ ich werde schon bald wieder kommen

4. _____ Vielleicht nächstes Jahr.

5. _____ Hoffentlich ist es noch nicht zu spät.

6. _____ Und du kannst jetzt noch leichter reisen.

7. _____ Als Geschäftsfrau.

8. _____ mein Lieblingsberuf

9. _____ Ihr seid herzlich eingeladen.

10. _____ Das werden wir tun.

11. _____ Wann kommt denn deine Schwester?

12. _____ Und schreib uns einen Brief.

13. _____ Es wird Zeit.

14. _____ lass uns zahlen

G. Was werden sie machen? Sabine, Lisa, and Julian tell what they would like to do after they finish their studies. Read through the list of statements or fragments. Watch *Szene 12* again and write in the letter of the person who says the statement or to whom it relates.

            a. Sabine   **b. Lisa**   **c. Julian**

1. _____ Ich denke, ich werde schon bald wieder kommen, nach meinem Abitur, und werde hier Medizin studieren.

2. _____ Ich möchte zum Beispiel nach London gehen und dort im Filmgeschäft arbeiten.

3. _____ Wenn ich fertig bin mit meinem Studium, dann könnt' ich in die neuen Bundesländer gehen und dort vielleicht als Ärztin Forschung betreiben.

4. _____ … Karriere machen im europäischen Parlament.

5. _____ Ich würde gerne nach Dresden, oder Halle, oder Leipzig, oder Jena gehen. Ich hab' gehört, das sind sehr schöne Städte.

6. _____ Als Geschäftsfrau.

H. Stimmt's? Read through the following statements. Then watch *Szene 12* again and check the statements that you think are true.

1. _____ Lisa wird Medizin an der Universität Hamburg studieren.

2. _____ Lisa möchte nach dem Studium in die neuen Bundesländer gehen.

3. _____ Lisa möchte etwas gegen die Umweltverschmutzung tun.

4. _____ Sie war schon eine Woche in Dresden und es hat ihr gefallen.

5. _____ Sabine findet, die Europäische Union tut viel für den Umweltschutz.

6. _____ Wegen der Europäischen Union kann man jetzt einfacher in die anderen Länder der EU reisen.

7. _____ Julian interessiert sich für das Filmgeschäft.

8. _____ Lisa lädt Sabine und Julian nach Hamburg ein.

9. _____ Lisa wird Sabine und Julian viele E-Mails schreiben.

I. Sie sind dran. In 4–5 German sentences give your opinion and impression of Sabine, Lisa, or Julian.

_____

_____

_____

_____

_____

Video Workbook

German-English Vocabulary

German–English Vocabulary

The German-English vocabulary contains most of the words and expressions that appear in the video and the video workbook. The definitions are limited to those that reflect the meaning of the words as used in the video.

ab•heben (abgehoben) to point out

das **Abitur** final exam and diploma **(Gymnasium)**

die **Aborigines** (*pl.*) native people (Australia)

der **Abschied** farewell, departure

ab•schließen (abgeschlossen) to conclude, finish

absolut absolutely

absolvieren to complete (one's studies)

ach oh; ~ **was** really!

ade good-bye

adelig noble

Afro-Brasil Afro-Brazilian

die **Ahnung** idea; **keine ~** no idea

akademisch educated

aktiv active

die **Alemannen** (*pl.*) Germanic tribe

als (*conj.*) than; when

die **Altstadt** old town

die **Anatomie** anatomy

an•bieten (angeboten) to offer

andererseits on the other hand

ändern to change

anders different

an•fangen (ä; angefangen) to begin

an•fassen to touch, handle

an•gucken to look at

an•haben to have (clothes) on

sich an•hören to sound; **es hört sich gut an** it sounds good

die **Anlage, -n** stereo unit or system

an•nehmen (nimmt; angenommen) to assume

annoncieren to advertise

an•schauen to look at

anständig proper, respectable

die **Anstellung, -en** position, employment

an•stoßen (ö; angestoßen) to drink a toast

anstrengend exhausting

die **Anzeige, -n** advertisement

der **Apfel, ¨** apple

die **Aprikose, -n** apricot

apropos by the way, in respect to

der **Ärger** annoyance

arm (ä) poor; **du Arme(r)** you poor thing

die **Armbanduhr, -en** wristwatch

die **Art, -en** kind

auf•brechen (i; aufgebrochen) to depart; **brechen wir auf** let's go

der **Aufenthalt, -e** stay

auf•führen to perform (theater)

aufgeregt excited

auf•schneiden (aufgeschnitten) to cut open, dissect

auf•setzen to put on (hat)

der **Auftritt, -e** appearance, scene (theater)

auf•wachsen (ä; ist aufgewachsen) to grow up

das **Auge, -n** eye

ausführlich detailed, thorough

sich aus•kennen to know all about

das **Ausland** foreign country; **im ~** abroad

aus•sehen (ie; ausgesehen) to appear

außerhalb (+ *gen.*) outside of

der **Austauschschüler, -/die Austauschschülerin, -nen** exchange student (secondary school)

die **Auswirkung, -en** effect

der **Bahnhof, ¨e** train station

der **Balkon, -s** *or* **-e** balcony

die **Bank, ¨e** bench

der **Bauer, -n, -n/die Bäuerin, -nen** farmer

sich bedienen to serve oneself; **bedient euch** help yourselves

sich beeilen to hurry

begegnen (ist begegnet) to meet, run into

behilflich helpful

das **Behindertenzentrum, -zentren** center for the disabled

beige beige

beliebt popular

benötigen to require, need

der **Bereich, -e** area (of interest)

bereisen to tour (a country)

beruflich professional, vocational

berühmt famous

der **Bescheid** information; **~ wissen** to know the answer

besetzt on duty; occupied

besichtigen to look at, view

besitzen (besessen) to own

bestellen to order

der **Betrieb** business; activity

bewölkt cloudy

der **Bezug** case; **in ~ auf** in regard to

der **Bildband, ¨e** picture book

die **Biochemie** biochemistry

der **Biologe, -n, -n/die Biologin, -nen** biologist

die **Biologie** biology

der **Biologieleistungskurs** advanced course in biology

bis gleich until later

bitte schön please

bitter bitter

der **Blick, -e** look, view

blond blond

die **Blume, -n** flower

das **Boot, -e** boat

die **Boutique, -n** boutique

der **Brauch**, ⁻e custom
die **Brille**, **-n** glasses; **eine ~** a pair of glasses
das **Brot**, **-e** bread
die **Brücke**, **-n** bridge
der **Bruder**, ⁻ brother
brünett brunette
die **Büchertasche**, **-n** bookbag
der **Buchladen**, ⁻ bookstore
büffeln to cram (for a test)
der **Bund**, **-e** bunch (keys)
das **Bundesland**, ⁻er state (Germany); **die neuen Bundesländer** the new states (Eastern Germany)
die **Burg**, **-en** fortress
der **Bürger**, **-**/die **Bürgerin**, **-nen** citizen
das **Büro**, **-s** office
die **Büroarbeit** office work
der **Bus**, **-se** bus
die **Bushaltestelle**, **-n** bus stop

das **Café**, **-s** café
die **Chance**, **-n** chance
chaotisch loose, disorganzied
der **Chef**, **-s** boss
die **Chemie** chemistry
ciao (Ital.) so long; *the Germanized term is* **tschau**
die **Cola**, **-s** cola
der **Couchtisch**, **-e** coffee table
creme cream (color)

dabei with me (him, her, etc.)
das **Dach**, ⁻er roof
dadurch in this manner, thereby
dahinter behind it, at the back
damalig former, at that time
damals then, at that time
damit thereby
der **Dank** thanks; **Gott sei Dank** thank goodness
danken to thank; **danke schön** thank you
daraufhin thereupon, after that
der **Daumen**, **-** thumb; **~ raus** thumb out; **wir drücken dir die ~** we'll cross our fingers for you
denken (gedacht) to think; **denk dran** think of it, remember
deutschsprachig German-speaking
der **Dichter**, **-**/die **Dichterin**, **-nen** poet

das **Ding**, **-e** thing; **vor allen Dingen** above all
direkt direct, immediate
der **Direktor**, **-en**/die **Direktorin**, **-nen** director
der **Dolmetscher**, **-**/die **Dolmetscherin**, **-nen** interpreter
das **Dorf**, ⁻er village
dran on it
draußen outside
dreidimensional three-dimensional
dringend urgent
drinnen inside
die **Drogerie**, **-n** drugstore
drüben over there; **da ~** over there
drücken to press; **wir ~ dir die Daumen** we'll cross our fingers for you
das **Drum und Dran** everything; **mit allem ~** with all the trimmings
drunter underneath

die **E-Mail** E-mail
echt real, really
die **Ecke**, **-n** corner; **um die ~** around the corner
Edamer type of cheese
egal equal; **das ist ~** it makes no difference
das **Ei**, **-er** egg
eigentlich really, actually
das **Eigentum** property, possession
eilen to be in a hurry; **es eilt nicht** no hurry
der **Eindruck**, ⁻e impression
einerseits on the one hand
einfach simple
der/die **Einheimische** (noun decl. like adj.) local person
die **Einheitswährung** a single currency (euro)
einige some
die **Einkaufstasche**, **-n** shopping bag
ein·laden (ä; eingeladen) to invite; to treat
einmal once
ein·packen to pack up
einschreiben (eingeschrieben) to enroll; to register
ein·setzen put into; put into action; **sich ~** to stand up for

ein·steigen (ist eingestiegen) to get in/on (a vehicle)
der/die **Einzige** (noun decl. like adj.) the sole person
die **Eltern** (pl.) parents
das **Ende**, **-n** end; **am ~** at the end
sich engagieren to commit oneself to
entlang (+ acc.) along
sich entschließen (entschlossen) to decide
entschuldigen to excuse; **entschuldige bitte** excuse me
entstehen (ist entstanden) to emerge; to originate
entweder ... oder either . . . or
entwickeln to develop
die **Erdbeere**, **-n** strawberry
erfahren (ä; erfahren) to find out, to learn, to experience
erkennen (erkannt) to recognize
das **Erlebnis**, **-se** experience, event
erledigen to take care of
eröffnen to open up
errichten to erect
erst first; **~ mal** first of all
der **Euro** euro (European currency)
europäisch European

das **Fachwerkhaus**, ⁻er half-timbered house
das **Fahrrad**, ⁻er bicycle
die **Fahrradtour**, **-en** bike trip
die **Fahrt**, **-en** trip
die **Fakultät**, **-en** department of university
der **Fall**, ⁻e case; **auf jeden ~** in any case
die **Farbe**, **-n** color
fast almost
faulenzen to loaf
felsenfest absolutely
das **Fenster**, **-** window
der **Ferienort**, **-e** vacation spot
fertig finished
fest firm; **fester Freund** steady boyfriend
die **Finanz** finance
der **Fisch**, **-e** fish
fit fit
der **Fjord**, **-e** fjord
fließend fluent
der **Flughafen**, ⁻ airport

der **Fluss, -̈e** river
Folgendes the following
die **Forschung** research; **~ betreiben** to do research
fortgeschritten advanced
der **Fortschritt** progress
das **Foto, -s** photo
der **Fotoapparat, -e** camera
fotografieren to photograph
französisch French
die **Frau, -en** woman; wife
die **Freilichtbühne, -n** open-air theater
das **Fremdenverkehrsbüro** tourist agency
die **Fremdsprachenkenntnisse** (*pl.*) knowledge of foreign languages
freuen to be pleased; **freut mich** pleased to meet you; **sich ~** to be glad
der **Freund, -e**/die **Freundin, -nen** friend
freundlich friendly
die **Freundschaft, -en** friendship
fröhlich cheerful
frühstücken to eat breakfast
führen to lead
füllen to fill
die **Fußgängerzone, -n** pedestrian zone

ganz complete; **~ schön früh** rather early
der **Garten, -̈** garden, yard
die **Gasse, -n** narrow street
das **Gebäude, -** building
geben (i; gegeben) to give
das **Gehalt, -̈er** salary
gehen (ist gegangen) to go
gelb yellow
der **Geldbeutel, -** wallet, purse
das **Geldwechseln** changing money
gell (*colloq.*) isn't it?
gemeinsam joint, common, together
der **Gemüsehändler, -**/die **Gemüsehändlerin, -nen** vegetable dealer
genau exact(ly)
genügend sufficient
gerade straight, even; just; **doch ~ erst** just now
die **Germanistik** study of German language and literature
gern(e) gladly, with pleasure
die **Geschäftsfrau, -en** business woman
das **Geschenk, -e** gift
geschieden divorced
die **Geschwister** (*pl.*) brother and sister
das **Gespräch, -e** conversation; **ins ~ kommen** to start a conversation
die **Gesundheit** health
der **Gewölbekeller, -** cellar with vaulted ceiling
gleich same; immediately
der **Gott** God; **~ sei Dank** thank goodness
Gouda type of cheese
der **Graf, -en, -en** count
das **Gramm** gram
die **Grenze, -n** border
groß (ö) large; tall (people)
die **Grundbedingung, -en** basic condition
grün green; **mit dem Grünen** with the green (tops) on it
der **Grund, -̈e** reason; **im Grunde** basically
gründen to found, establish
die **Gruppe, -n** group
gucken to look
die **Gurke, -n** cucumber
die **Güte** goodness; **meine ~** good heavens

das **Haar, -e** hair
die **Haarbürste, -n** hairbrush
hallo hello
halt (*colloq.*) just; you know
halten (ä; gehalten) to stop
die **Haltestelle, -n** bus stop
die **Hand, -̈e** hand
der **Handwerker, -** craftsman, artisan
hässlich ugly
hätte (*subjunctive of* **haben**) would have
die **Hauptsache** main thing
hauptsächlich main(ly)
die **Haustür, -en** front door
heiraten to marry
heiß hot
heißen (geheißen) to be named
hell bright; light (color); daylight
hellbraun light brown

her here; **lange ~** a long time ago
herum•führen to show around
hervor•gehen (ist hervorgegangen) to emerge; to become clear
herzlich cordial
hilfsbereit helpful
hin•bringen (hingebracht) to take there
hin•führen to take there
sich hin•setzen to sit down
hinten in the back
hoch•kommen (ist hochgekommen) to go up
die **Hochzeit, -en** wedding
hoffentlich hopefully; I hope
der **Hörsaal, -säle** lecture hall
die **Hose, -n** slacks
das **Hotel, -s** hotel
das **Hotel- und Gaststättengewerbe** hotel and restaurant industry
der **Hut, -̈e** hat

ideal ideal
immer always; **was auch ~** whatever
immerhin at least
die **Informatik** computer science
die **Insel, -n** island
interessieren to interest; **sich ~** to be interested
irgendein any
irgendetwas something
irgendwann sometime
irgendwas something
irgendwoanders somewhere else
irgendwie somehow

die **Jacke, -n** jacket
der **Jazzkeller** jazz cellar
die **Jeans** (*pl. or sg.*) jeans
der **Job, -s** job
der **Jogger, -**/die **Joggerin, -nen** jogger
journalistisch journalistic
die **Jugendherberge, -n** youth hostel
der/die **Jugendliche** (*noun decl. like adj.*) young person
jung (ü) young

der **Kaffee** coffee

die **Karotte, -n** carrot
die **Karriere, -n** career
die **Kartoffel, -n** potato
der **Käse** cheese
das **Kaufhaus, ̈er** department store
kaufmännisch commercial
die **Kenntnis, -se** knowledge
der **Keller, -** cellar
das **Kind, -er** child
der **Kinderarzt, ̈e/die Kinder-ärztin, -nen** pediatrician
die **Kirsche, -n** cherry
der **Kittel, -** smock
klappen to work out, go smoothly
klar clear
die **Klasse, -n** class, grade
die **Klausur, -en** test
das **Klavier, -e** piano
das **Kleidungsstück, -e** article of clothing
klein small; short (people)
die **Klinik, -en** clinic
kommen (ist gekommen) to come
der **Kontakt, -e** contact
der **Kopfsalat, -e** lettuce
körperbehindert physically impaired
der **Kran, ̈e** crane
die **Krawatte, -n** tie
der **Krimi, -s** mystery (novel or film)
die **Kultur, -en** culture
die **Kunsthalle, -n** art gallery
kurz (ü) short
die **Kusine, -n** cousin (female)
der **Kuss, ̈e** kiss
küssen to kiss

das **Labor, -s** lab
die **Laborübung, -en** lab experiment
lang (ä) long
lange long; **~ her** a long time ago
lassen (ä; gelassen) to permit; to let; **lass uns (gehen)** let's (go)
die **Laufbahn, -en** career
leben to live
der **Lebenslauf, ̈e** résumé
lecker tasty, delicious
der **Lehrauftrag, ̈e** teaching assignment
die **Lehre, -n** apprenticeship

der **Lehrer, -/die Lehrerin, -nen** teacher
die **Leiche, -n** cadaver
Leid: es tut mir ~ I'm sorry
leider unfortunately
der **Leiter, -/die Leiterin, -nen** manager
leihen (geliehen) to lend
leiten to lead, manage
lieber rather
der **Liebling, -e** favorite; **Lieblings-** (prefix) favorite
liebsten: am ~ prefer most of all
Limburger a type of cheese
die **Locke, -n** curl
lockig curly
sich lohnen to be worthwhile
lose informal; **lose Freunde** just friends
los•fahren (ä; ist losgefahren) to depart
los•gehen (ist losgegangen) to go off ; to begin
die **Lösung, -en** solution
die **Lücke, -n** blank
die **Lust** desire; **~ haben** to feel like
lustig merry, in good spirits

machen to do; to make; **machen wir es so** let's do that; **kann man nichts machen** can't be helped
der **Manager, -/die Managerin, -nen** manager
der **Mann, ̈er** man; husband
der **Mantel, ̈** coat
der **Markplatz, ̈e** market square
die **Mauer, -n** wall
die **Medienwissenschaften** (pl.) media studies
die **Medizin** medicine (branch of science)
der **Mediziner, -/die Medizinerin, -nen** doctor of medicine
mehrere several
melden to inform; report
die **Metzgerei, -en** meat market, butcher shop
die **Milch** milk
mischen to mix

der **Mitarbeiter, -/die Mitarbeiterin, -nen** employee; fellow worker
mit•haben to have along
mit•kommen (ist mitgekommen) to come along
mit•nehmen (i; mitgenommen) to take along
mögen (mag, gemocht) to like
die **Mohrrübe, -n** carrot
mollig plump
momentan at the moment
die **Morgenstelle** name of the Tübingen University building where physics and chemistry are taught
das **Motorrad, ̈er** motorcycle
das **Museum,** pl. **Museen** museum
die **Mutter, ̈** mother
die **Mütze, -n** cap

na well; **~ ja** oh well
nachdem (sub. conj.) after
nach•kommen (ist nach-gekommen) to join later
nah (ä) near
die **Nähe** proximity; **in der ~** close by
nämlich to be sure, indeed
die **Natur** nature
natürlich naturally
die **Naturwissenschaft, -en** natural science
nebeneinander next to each other
nee no
nehmen (i; genommen) to take
die **Nektarine, -n** nectarine
nervös nervous
nett nice
nichts nothing
nirgends nowhere
der **Nobelpreis, -e** Nobel Prize
noch still; **~ immer** still; **~ nicht** not yet
nochmal once again
nochmals once again
das **Nordkap** North Cape
normalerweise normally
nötig necessary
der **Numerus clausus** limited number of university openings for study in certain subjects

oben above; upstairs; **nach ~** to go upstairs

die **Oberstadt** upper part of old Tübingen

der **Obsthändler, -**/die **Obsthändlerin, -nen** fruit seller

der **Opa, -s** grandpa

orange orange

das **Organ, -e** organ (body)

organisieren to organize

die **Ostsee** Baltic Sea

das **Ozonloch, ¨er** hole in the ozone

paar: ein ~ a few

packen to pack

der **Papa, -s** papa, dad

der **Park, -s** park

das **Parlament, -e** parliament

passieren (ist passiert) to happen

die **Person, -en** person

die **Perspektive, -n** perspective

der **Philosoph, -en, -en**/die **Philosophin, -nen** philosopher

die **Physik** physics

das **Physikum, -s** preliminary medical examination (taken after six semesters)

das **Plakat, -e** poster, placard

das **Portemonnaie, -s** wallet

das **Praktikum, -ka** internship

der **Präparationskurs, -e** histology (slide preparation) course

prima great, excellent

das **Problem, -e** problem

prosit! cheers (as a toast)

das **Publikum** public

der **Pullover, -** sweater

die **Radtour, -en** bike tour

raten (ä; geraten) to give advice; to guess

das **Rathaus, ¨er** city hall

rauf up

rauf·gehen (ist raufgegangen) to go up

der **Raum, ¨e** space; area; district

die **Räumlichkeiten** premises, rooms

raus out

reagieren to react, respond to

rechnen to calculate; to count on

recht right; **~ sympathisch** very nice

der **Recycling-Container, -s** recycling container

reden to speak, to converse

das **Regal, -e** shelf

der **Regenschirm, -e** umbrella

regnen to rain; **es regnet** it's raining

rein·gehen (ist reingegangen) to go in

rein·kommen (ist reingekommen) to come in

rein·legen to put in

rein·tun (reingetan) to put in(to)

die **Reise, -n** trip; **auf Reisen** on a trip

reisen (ist gereist) to travel

der/die **Reisende** (*noun decl. like adj.*) traveler

reizen to attract

respektieren to respect

das **Restaurant, -s** restaurant

richtig right

die **Richtung, -en** direction; **in der ~** in the direction of

die **Rolle, -n** role; **eine ~ spielen** to be important

die **Romanistik** study of Romance languages and literatures

rücken to move; **es rückt näher** the time is getting close

der **Rucksack, ¨e** backpack

die **Rucksacktour, -en** backpacking trip

ruhig quiet, calm; free to do/say something

rund round; around

rundherum all around, round about

runter down

runter·laufen (äu; ist runtergelaufen) to run down

sagen to say; **sag mal** tell me

der **Salat, -e** lettuce; salad

satt satisfied; **ich bin ~** I've had enough, I'm full

sauer sour; **saurer Regen** acid rain

schaffen to produce; to manage, succeed

die **Schale, -n** bowl; tray; cup

schauen to look

der **Schauspieler, -**/die **Schauspielerin, -nen** actor

die **Schauspielschule, -n** acting school

der **Scheck, -s** check

die **Scheckkarte, -n** ATM card

schick chic

der **Schirm, -e** umbrella

die **Schlange, -n** snake; line; **~ stehen** to stand in line

schlank slender

das **Schloss, ¨er** castle

der **Schlüssel, -** key

der **Schlüsselbund, -e** bunch of keys

der **Schnarrenberg** name of hill on which the Tübingen University clinics and natural science buildings are located

schneiden (geschnitten) to cut

schon already; (*flavoring word*)

das **Schuhgeschäft, -e** shoe store

schwarz (ä) black

die **Schwester, -n** sister

sehen (ie; gesehen) to see

die **Sehenswürdigkeit, -en** sightseeing attraction; (*pl.*) sights (of a town)

sehr very

seit since; **~ 5 Jahren** for 5 years

selber oneself

der **Sezierkurs, -e** anatomy course

sicher sure, certain

singen (gesungen) to sing

die **Sitte, -n** custom, manner

sitzen (gesessen) to sit

die **Skifreizeit** ski outing

die **Slawistik** study of Slavic languages and literatures

so genannt so-called

sollen should, ought to

die **Sorge, -n** worry; **mache dir ja keine Sorgen** don't worry

die **Sorte, -n** kind

soweit as far as

sowieso in any case

spannend exciting; suspenseful

der **Spaß, ¨e** fun; **es macht ~** it's fun

spät late; **wie ~ ist es?** what time is it?

spielen to play

der **Sportverein, -e** sports club

sprachbehindert speech-impaired

die Sprache, -n language

die Sprachübung, -en language exercise

die Sprechstunde, -n office hour

statt•finden (stattgefunden) to take place

stecken to stick, put into

stehen (gestanden) to stand

die Stereoanlage, -n stereo system

die Stiefmutter, ⸚ stepmother

stimmen to be true; **es stimmt** it's right

die Straße, -n street

die Straßenbahn, -en streetcar

der Straßenmusiker, -/die Straßenmusikerin, -nen street musician

das Studentenwohnheim, -e dormitory

der Studienplatz, ⸚e opening at the university

studieren to study

das Studium, *pl.* **Studien** studies

der Stuhl, ⸚e chair

surfen to surf; to go windsurfing

die Szene, -n scene

der Tag, -e day; **Tag!** hello!

die Tasche, -n pocket; purse; shoulder bag

die Tat, -en deed; **in der ~** actually

tätig active

die Tätigkeit, -en activity; responsibility

das Taxi, -s taxi

das Telefon, -e telephone

die Theke, -n counter

der Tisch, -e table

der Titel, - title

die Tomate, -n tomato

total total

die Tour, -en trip; tour

der Tourismus tourism

der Tourist, -en, -en/die Touristin, -nen tourist

tragen (ä; getragen) to wear; to carry

trampen to hitchhike

das Trampereck place to hitchhike from

traurig sad

treffen (i; getroffen) to meet; **treffen wir uns** let's meet

trinken (getrunken) to drink

die Tür, -en door

türkisch Turkish

der Turm, ⸚e tower

typisch typical

überhaupt generally, actually

sich überlegen to consider, to reflect upon

überzeugen to convince

übrigens by the way

die Uhr, -en watch, clock; **es ist [11] ~** it's [11] o'clock

um•gehen (ist umgegangen) (mit) to deal with

um•gucken to look around

umsiedeln to resettle

der Umstand, ⸚e circumstance; **unter Umständen** under certain circumstances

die Umwelt environment

der Umweltschutz protection of the environment

die Umwelttechnik environmental technology

die Umweltverschmutzung environmental pollution

die Umweltzerstörung destruction of the environment

um•ziehen (ist umgezogen) to move; **sich ~ (hat sich umgezogen)** to change one's clothes

unbedingt absolutely

unentschlossen undecided

unfreundlich unfriendly

ungefähr approximately

unheimlich tremendous

die Uni, -s university

die Universität, -en university

unterbringen (untergebracht) to place, accommodate

die Unterlagen (*pl.*) documents; references

unternehmen (i; unternommen) to undertake

die Unterstadt lower part of old Tübingen

unterteilt divided

unterwegs on a trip; away

der Vater, ⸚ father

die Verabredung, -en appointment, date

sich verändern to change

verbinden (verbunden) to combine, connect

verdienen to earn

der Verein, -e club

vergessen (i; vergessen) to forget

vermissen to miss; regret

verreisen (ist verreist) to go on a trip

verschieden various

sich verständigen to make oneself understood in a foreign language

verstehen (verstanden) to understand

der Versuch, -e attempt, experiment

verwinkelt crooked, with lots of corners (street)

verzichten to do without

viel much; **viele** many

vielleicht perhaps

vielseitig many-sided

der Vierer bus line 4

vollenden to complete

vor before; **~ [5] Jahren** [5] years ago

vorbei•gehen (ist vorbei-gegangen) to go past

vor•bereiten to prepare

vorher previously

die Vorlesung, -en lecture; **eine ~ halten** to give a lecture

vorne in front; **~ dran** up in front

vornehm first class, fashionable

vor•schlagen (ä; vorgeschlagen) to suggest

vor•stellen to introduce

sich vor•stellen to imagine

das Vorstellungsgespräch, -e job interview

der Vorteil, -e advantage

der Wagen, - car

wählen to choose

wäre (*subjunctive of* **sein**) would be

warm (ä) warm

warten to wait

warum why

wär's: das ~ dann schon that will be all
was = etwas something
wechselhaft changeable
wechseln to change
weg away; gone; off
wegen (+ *gen.*) because of
der **Weinbauer, -n, -n**/die **Weinbäuerin, -nen** wine-grower
weiß white
wer who
wesentlich essential
die **Weste, -n** vest

das **Wetter** weather
wichtig important
wie how
Wiederschauen: Auf ~. Good-bye.
das **Willkommen** welcome
die **Wirtschaft** economy
wo where
woanders elsewhere
woher from where
das **Wohl** well-being; **zum ~!** to your health!
wunderbar wonderful
wunderschön very beautiful

zahlen to pay
zeigen to show
die **Zeitschrift, -en** magazine
die **Zeitzone, -n** time zone
zerstören to destroy
das **Zimmer, -** room
das **Zimmertheater, -** small private theater with only a few seats
der **Zoo, -s** zoo
zusammen•packen to pack up